D1222810

STRANGER THAN FICTION

THE MACMILLAN COMPANY
NEW YORK · BOSTON · CHICAGO · DALLAS
ATLANTA · SAN FRANCISCO

MACMILLAN & CO., LIMITED
LONDON · BOMBAY · CALCUTTA
MELBOURNE

THE MACMILLAN COMPANY
OF CANADA, LIMITED
TORONTO

STRANGER THAN FICTION

A SHORT HISTORY OF THE JEWS
FROM EARLIEST TIMES TO
THE PRESENT DAY

BY

LEWIS BROWNE

WITH FIFTY ANIMATED MAPS BY THE AUTHOR,
GIVING A PICTORIAL HISTORY OF
CENTURIES OF WANDERING

New York
THE MACMILLAN COMPANY
1932

Set up and electrotyped. Published March, 1925. Reprinted June, September, December, 1925; March, October, November, 1926; February, June, October, 1927; February, October, 1928; March, 1929; April, 1930; November, 1931; August, 1932.

PRINTED IN THE UNITED STATES OF AMERICA
BY BERWICK & SMITH CO.

TO THE MEMORY

OF

A GREAT HISTORIAN

MY MASTER

GOTTHARD DEUTSCH

THIS IS THE STORY OF THE JEW, THAT STRANGE MAN WHO WILL NOT DIE

Through thirty and more centuries he has wandered about on earth, despised and rejected, bruised and beaten, yet all the time wandering on.

He has seen far-flung empires crack and crumble, and mighty peoples dwindle to naught. Egyptian, Canaanite, and Philistine; Assyrian, Chaldean, and Persian; Greek, Roman, and Saracen: all these and more have marched over him in pride. With their kings and priests, their tyrants and princelings, they have marched over him in vainglorious pride—only to fall and die by the roadside.

But he, the Jew, still lives on. Obstinately he fights off Time and Man, pressing along on his own path, keeping his own counsel, cherishing his own dreams, living his own life in his own way.

A strange man he has been, and a strange man he remains—and a stranger story than that of his life no tongue has ever recounted. . . .

TABLE OF CONTENTS

ILLUSTRATIONS AND CHARTS

STRANGER THAN FICTION

PROLOGUE

42 Washington Sq.,
New York City, Nov. 1, xxiii

The proper way to write a book—at least, so I've been told—is to buy a ream of clean white paper, a stock of pens, a large bottle of ink—and begin.

And I did all that to-day. I bought the paper, the pens, the ink; I even bought the wire clips with which to fasten the loose pages, and the pressboard folder in which to bind the whole manuscript. And seven hours ago I came up to my workroom, arranged the materials on the table, took the best pen in hand, and made ready to write.

I am still making ready to write. It is already long after midnight, and the noises of the street have died down to a creepy silence. Even whirling, frenzied, fevered New York has tired at last, and fallen asleep. But still in vain do I make ready to write.

By this time I should have been nearing at least the end of the first chapter—and I have not so much as begun! In a brave flourishing hand I have written across the top of a blank sheet:

Stranger Than Fiction
A Short History of the Jews

by Lewis Browne

CHAPTER I

—and no more.

For now that I am ready to begin, my mind is overawed. Hundreds of volumes crowd the sagging shelves that range the walls. Scores of other volumes litter the tables, the chairs, the floor. Encyclopedias and text-books and learned monographs are scattered around, and among them all sorts of pamphlets and clippings. They are in many languages, and they are cluttered with references to other writings in still other languages. And most of them tell at endless, at exhausting length, only a paragraph, perhaps even but a sentence, of the long story I would recount.

And the sight of all those enormous volumes is appalling. Their story is so long! . . . So bewilderingly involved! . . . And already it has so often been told.

Yet it cries out to be told still again. From beginning to end it pleads to be retold, and not as a list of names and dates, but as a wild adventure, as a romance. For the whole history of the Jewish people *is* a romance; the strangest, the most colorful in the saga of all mankind.

And it deserves to be retold because so few in the land have ever heard it. Both Jews and Gentiles—save they be historians—know exceedingly little of that romance. Perhaps the first chapters of it, those contained in the Bible, are familiar to most people—but even they are far from rightly known.

The Bible is a whole vast world of wisdom, beauty, and moral truth—but it is not a literal history. Its episodes and chronicles were in the mouths of desert tribesmen for long centuries before ever they were written down. For long centuries they were passed on from father to son, growing grander and more wonderful with each generation. So that by the time they were set down in writing, the literal truth in them, like the vein of gold in a mountain, was crushed and tortured and broken in a thousand places.

We know all that because for over a hundred and fifty years great Bible scholars have been exploring for that truth. They have toiled endlessly, examining manuscripts, comparing texts, digging around for buried clews, spinning out theories and then destroying them again—all to discover just where in the Bible the literal truth breaks off, and where legend begins.

Five generations of scholars have been toiling at this "Biblical Criticism," and through their labor we have come to a new and nobler understanding of all the early history of the Hebrew people.

But too few among us are possessed of that new understanding. To most of us the Bible is still a book every word of which is literal fact. We try to swallow it whole, to believe it without understanding it. As a result, its history often seems but a monotonous and meaningless round of unbelievable miracles and incredible facts: a long, rambling chronicle of imaginative but suspicious wonders. There is no grand swing in it, no dramatic surge up, up, up toward the heights.

So the first chapters of the story of the Jews must be retold in the light of the new understanding. They must be shown to be what they truly are: the immortal epic of a people's confused, faltering, insatiable hunger for a nobler life in a happier world.

And the rest of the chapters must naturally be retold as a continuation of that epic. For the Jews did not cease hungering for the Kingdom of God on Earth when they closed the Bible era. They went on and on—as perhaps they still go on to-day.

That is the true wonder of their story. There has been no end to the march of the Jews. They have gone on and on, ever refusing to halt where the world halted, ever pressing on in their own stubborn, headstrong, singular way. Of course, they have faltered at times; for decades, for generations, they have stood still. At times they have even retreated. But never for long. The slightest lifting of the yoke laid on them by a slow-moving world and on they have plunged—on, on, in the strangest, the wildest, the most fantastic career ever essayed by a people.

It is the story of that career that I want to tell—that I have been trying to begin to tell all this night.

Perhaps I'm too tired now to begin, too worn out from long wondering how. . . . Dawn is stealing up behind the blackened chimneys in the east. The city is awaking. There is a feeble stir in the streets, a rattling of milk wagons and a rumbling of trucks. Workmen with lunch boxes under their arms, their hair frowsy, their faces still swollen with sleep, clump along over echoing pavements.

But in the east, over where the roof tops dully gleam in the morning light, there is a greater stir, I know. Old men with matted beards, and young men and boys, crawl out from under feather beds and shiveringly don their clothes. They touch their hands and faces with water from kitchen faucets, whisper a prayer, and then hurry out into the streets.

Where are they going? . . . But where *should* pious Jews go so early in the morning? . . . To the synagogues, of course!

So they go, hundreds of them, old and middle-aged and young. They go to their little synagogues hidden away in basements, there to pray as their fathers have prayed these two thousand years or more.

For there in the east, where now the roof tops are turning from black to pearl in the growing light of the dawn, lies the great ghetto of New York. More Jews are huddled there than ever were seen in old Jerusalem—more probably than were known in all the world when Solomon was King in Zion.

What are they doing there? How did they come? And why? . . .

It is almost four thousand years since they were born, and fully five thousand miles from their birth-place. What have they seen and thought, what have they lived through and learnt, in all that long trek through time and space?

But that is just the story I have been wanting to tell all along, the story I *will* tell—so soon as I can begin.

Only I am too tired now.

Perhaps a little later, after I have slept, I shall be able to begin. . . .

CHAPTER I

THE STORY OF CERTAIN HALF-SAVAGE SHEPHERD TRIBES WHO STRUGGLED OUT OF THE ARABIAN DESERT INTO THE FERTILE CRESCENT

Far to the east of us, pinched between Africa and Asia, lies a vast and barren region called the Arabian Desert. It is a cruel, forbidding place: an endless sheet of dry rock that by day is scorchingly hot, like a lead roof under the rays of the sun, and by night is piercingly cold. Here and there across the plain are reaches of hard-packed gravel, or of drifting sand that can be swept up blindingly by the winds. And only at long intervals are hidden thin springs of water that soak the soil and relieve the grayness with a touch of green.

Four thousand years ago—even as in our day—countless tribes of wild shepherds roved hungrily across that dry waste. They were constantly moving about, swarming with their bedraggled flocks of sheep and goats from one oasis to another as the springs dried up or the grass was nibbled away. They had no homes save their goatskin tents; they had no possessions save the stone weapons in their hands, the rags on their backs, and the tribal flocks and herds. The only law they knew was the word of the Patriarch, the Old Man of the Tribe. They had no knowledge of reading or writing, and probably they could not count above ten.

Such were the early Semites, from whose loins sprang the Jews.

Because they did not yet know the use of metals, but made their tools and weapons of stone, we speak of them as living in the Stone Age.

They were probably far unhappier than we are to-day, for their life was crowded with all sorts of fears. The whole world seemed to them to be peopled with terrible demons and spirits. In every tree and stone and tiny spring, in the thunder and lightning, in the wind and the night, those demons were thought to dwell; and the shepherds were greatly afraid of them. They used to utter magic incantations and go through all sorts of weird ceremonies in their efforts to win the favor of those spirits. They used to offer sacrifices to them, burning the firstborn of their flocks, and often even of their own children, so that those spirits might be pleased and give to the worshipers many more sheep and children.

2

These Semite shepherds were divided into many groups, and each of these groups consisted of several tribes or clans. Each tribe had its favorite spirit which—so the people believed—went with it and helped it fight the other tribes. But often these clans found it necessary to change favorites, for each demon was believed to have power only over a certain bit of desert. Therefore when a clan moved a long distance it usually threw over the old spirit, and took up a new one.

Idols of wood and stone were set up to represent

those spirits. And in time these idols came to be thought of as real gods.

There was constant warfare between the tribes, for there were exceedingly few springs of water in the desert, and many flocks to drink them dry. The tribes fought for the possession of those springs of water just as nowadays the nations fight for the possession of wells of oil or mines of coal. There was no law regulating the conduct of the clans, and always they were stealing sheep and wives and children from each other. They murdered or enslaved their defeated foes, they stole and cheated, they sweltered and froze to death, they hungered and went mad from thirst.

Their life was hard and unhappy because of the barrenness of the soil on which they lived.

3

Only far to the north of the great desert is there a moist and less ungenerous region. For want of a better name, modern historians have called it the Fertile Crescent, for it is shaped somewhat like a quarter-moon. Of course, that Crescent acted like a magnet upon the thirsting Semites in the wilderness. They were forever struggling to reach it, plunging out one after the other, scrambling desperately to get a foothold in the rich soft soil, falling back, trying again, falling back, trying still again—and finally beating their way in and remaining there. Like hot oil spluttering out of a frying pan, so were those famished and desperate tribes as they came charging out of the desert.

They began coming out many thousands of years

1.—On to the Fertile Crescent

ago, and by the time of the dawn of history certain of them had already grown very old in the rich Crescent lands. Indeed, when one little group of those tribes, the group which we have since come to call the Hebrews, belatedly attempted to invade that Crescent, they found it already overcrowded with inhabitants.

There were first of all the non-Semitic peoples who had drifted there from many directions, and had very early begun to cultivate the soil and develop some sort of civilization. Along the Nile there were the Egyptians with an amazingly high culture. Far to the north, in what we now call Syria, there were the Hittites. Along the garden lands of the Tigris and Euphrates rivers there were remnants of the Sumerians, a strange and at present little known people, who were among the first to invent a method of writing. And in and among these non-Semitic people were the hordes of early invaders from the desert: the Amorites, or Canaanites, or Phœnicians, or Babylonians, as they were called in different places.

4

It was not easy for the still half-barbaric Hebrews, with their clumsy stone weapons and feeble strength, to fight their way into those well-settled lands. Many times they tried, hurling themselves with all their might against the fortifications in their path. Their particular goal seems to have been that narrow strip of land we now call Palestine, and desperately they fought for its possession against the Canaanites who lived there. Several times the invaders, led by patriarchs like Abraham, Isaac, and Jacob, managed to break their way in; but they were not allowed to remain in peace. The wells which they dug were filled with stones and rubbish by their enemies; their sheep were stolen; and occasionally they themselves were massacred.

Then, to add to all these hardships, there seems to have come a great famine in the land. The wells became utterly dry and the flocks began to dwindle for lack of food and drink. Death stared those harassed Hebrews in the face. All about them were their foes, the Canaanites, swooping down on them in surprise attacks and carrying off what famished sheep and goats were left to them. There was no sense in remaining longer in the land, especially since the rumor had reached them that far off in Egypt there was drink aplenty, and also much grain stored away. It was a tremendous distance to the lands of the Nile, a journey for them of many weeks—though a train now can cover it in little more than half a day—but nevertheless many of the Hebrews turned to go there. They folded their tents, gathered together the remnants of their lean and sunken-eyed flocks, and began the long journey toward Egypt.

And with that journey the ancient Hebrew shepherds enter into the realm of history.

CHAPTER II

HOW THE HEBREWS LOST AND REGAINED THEIR FREEDOM, TOOK UNTO THEMSELVES A GOD, AND TRIED AGAIN TO SETTLE IN THE FERTILE CRESCENT

Just what happened when those Hebrew wanderers straggled into Egypt we can only vaguely guess. All the hundreds of Egyptian records thus far unearthed tell us nothing of the episode; and the account in the Bible is not altogether clear on the subject. No doubt the scholars now busily digging away in the pyramids and mounds of Egypt will soon have all sorts of new secrets to tell us, so that in a little while it may be possible to make this chapter in the story of the Jews far less brief and sketchy than it must be left to-day.

All we can say now with any certainty is that the Hebrew shepherds who wandered to Egypt in search of food did not have to penetrate far into the land. They stopped in a large tract of meadows called the Land of Goshen, in the eastern part of the Nile delta, and there they settled down. But then, after a lapse of years, a powerful king arose in Egypt, and marching down on the little settlement of aliens, he took them all into slavery. That king, or pharaoh as he was called, was probably Ramses II, who lived some thirty-two hundred years ago and was a little crazy with the desire to build huge temples and palaces and monuments to himself and his many gods.

To satisfy this frenzied desire he needed myriads of slaves, for there were huge tracts to clear and vast foundations to dig, and all sorts of quarrying and hoisting and dragging to be done. Even to-day, when we have steam-shovels and pile-drivers and innumerable other labor-saving devices, we are constantly in need of unskilled laborers in very large numbers. One can easily see how much greater the need must have been in days when hardly the simplest of machinery had yet been invented.

2

So the wild Hebrews, men who all along had lived the free and foot-loose life of desert nomads, suddenly discovered themselves the most abject of slaves. All their days they had to cringe beneath the lash of the taskmasters while they sweated at making bricks or quarrying stone. For those Hebrews it was the first taste of a misery which their descendants were to experience many times over, and the bitter memory it left in their minds was never allowed to fade away.

The oppression lasted many years, for Ramses II reigned a long time. But soon after his death the power of Egypt began to crumble. That foolish pharoah had exhausted his empire with his extravagance, and from all sides the enemies began to sweep down on the prostrate land. Hordes of barbaric invaders came charging in from Libya, and bands of ravenous pirates sailed down from the islands of the Mediterranean Sea. Desolation and distress covered the face of all Egypt. To the simple-minded Hebrews it seemed as though an angry and avenging god were visiting fell plagues on the land for its sins.

And in the confusion, while the Egyptians were straining with all their might to fight off the savage invaders, the Hebrew slaves got away.

Their leader in the rebellion and escape was a young Hebrew named Moses. According to the Bible story, Moses had been adopted as a child by an Egyptian princess, and brought up in the royal court. He had never been a slave, and therefore was able to appreciate the more clearly how bitter was the plight of his brethren. But instead of cutting himself off completely from them and enjoying his own good fortune, he seems as a young man to have taken their part against their taskmasters, with the result that finally he had to flee from the land. He wandered about in the wilderness with a tribe of Kenites—a people related to the Hebrews—and tasting among them the joys of free nomad life, he felt the call to go back and deliver his brethren.

Without a leader like Moses it is doubtful whether the Hebrews, grown timid and cowardly under the lash of the Egyptians, would ever have been able to free themselves. The worst evil of continued oppression is not so much that it cripples the bodies of the victims, as that it crushes their souls. It robs them of courage and self-reliance. Even after Moses succeeded in getting his brethren to flee from Egypt, it was all he could do to keep them from running back again. In the desert they were faced with hardships they had not known in Goshen—lack of food and water, for instance—and many of them were ready to barter every bit of their new freedom for the greasy "fleshpots of Egypt."

3

Compared with enormous revolutions like that in France in the eighteenth century, or the one in Russia in recent years, the uprising of those few Hebrew slaves three thousand years ago in Egypt appears a quite trivial incident. Yet, because of the hold the story of that uprising took on the minds of succeeding generations, the event itself looms up as one of the most important in all history. Again and again in these three thousand years, rebels against oppression and tyranny have turned for courage to that old story of the Exodus from Egypt.

4

Moses undertook no easy task when he attempted to lead those slaves to freedom. First of all he had to get them safely out of Egypt, and that meant avoiding the caravan routes—for they were infested with pirates, or were guarded by Egyptian garrisons. Then he had to give them a religion, so that they might have the courage to withstand the hardships of the desert. In Egypt the Hebrews had forgotten the god they had worshiped when they were shepherds. They had no doubt accepted the gods of the Egyptians in his place. But now, out in the wild places once more, they believed those Egyptian gods were not present, and they were therefore left without any faith.

Moses quickly felt his people's need, and as soon as he could he led them to a certain mountain called Sinai or Horeb, which was believed by his Kenite friends to be the dwelling-place of their god Yahveh.* At that holy mountain the Hebrews solemnly swore to accept Yahveh as their one and only god, and it was believed that in return Yahveh would be their special protector. The people's duties in this covenant were expressed in certain commands which were easily remembered because they were ten in number, and could be ticked off on one's ten fingers. A wooden shrine called the Ark was made to symbolize the shielding protection of Yahveh, and wherever the Hebrews wandered, there went also that Ark. For, being still a primitive folk, they could firmly believe that the presence of the Ark brought them safety!

5

But even after this acceptance of the protection of Yahveh, the runaway slaves still remained cowed and frightened. It had been Moses' plan to go directly from the Holy Mountain up to Canaan in the Fertile Crescent. But when his followers heard of the prowess and might of the inhabitants of that region, they refused to attempt to invade it. Instead they wandered about in the desert lands just

* Through the mistake of an ignorant translator of the Bible, we have come to speak of this god as Jehovah, but his real name was Yahveh, which may have meant "The Creator," or perhaps "The Thunderer."

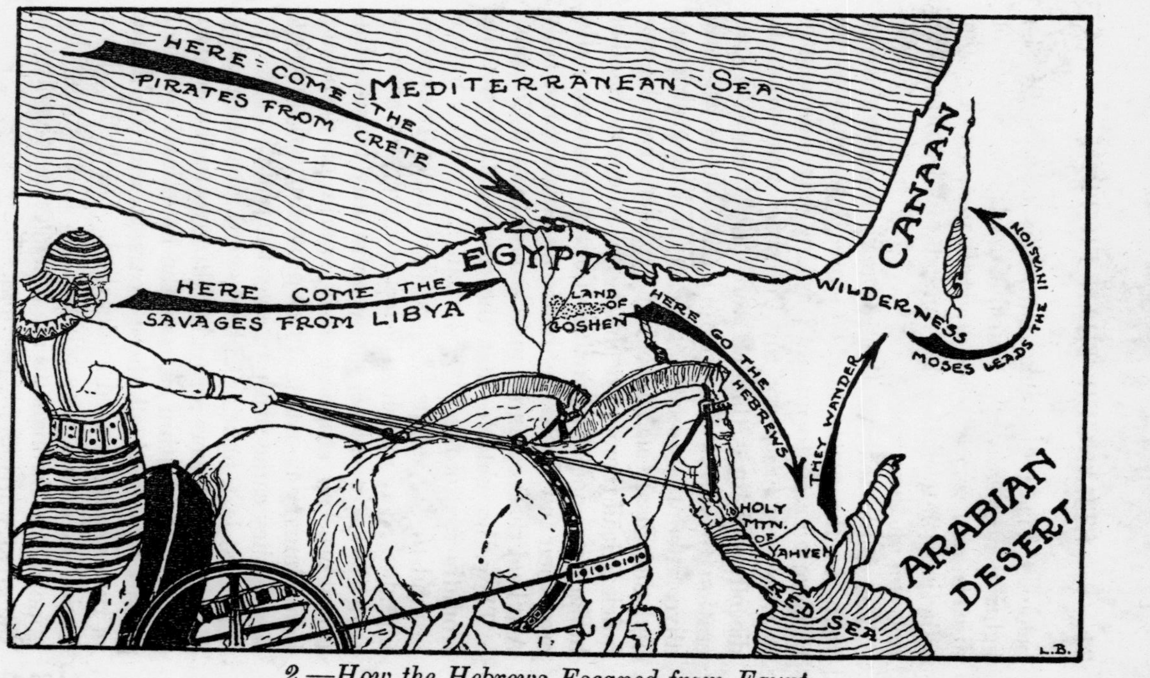

2.—*How the Hebrews Escaped from Egypt*

below Canaan, tending their flocks and herds, fighting hostile tribes, starving at times, dying of disease and snake bites and all manner of other afflictions, but not daring to strike out toward the rich soil on the north.

The Bible tells us the Hebrews wandered forty years in the waste lands before they plucked up courage enough to invade the Crescent. Evidently it was first necessary for the slave generation to die off, and for a tougher and more desperate generation to arise. We are told that Moses was still alive when that second generation had grown up, and though already an old and broken man, he was quick to lead them in the invasion. The little band of hungry wanderers packed up their belongings, gathered their few flocks and herds, and letting the Holy Ark lead their columns, marched off toward Canaan.

They thought to enter the coveted little domain from the east of the River Jordan, and so they moved around to the steppe-land on that side. They were not allowed to march in peace, however, for at every turn they were attacked by unfriendly tribes. But there was no stopping that swarm of desperate, home-hungry nomads. They proved utterly irresistible as they came sweeping over the plain.

And at last, fighting almost every inch of the way, Yahveh's followers struggled through to the Jordan.

But there, within sight of the little land to which Moses had tried all those years to lead his horde of runaways, the aged leader died. He died and was buried no one knows where; but his memory has gone down throughout all the ages as the first of the great warriors for freedom.

CHAPTER III

THE BRAWLING, ILL-ORGANIZED STRUGGLE OF THE HEBREWS TO MAKE CANAAN COMPLETELY THEIR OWN

The invasion and conquest of Canaan was a long, difficult, and bloody affair. The Hebrews were poorly armed, for they still used flint knives and stone hatchets; and they were utterly untrained in organized warfare. The odds were heavily against them, for the Canaanites used chariots and fought with metal weapons and were always able to take refuge in one or other of their many fortresses. Only the ferocity and desperation of the invaders made it possible for them to conquer at all. They had come to hate with all their being the arid desert and the wanderer's life. They craved a bit of this land that—to use their own metaphor—"flowed with milk and honey"; and they were ready to go to any extremes to satisfy that craving.

People nowadays are greatly shocked when they read the Biblical account of the conquest of Canaan. When those ancient Hebrews conquered a city they followed the custom of the time and "devoted" it to their god: that is, they stole all the gold and silver, butchered all the cattle and human beings, and then burnt the whole place to the ground. They plundered and pillaged right and left, razed fortresses, and decimated whole tribes. They were like ravenous beasts out of the wilderness! But we need hardly urge in their defense that they were still half-savages. We need only remember that invading armies even in our own time behave not one whit less bestially. . . .

2

The invasion was not accomplished by all the tribes united in one definite campaign. They fought their way into the land separately, and then settled down in different localities. For instance, the tribe called Judah and that called Simeon went to the southern part of Canaan. With them went also the Kenites, among whom Moses had lived as a young man. The tribe of Ephraim and half the tribe of Manasseh settled down in the center of the land; and the other tribes wandered off to the north and almost lost themselves among the Canaanites there.

It was a wildly daring and dangerous undertaking—that invasion of Canaan by the Hebrews. Once they got into the land they found themselves surrounded by enemies on every side. And worse still, they were cut off from each other by lines of Canaanite fortresses. Clearly they had to kill or be killed. They had to crowd out and murder their foes, or else be crowded out and murdered themselves.

3

Then there was another difficulty: the Hebrews, who were wanderers and shepherds by long training, suddenly had to settle down and become farmers.

They had to give up their life in open tents and take instead to huddled, ill-smelling stone villages inclosed by thick high walls. They had to take up the life of the very people against whom they were fighting.

Of course, there was grave danger that in taking up the life of the enemy, the Hebrews might also take up his gods and morals. And many of the Hebrews succumbed to that danger. Yahveh belonged to the desert, and therefore many of the Hebrews feared his power did not extend to this fertile land they had entered. They imagined they had to worship the gods of this new country, the Canaanite gods, the Baalim as they were called. Every hill and field and spring had its little Baal to be fed with human or animal sacrifices, and honored at festivals which often were little more than drunken debauches. If this was not done it was imagined that the field would not yield a crop, or the spring would dry up. The sun, moon, and stars had to be worshiped because they were believed to control the weather, and the household idols—which were a little like the totem-poles of the American Indians—had to be respected because they were supposed to localize the spirits of dead ancestors.

The natives believed that every accident or misfortune was a sign that some little local god or other had been slighted; and the Hebrews were not long in accepting that belief. They made very poor farmers and their crops often failed; but instead of laying the blame for the failure on their ignorance of husbandry, they laid it on their neglect of the native idols. So in many sections we find the conquerors, although still worshiping Yahveh, "played safe" by sacrificing also to a dozen other gods.

In districts where that practice of "playing safe" was most common, it was almost impossible to tell who were the conquerors and who the conquered. The mingling of gods was often followed by the mingling of families, and in certain regions the Hebrews and their enemies became practically one people. Thus the half of the tribe of Manasseh that had been left on the east side of the Jordan was almost completely absorbed by the Arameans there, and the tribe of Reuben almost lost itself among the Moabites. Asher took to the sea and became very largely Phœnician.

After all, there was no great difference in blood between the Hebrews and these other peoples. They were all Semites who at one time or another in the past had been nomads in the great Arabian Desert. They all belonged to the same cultural stock, and spoke more or less the same language.

4

And yet, for reasons we cannot quite understand now, those Hebrews did not lose themselves entirely in their Canaanite surroundings. Perhaps it was because they had not yet been in the land long enough to be completely assimilated; or perhaps there was something in the mental make-up of those invaders, memories of their hard past in Egypt and of their covenant with Yahveh at the Holy Mountain in the wilderness, that rendered them incapable of complete assimilation.

Whatever the reason, the fact remains that they

persisted as a separate people. Divided as they were into many little tribes, each with its own chieftain—or judge, as he was called—and surrounded by overwhelming hosts of the enemy, they still preserved their identity.

Their judges were not drawn from any one particular class, for there were no class distinctions among the Hebrews at that time. There were neither learned nor ignorant among them, for none at all could read or write. There were no rich or poor, for there was practically no private property. One man was as good as another, and flocks, herds, and lands belonged to all the members of the tribe together.

Their social life was completely democratic. In time of danger, when the enemy pressed down on them, they usually picked the most daring fighter in the tribe to be their leader in battle. And when the battle was over, this leader often continued as head of the tribe for a time. But there was nothing permanent about the office—which was just as well, considering the type of man who sometimes became leader. For instance, Jepthah who led the Gileadites in a successful sortie against the Ammonites, was a wild half-breed outlaw before his election. Samson, of the tribe of Dan, was little more than a burly, untamed strong-man with enormous muscles but pygmy sense. And no doubt other of the judges during this period were men of like inferior quality.

5

The years passed. One generation died and another arose. But still no peace came to the Hebrews.

The people whom they had dispossessed, the Canaanites and Moabites and Ammonites, kept returning year after year, raiding, pillaging, and burning the little settlements. And only the lack of union among those marauders saved the disunited Hebrews from utter destruction.

But then came the Philistines.

The Philistines were not a Semitic people. They had not come up from the desert of Arabia, but down in ships from the islands of the Mediterranean. They had been among those pirate bands that had raided the coast of Egypt when the Hebrews escaped from slavery, and now they were settled along the shore of southern Canaan. Gradually they had begun to creep inland, beating down the Canaanite farmers in their path, until their talons were fastened on the foothills right below the Hebrew settlements.

It was inevitable of course that they and the Hebrews should meet and clash. Both were trying to conquer the land from opposite directions at the same time. There had been skirmishes between them in the days of Samson, but the Hebrews had not then realized the danger of this new enemy. They had trusted to the tribes nearest the Philistines to fight them off unaided.

When the Philistines massed their troops, therefore, and made their first real attack, it brought the Hebrews very rudely to their senses. They went down to a crushing defeat, and then ran helter-skelter to get the Holy Ark of Yahveh which they had left behind them in one of their new cities. Thinking the Ark would lead them to certain vic-

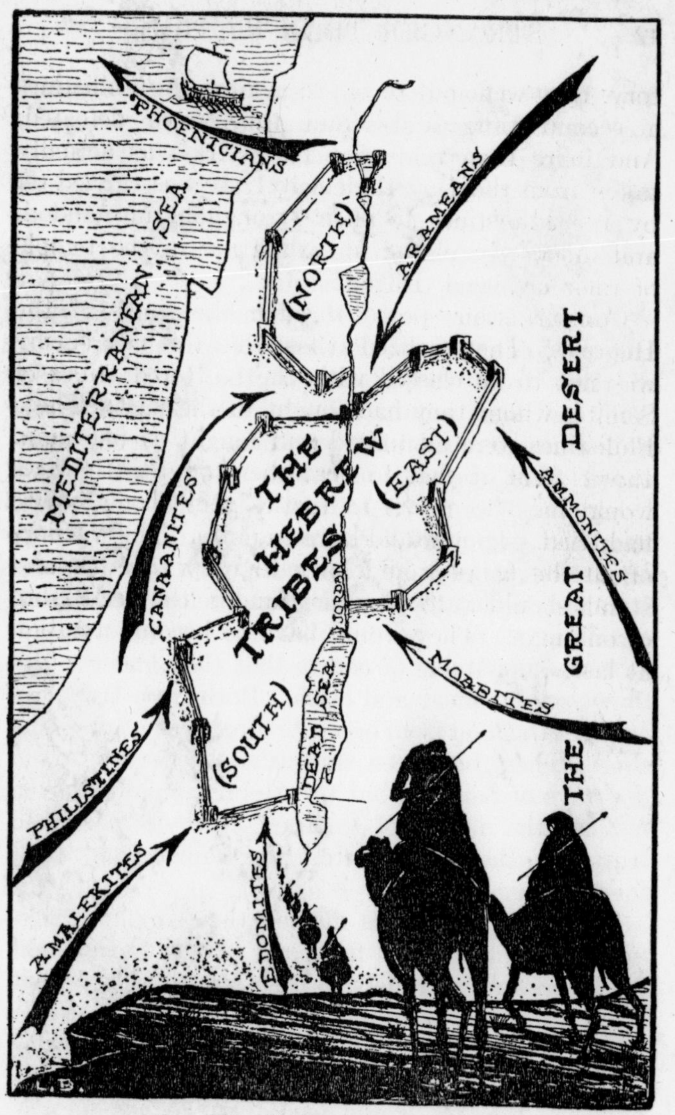

3.—*The Struggle for a Home*

tory, they went out to battle against the Philistines a second time—and again they were defeated. And more than that—the Holy Ark was actually taken from them by the enemy! It was carried off by the Philistines to their stronghold in Ashdod, and mockingly placed on exhibition in the temple of their own god, Dagon!

Consternation spread through the ranks of the Hebrews. They realized at last that this new enemy was not to be classed with the scattered tribes of Semites whom they had fought in the past. These Philistines were all united and fought as one man. It was evident that to beat them off the Hebrews would have to resort to tactics they never before had tried. They would have to unite. The warriors of all the tribes would have to rally together and stand shoulder to shoulder under the leadership of one man. They would have to become a nation at last. . . .

CHAPTER IV

CONTINUED OPPOSITION FORCES THE HEBREW TRIBES TO UNITE AT LAST UNDER A SINGLE KING

The Philistines to the west were pressing on into the land, creeping over the Hebrew fields and fortresses like the incoming tide over the rocks on a beach. And to add to the distress, an old foe, the Ammonite people, began to sweep in upon them from the desert to the east. The little Hebrew people seemed about to be drowned in the sea of its enemies.

Just in time, however, there arose a leader quick and courageous enough to avert the doom. He was a farmer named Saul, a fearless, quick-tempered man who belonged to one of the northern tribes. When the news reached him that the Ammonites had captured a Hebrew stronghold on the east side of the Jordan, he gathered the warriors of all the tribes, and with a threat of cruel vengeance if they refused to follow, went forth to repel the invader.

All night he marched eastward, and when dawn came and the astounded Ammonites saw the united Hebrew army pouring out of the dark to attack them, they broke and fled in panic. Taken thus completely unawares, the Ammonites could not but go down to utter defeat.

Saul was the hero of the hour. With one accord

the elders turned to him as their leader. And at a holy place called Gilgal, high up in the hills of central Canaan, amid sacrifices to Yahveh, Saul was solemnly anointed King of the Hebrews.

2

Then began a new chapter in the struggle with the Philistines. Saul gathered his forces and prepared for attack. At first he was repulsed, and half his followers deserted him in terror; but in a little while he regained the offensive. Full at the enemy he hurled his men, slashing right and left—and then it was the Philistines who turned and fled. Back they fled westward, over hill and down dale, until at last they reached their own lands by the sea.

Thus was the Philistine menace overcome.

But still there was no peace. The Ammonites and Moabites and Amalekites were still there on the borders of Canaan, ready like hungry wolves to pounce down on any unprotected village. And the Philistines, for all that they had been so thoroughly beaten, continued to raid and plunder along the frontier.

King Saul's only palace was a tent; his scepter was a sword; his courtiers were all hard-fighting soldiers. His whole reign was one unending war against his enemies.

3

Unfortunately, Saul was not so good a statesman as he was a warrior, or he might have been rewarded with greater success. He could not deal well with men. He had always had a violent temper, and as the years passed he began to suffer more and more from queer spells of moodiness. To make matters worse, he assumed high and haughty airs. The result was that in the end he broke with one of his most powerful supporters, an old prophet and priest named Samuel.

In those days there were to be found in all the Hebrew tribes, bands of religious zealots who went up and down the country shouting and singing excitedly about the glories of their god, Yahveh. (Nowadays the "Holy Rollers" and evangelists in our country carry on in very much the same way.) Those zealots were called in Hebrew *neviim*, which came to be translated "prophets," although in the beginning it may have meant no more than "shouters." Most good Hebrew farmers probably thought those "shouters" a little crazy, but nevertheless they stood in great awe of them. The neviim were supposed to possess all sorts of magic powers, and Samuel had great influence in the land because he was recognized as the chief of them. So it was a sorry day for Saul when he lost the old priest's friendship.

Nor was Samuel the only person whom the king antagonized. A certain gifted young musician named David had once been brought to cheer the king out of one of his frightful spells of melancholy. The minstrel succeeded, and so well that Saul asked him to remain on in the camp. And later, when he discovered the lad was as brave a soldier as he was a talented musician, Saul made him the royal armor-bearer.

But as the months passed, and this David's prowess as a soldier came to be talked of among the people, Saul grew almost insanely jealous. Several times in his rage he even attempted to take the young man's life.

So David had to flee from the court.

He fled to his own home in the south, in the land of Judah, and there he gathered his clansmen, and set up in a cave as a robber chieftain. Saul and his army pursued him, and after a series of flights from one place to another, David was compelled to take refuge finally with the Philistines. Of course, the Philistines, still the bitter enemies of Saul, received the outlaw with open arms. They were determined to wreak their vengeance on the man who once had so utterly defeated them, and now they thought the chance was theirs. By now Saul's insane temper had become very like a disease, and it had robbed him of his bravest warriors. Many of his old chieftains had deserted him, and those fanatical Yahveh worshipers, the neviim, refused any longer to rally the people to his support.

4

All hope and courage seeped out of the king's heart as he learned the Philistines were making ready for a new attack. Even though he was securely intrenched up on Mount Gilboa, Saul felt himself beaten before the enemy came in sight. And his troops, on seeing his despondency, also lost all heart. Fiercely the Philistines attacked, and the Hebrews crumbled under the blow. Desperately Saul tried to hold his lines—but in vain. The

Hebrews flinched under the hail of arrows from the Philistine archers. Their ranks wavered, broke; and pellmell they fled before the enemy.

The rout was complete. The three sons of Saul died fighting like lions, and the father, badly wounded, took his own life to escape capture. The next day the patrols of the Philistines, in their work of stripping the bodies of the slain, came across the dead king. They cut off his head and fastened the corpse to the walls of the city of Bethshean. And there it remained until certain Hebrews from the east side of the Jordan, remembering how years earlier Saul had delivered them from the Ammonite invaders, went at the risk of their lives and rescued the mutilated corpse. They brought it back to their own village, and there reverently they buried it under the village tree.

So ended the life of Saul, the first king of the Hebrews. He had been a brave soldier and a loyal follower of Yahveh—but unfortunately he had also been just a bit unbalanced.

CHAPTER V

THE SECOND KING, DAVID, LEADS THE TRIBES TO VICTORY, AND WINS FOR THEM AN EMPIRE

As soon as the news was brought to the outlaw, David, that Saul was dead, he took his men and marched quickly up into Judah to make himself the new king. But only the southern tribes would take part in his coronation. The northern tribes had all along felt themselves different from those in the south, and they now set up a king of their own, a son of Saul named Ishbaal.*

The Philistines must have been highly satisfied with this arrangement, for they knew that so long as the Hebrews were divided, they were helpless prey. But David knew that too, and immediately he set himself the task of winning over the northern tribes to his standard. Full eight years passed before that task was accomplished, eight years of spying and bribing, of flattery and bloodshed. But finally David attained his end. Ishbaal was assassinated by two of his captains, and young David—he was still only thirty years of age—was for the second time crowned king. And not two now, but all twelve of the Hebrew tribes took part in the coronation.

No sooner was David re-crowned, however, than

* See how popular the Canaanite god, Baal, had become among the Hebrews. Even the king's son was named after him!

the Philistines became troublesome again. They had had no fear of the young man so long as he was an outlawed freebooter, or the leader of a few roving clans; but now that he was king of all Israel, they thought it well to snuff him out immediately. So down marched a great army on him, and he was forced to beat a retreat. But recklessly they pushed on after him, and then of a sudden they discovered themselves trapped. David had lured them into a most unfavorable strategic position, and then turned and attacked. Of a sudden he came crashing back at them, and in utter bewilderment they were forced to recoil. A second time his little army struck them a smashing blow, routing them completely. And then in terrible confusion the Philistines fled back to their own lands.

2

David was too wise to repeat their mistake and pursue his enemies. Instead he let them escape, and addressed himself to making his own throne completely safe. He realized that his first need was a capital, but no city already in his possession could possibly fill the need. Favoring one city would certainly have aroused the jealousy of all the rest; establishing his throne within the land of one tribe would immediately have brought him into disfavor with all the others. There was anything but a feeling of complete union among the Hebrew clans, and the antagonism—especially between the north and south—seemed ready to break out into open dissension on the least provocation.

Early in the history of the United States a capital

had to be chosen, and it was found necessary, in order to avoid all jealousies, to build an entirely new city: Washington. That was a recurrence in a measure of David's experience, except that the Hebrew king did not build a city—he and his people were altogether too poor for that—but captured one.

In the midst of the kingdom lay a certain little fortress which from the very beginning of the invasion of Canaan had withstood all the attacks of the Hebrews. It was called Jerusalem, which may have meant "City of Peace," or more probably "City of Shalim," a Canaanite god. It was built high up on a spur, and for that reason was almost unconquerable by ordinary methods of attack.

Only by climbing with his men up into the very heart of the city through the huge stone water-tunnel, was David able to get at its inhabitants and force them to surrender. And this city, Jerusalem, he made his capital.

3

With that matter attended to, David was now free to turn on the ring of foes surrounding his people. First he attacked the Philistines, marching right through their lands and taking Gath, their chief city. The Holy Ark of Yahveh which had been in Philistine hands so many years, was at last retaken and brought in triumph to the capital, Jerusalem. And Yahveh was thus recognized officially and formally as the god of the Hebrew Kingdom.

The Philistines quite thoroughly shown their place, David next turned on the Moabites and

4.—The Empire of the Robber Chieftain

trampled them into harmlessness. (We are told he slaughtered two out of every three men in all the Moabite army!) Next the Ammonites were assailed, and after they were decisively beaten in battle, their soldiers were all condemned to captivity. Then the Arameans, and a little later the Edomites, and finally the Amalekites were all thoroughly subdued. Only the Phœnicians on the north were spared, for they had always been too busy as seafaring traders on the Mediterranean ever to trouble the Hebrews.

4

David now felt in a position to devote himself to internal affairs. First he undertook the task of beautifying his capital, for his victorious wars had filled his storehouses to overflowing with all manner of precious booty. He had gold and silver and brass and precious wood aplenty; also he had many captives to slave in his labor-gangs as once his own forefathers had slaved in the labor-gangs of the Egyptians. All he lacked was a knowledge of what and how to build. He and his people had always been poor and struggling. Until very recently they had lived in tents, and had eaten and slept and worshiped like barbarians.

But now David wanted to bring a measure of beauty and civilization into the life of his people. He wanted to erect a great palace and a great temple, and adorn them with all the treasures whereof he was master. He wanted to show the world of his time—and also his own followers—that he was no longer a robber-chieftain but a rich and mighty monarch.

It was to the Phœnicians, of course, that he had to turn for help. They were men of the world, great travelers who were well acquainted with the monuments and palaces of distant emperors and princes. They claimed to know all about architecture and decoration, and were glad to sell their services to this newly-rich neighbor of theirs.

5

When David took hold of Jerusalem, it must have been much like any other Canaanite town. From end to end its length was probably that of ten of our city blocks, and surrounding it was a tremendously high wall of stone. Between two massive towers projecting from this wall was a narrow entrance closed by a wooden portcullis. This entrance was paved with uneven cobblestones, and spread like a fan into a maze of crooked little lanes running all through the town. The houses were flat-roofed, one-story huts of stone plastered with mud; and there was no furniture inside them. The people ate and slept on the ground, and the animals ate and slept there with them. Horrid smells filled every corner of the town, for of course there were no sewers and no street-cleaning department. Nasty insects buzzed around everywhere, for refuse rotted in front of every house. Savage, half-starved dogs prowled about, and here and there dirty little children, naked save for the good-luck charms hung around their necks, with bellies swollen from drinking foul water, and faces covered with sores and scars, played amid the filth or ran errands.

Such was the Jerusalem that became the capital

of David's empire. There he established his harem of twenty or thirty wives — and right proud he must have been of it, for in those days the might of a monarch was largely judged by the size of his harem— and there he served as high priest and chief justice and king. There, too, his appetite grew and he began to usurp more and more privileges and perquisites. He began to forget that he was king only because his people had elected him to that office. He began to make himself almost a tyrant, like the kings of all the other peoples of the Orient. Once he even stole away the wife of one of his soldiers, and afterwards had the man killed to get him out of his sight. His new-found glory went to his head, and he grew lax in performing his duties as ruler.

6

The people in their turn grew restive and rebellious. Absalom, one of David's own sons, started a civil war that almost swept the old man from his throne. The whole country seethed with plots and conspiracies and rumors of revolution. Within the capital there was constant whispering and spying, for as the king aged, each of his many sons began scheming to make himself the successor. The unity among the tribes which David had managed with such great effort to bring about, began rapidly to break down again. And on all the borders the defeated and subject foes watched with vengeful eyes for their chance to regain their freedom.

And just then, when the new and hastily built empire seemed about to topple down and be destroyed forever, David, its builder died.

A romantic figure is this second king of Israel, a man who could think quickly, fight courageously, and love intensely. If he did not achieve more with his tremendous talents, it was probably because to his dying day he still retained the mind of—a robber-chieftain.

CHAPTER VI

THE THIRD KING, SOLOMON, LOSES THE EMPIRE THROUGH HIS EXTRAVAGANCE, AND BRINGS RUIN TO HIS PEOPLE

There had really been two different Davids on the throne of Israel: first the attractive young chieftain struggling to win peace and security for his people, and later the slack old king desirous of nothing so much as pleasure and power for himself. Had his successor chosen to follow the first David, much of the sad history I am about to relate might never have occurred. As it was, however, the successor chose rather to emulate the second David, and ill-fortune had to follow.

The successor was David's favorite son, Solomon, and to this day he is usually spoken of as a person of surpassing wisdom. Judged by his life and work, however, the real Solomon was rather a person of unrestrained cruelty, thoughtlessness, and self-indulgence. There is no gainsaying that he was clever; he could coin smart proverbs and solve riddles. Nevertheless he was far from wise, for his rule in Israel brought little to his people save idolatry, corruption, misery, and debt.

The whole trouble, of course, was that Solomon desired only to imitate the extravagant, loose-living Oriental monarchs around him. His dream was to make his reign magnificent and splendid in that loud, garish, and despotic fashion toward which his father had leaned in his latter days. But David had been held back from going to extremes by his fear of the neviim, or perhaps by an innate simplicity. Try all he might, the robber-chieftain's imitation of a grand Oriental emperor could not be more than a rather sorry and feeble failure. It took a man born to the purple to show how far such imitation could be carried.

2

One of the first things the young king decided on having was a grand palace; and very soon tens of thousands of slaves were at work, felling trees far north in Lebanon, and quarrying limestone near Jerusalem. Phœnicians were called in to serve as architects, and to pay for their hire Solomon had to provide their king annually with tremendous quantities of grain and other food-stuffs. Throughout the land there was a great bustle and turmoil and confusion; in the fields, the forests, down in the quarries, and up on the highroads, there was great groaning because of the travail. Everywhere slaves were writhing beneath the lash of Solomon's taskmasters, and freemen were muttering because of the demands of Solomon's taxgatherers. But still the work went on.

The subject peoples on the borders, seizing their long-awaited chance, openly rebelled. The Edomites broke away from the Hebrew empire and proclaimed their independence; so did the Moabites and the Arameans. And Solomon, who was anything but a warrior, let them go. He realized their revolt meant a great loss in revenue to him, but rather than attempt to recapture them, he preferred to crush his own people more severely. First he forced all the Canaanites still living in Palestine into slavery; later he compelled even the Hebrew freemen to become his slaves for one month out of every three. And from every field that was harvested and every flock that was sheared, a rich portion was taxed away to fill the coffers of the ambitious king.

3

At last, after many years, the palace was completed. It stood on a hill hard-by the old fortress of Jerusalem, and no doubt it appeared a thing of almost incredible magnificence to the simple Hebrews. Of course, compared with the tremendous palaces of the emperors of Egypt and Babylon and India, this one of Solomon's was a rather tiny and tawdry affair. It had been designed by men who were not artists but merely mechanics trying vainly to imitate artists; and all the realms of the monarch who built it, could have been tucked away in the narrowest corner of a really full-sized empire. But to those children of a primitive desert-folk that had lived in goatskin tents throughout its history, the palace on Mount Moriah must have seemed the most wondrous thing ever built by men.

The palace consisted of several buildings: an armory, an assembly hall, a throne room or court of justice, and a harem large enough to house the king's many hundreds of wives. There was also a temple, a small building only one hundred feet long by about thirty feet wide, in which the Ark of Yahveh was housed. It is hardly possible that this temple meant as much to Solomon as did the palace, for he spent only half as much time building it. Perhaps he looked on it more as a royal chapel than anything else.

But as it happened, that temple, with the priests it attracted, proved in after years to be the salvation of Solomon's dynasty; and during many centuries the memory of it did more to perpetuate Israel on earth than perhaps any other earthly thing. Undoubtedly that little temple, smaller by far than any one of a hundred city synagogues in America to-day, smaller even than many village churches scattered in every corner of our world—that little temple has proved infinitely the most significant building ever erected by the hands of man.

4

Solomon lavished his people's money on other things also: roads for his chariots and horses, store-depots, and fortresses. Once when he managed to win the daughter of the mighty pharoah of Egypt for one of his wives—she was a great "catch" for Solomon!—he built her a special villa on the highest spot in the palace grounds. His expenses mounted at a mad rate, and his people were ground down until not another penny could be got out of them. So the king took to "trading," which in those days really meant piracy, and sent a fleet of ships to far distant parts of his world in search of gold and silver.

Even then the income of the spendthrift king could not keep pace with his outlay, and he had to resort at last to borrowing. Hiram, the rich king of the Phœnician city of Tyre, after lending him millions and millions, finally grew frightened and suddenly demanded his money back. Solomon, of course, was completely out of cash, and all he could do was to offer Hiram twenty of his cities. Hiram accepted, but when later he came to look at those cities, he found he had been cheated. They were not worth nearly the amount of money he had advanced to Solomon. But Hiram had in his day himself done a tidy bit of cheating, and he did not dare to make much of a fuss.

5

And so, by tyranny and oppression, by piracy and fraud, Solomon managed to carry out his ambitious schemes. Perhaps he thought he was succeeding admirably in winning the respect of the great nations roundabout. But a more ruinous success it would have been difficult to imagine. The many foreign princesses he took into his harem brought with them their strange gods and priests. Yahveh was no longer the sole god of Israel; even his own temple on Mount Moriah he had to share with the foreign idols. And the religious practices most in favor throughout the land were low and lewd and unclean. Poverty and distress stalked everywhere among the people, and only dread of the harshness of that petty tyrant on the throne kept thousands of embittered Hebrews from leaping to arms. The neviim went up and down the land seeking to stir the people to rebellion, but only once was there an uprising, and Solomon crushed that in an instant.

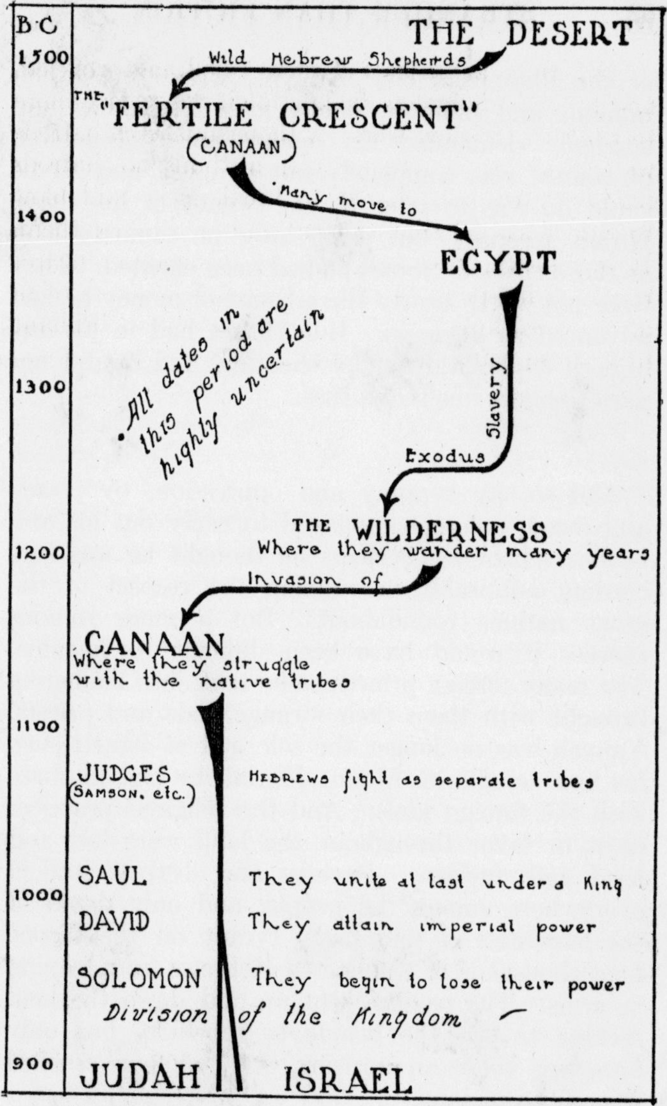

Chart A. The Adventures of the Jews. Part I

And thus in peace Solomon ruled and reveled, and in peace Solomon died. But it was peace more terrible by far than war. A thousand fierce hatreds were pent up in the people, a thousand hatreds ready at the first chance to break loose and blow to fragments all that so long had smothered them. It was peace, yes—but only the peace ever nearer the breaking-point of war. And such was the reign of the third king in Israel, the reign of that brilliant fool whose name was Solomon.

CHAPTER VII

CIVIL WAR RENDS THE NATION INTO TWO KINGDOMS, BOTH OF WHICH ARE SWALLOWED UP BY THE NEIGHBORING EMPIRES

Revolution followed almost immediately. The northern tribes sent to ask the new king what policy he intended to pursue, and when the silly youth boasted that he would rule with even greater despotism than his father, the tribesmen murdered his overseer and declared their independence. They cut themselves loose from the south and took for their king the heroic man who had led that one attempt at revolution during Solomon's reign.

And from then on for many years there were two kings and two kingdoms in Palestine. There was Israel on the north, and Judah on the south; and rare indeed were the periods when they were not at each other's throats.

The division was not an even one, for the territory of Israel was three times as large as that of Judah. More than that, it contained many rich valleys and highroads, while the southern kingdom was rocky, dry, and cut off from everything save the raids of the desert savages. But the division, uneven as it may have been, was largely a natural one. The people of Israel inhabited a region so different from that of the people of Judah that their whole thought and life were different. The northerners were farmers or traders, and contact with alien peoples and customs had influenced them enormously. The southerners, on the other hand, were shepherds, and in many respects were still very like their ancestors who had roamed about in the desert. Their worship of Yahveh had changed less and been less corrupted than the worship in the north; and their respect for those queer neviim was greater.

2

But different as were the two kingdoms, their histories for over two hundred years were very similar. Like all the other little nations of the East, they spent much of their time anointing and assassinating their kings. Nadab, the second king of Israel, reigned one year and was murdered by his successor, Baasha; Baasha's successor reigned one year and was murdered by Zimri; Zimri reigned seven days and was driven to suicide by Omri. . . . And so it went on. Queen Athaliah of Judah seized the throne and murdered her own grandchildren in order to make her throne firm. But she in turn was soon murdered—as was her successor, Joash, and his successor, Amaziah. . . . Periods of peace and prosperity did occur—but they were rare and never lasted long. When the two kingdoms were not fighting their common enemies, they were insanely fighting each other.

And thus, quarreling, fighting, growing rich and corrupt, or poor and desolate, intriguing with one enemy to attack another and usually falling prey to both, the two little Hebrew kingdoms went down to their doom. Even had they been united they might not have been able to withstand the enemies roundabout; but divided as they were, they had not even a trace of a chance.

3

Palestine was the victim of almost incessant invasion, because it was a frail bridge between two continents, Asia and Africa. It was a tiny land, and so far as natural resources went, hardly worth conquering at all. But strategically, it was of the very highest importance. Every great empire builder and every ambitious trading king, had to thunder across it on his way east or west. And every great empire builder, and every ambitious trading king, *did* thunder across it at one time or another.

Living there in peace was as impossible as picnicking in peace in the middle of a crowded highway.

4

Egypt was the first to take advantage of the civil war in the little land, and soon after the division both North and South had to agree to recognize the overlordship of the Egyptian empire. Then came the Aramean suzerainty. Next, Assyria, the ancient empire at the other end of the Fertile Crescent, began to grow restive after its sleep of a century. Slowly it began to stretch and feel its strength, reaching out again and again to make a half-hearted clutch at Palestine. And finally, after a hundred and fifty years of such clumsy attempts, she came hurtling down on the land in earnest.

5. The Bridge Between the Empires

5

Israel was the first to go under. The king of Assyria, tired of the constant rebelliousness of the Hebrews, marched across its boundaries and laid siege to Samaria, the capital of the Northern Kingdom. The Israelites refused to surrender for three long and ghastly years. The Assyrian king died and his son succeeded him. But still the siege was continued. And at last, in the year 722 B. C., Samaria fell and the kingdom of which it was the capital was crushed never to rise again. All the wealthy and the learned, twenty-seven thousand of the best spirits in the ten northern tribes, were carried off into captivity. They were distributed throughout Assyria, and there gradually their identity was lost as they became inextricably mixed with the people around them.

To this day we still speak of them as the Lost Ten Tribes, as though those thousands marched off as one man and then lost themselves in the heart of some far romantic land. Many an explorer coming across some strange people in Central America or Greenland or Tibet, has rushed forth to declare that the Lost Ten Tribes have been found again.

But no explorer ever really found them, and no explorer ever will. Those tribes did not wander off together to any distant land, but simply dwindled out of existence right where they were set down by the Assyrians. Some few of them may indeed have gone off to the far ends of the earth on trading expeditions, and thus founded the little colonies we hear of in Abyssinia and China. And many of them must have joined and become mingled with the other two tribes of Hebrews. But it is quite clear that most of the exiled Israelites simply merged with the races dwelling in Assyria and Medea, and there faded out of history's picture.

And so ended the Northern Kingdom.

6

The Southern Kingdom, Judah, was spared for a while. By diplomacy and intrigue, by submission and bribery, it managed to drag out some extra days of life. But hardly a generation after the fall of Israel, Judah's territory had so shrunk that the Assyrians spoke of the kingdom as a mere "city." Gone was all the glory of David, and in the dust was all the pomp of Solomon. Judah, like a dormouse in a cage of fighting lions, was trampled on no matter who else won or lost. Assyria went down to destruction, but immediately Egypt laid its paw on Palestine. When Egypt was overthrown, Babylon began clawing the little land.

And then suddenly, in 597 B. C., Judah came to an end. Nebuchadnezzar, king of Babylon, angered by an attempt at rebellion on the part of Judah, came and laid siege to Jerusalem. After he had emptied its treasury, and despoiled its Temple, he wrecked the city utterly. All the better citizens, the men of influence and the soldiers and the craftsmen, were taken captive to Babylon. Only the ne'er-do-wells and the shiftless were left to take over the affairs of the city, a sorry lot of uneducated and incompetent varlets.

For a while there was quiet in the land of Judah,

but as the years passed and passion for freedom began to go to their heads, even this riffraff tried to rebel again. Down hastened Nebuchadnezzar in another great fury, and once more the dread battering-rams were to be heard thundering against the northern wall of Jerusalem. A whole year and a half the rams pounded away before a breach could be made—they were mighty walls around Jerusalem in those days—and then in poured the raging enemy. The wretched king of Judah was forced to look on while his sons were slaughtered in cold blood; and then his own eyes were gouged out. Seventy of the leaders were executed, and almost the entire population of Jerusalem was taken captive to Babylon.

And so ended the Kingdom of Judah.

7

Almost five centuries had passed from the time the Hebrew invaders of Canaan took unto themselves a king, five centuries of war and intrigue, of tyranny and corruption, of conquest and defeat. They were not at all unlike the centuries through which all the other little Oriental kingdoms had lived—except in one respect. The Philistines and Edomites, the Phœnicians and Moabites, had all of them experienced much the same run of life and met the same death.

But when those other peoples died, they died forever; the Hebrews alone lived on after death. Those other nations, great and small, are no more than names to us now; but the sons of the ancient Hebrews form to this day a mighty people on earth.

There was a reason for this.

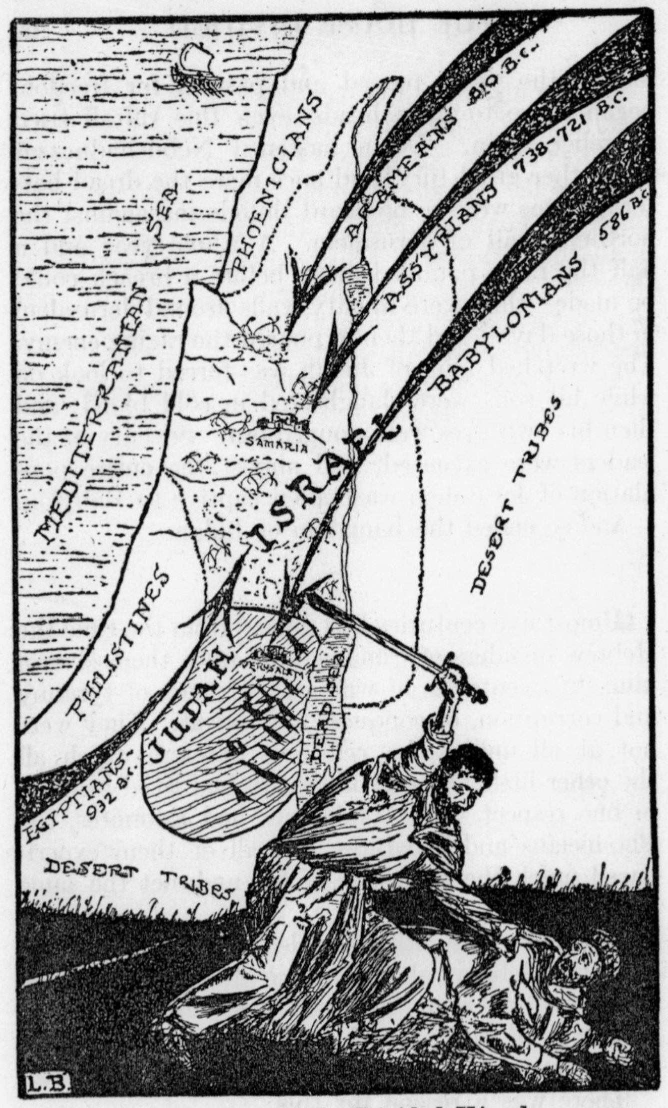

6.—The End of the Divided Kingdom

During all those five centuries in the history of the Hebrews, a spirit was sprouting and flourishing that was almost completely unknown to the peoples roundabout. That one thing made those five centuries in Palestine among the most extraordinary in all human history. Outwardly the Hebrews went the way of all the other nations, but inwardly they went a way which even to this day we cannot quite understand or explain.

And of that strange inward way I shall now have to tell at some length.

CHAPTER VIII

THE HEBREWS CONTINUE TO LIVE BECAUSE OF THE SPIRIT THE PROPHETS HAD BREATHED INTO THEM

The one element in those five centuries of Hebrew kingship which really makes their history worth telling, is the presence of the neviim, the "prophets."

No one quite like the ancient Hebrew prophet had ever before appeared among men. He was a new type in human society, a strange creature whose coming marked a revolution in the history of all civilization.

In *very* early times the "prophet" was apt to be a somewhat half-crazed man, perhaps an epileptic, who because of his queer actions was believed by the people to be a wonder-worker. The primitive Hebrews used to go to him whenever they were in trouble, for they imagined they could learn from him the mind of the god they worshiped. He was fortune-teller, medicine-man, and priest all in one. He would be consulted when a tribe thought of going to battle, for he was supposed to be able to foretell who would win. When the boy Saul was sent to find his father's asses, he went to the prophet-priest, Samuel, to learn where they had strayed.

As we have already seen, in the time of Samuel whole bands or guilds of these neviim began to appear. They went up and down the land clad in rough goatskins, and danced madly while they shouted out the might of their god, Yahveh. They loathed the Baalim of the Canaanites, and their whole aim seems to have been to keep the Hebrews true to that covenant which their fathers had once made at the Holy Mountain in the Wilderness. The fact that the Hebrews did not become Canaanites and lose their identity very soon after they reëntered the Fertile Crescent, was due largely to these roving agitators. They were frenzied patriots who were constantly reminding the people that they belonged to Yahveh, not to Baal.

2

As time went on, however, these neviim began to change altogether in their character and function. When Solomon built the temple and a horde of fussy, bustling priests began to minister there, the true prophets took very little part in the services. So long as Yahveh was worshiped in a tent in the field, or on a rough stone altar in the forest, the prophets were willing enough to perform the work of priests. But they were too wild and foot-loose a set of men to mess about for long within the four walls of what they might have described as a stuffy little ornamented temple. They liked to meet their god in the open, where the wind was sharp and all heaven was the roof above their heads. They did not take to the new-fangled ways which the Hebrews had learned from the city-dwelling people around them. They cried out constantly for a return to the stern, simple life of the desert nomad. Constantly, they clamored for a revival of the "old-time religion."

3

They were a courageous lot, those neviim. They were not afraid even of the king. When David grew drunk with power and stole another man's wife, the prophet Nathan went to the king and told him to his face he was an accursed criminal.

It was a prophet, Ahijah, who stirred up the one attempt at revolution when Solomon was on the throne.

And when Ahab, king of Israel, married an ambitious Phœnician princess named Jezebel, it was a prophet, Elijah, who alone kept her from ruining her husband's race. Jezebel sought to make Israel another Phœnicia, a land where vile practices and child-burning formed part of the worship of Baal Melkarth, and where the king was an unrestrained despot. Again and again, Elijah, a wild man with uncut hair and only a sheep-pelt to cover his nakedness, rushed out of the wilderness to decry her wickedness and that of the king. He was called the "troubler in Israel"—but it was desperately necessary trouble that he made. His whole career was one impassioned protest against the corruption, the luxury, and the vice which were engulfing the land. He championed the cause of justice against tyranny, of the common man against the king; and the spark of discontent he put into the people flared up a generation later in a terrible and bloody revolution.

4

It was probably the neviim, too, who set down in writing the first history of the Hebrew people, and thus laid the foundation of that monument of literature which we call the Bible. Some time in the ninth century B. C. a group of writers in Judah gathered together many of the old songs and tales current among the people, and tried to arrange them so that they would tell a connected story. The aim of these writers was to prove that Yahveh, and Yahveh alone, had protected the Hebrews from the beginning, and that he would continue to protect them if they but kept his commandments.

Fragments of that ancient history are to be found scattered through the first four books of the Bible, and scholars after much travail have succeeded in piecing them together. The resulting document reveals most strikingly just what the ancient Hebrews thought of Yahveh: how he seemed to them a being who walked and talked with man, and who came down to earth every now and again to see for himself just what was going on here. After all, those ancient Hebrews were still a primitive people; even their prophets were primitive. And their ideas of a god could not but be primitive also. Yahveh to them was a god of war, a fiercely jealous and tyrannical Lord of Hosts. Yet for all that, this document of theirs registers a real advance in human thinking. Yahveh is still a dread spirit who greatly hungers for sacrifices and burnt-offerings, but amazingly, he begins to show an interest in something else as well—in morality. He commands his worshipers not alone to bring him fatlings and first fruits, but also to be hospitable to the stranger, to be faithful to one's human master, to respect the marriage relation.

Of course, this most ancient Hebrew document contains many half-savage doctrines. Because it was broken up and scattered here and there throughout the Pentateuch, it serves to lower the tone of much of the Old Testament. But when one remembers how far more horrible were the doctrines of the other peoples of the world in the ninth century B. C., one realizes that this "Yahvist" history is after all a most significant work. It marks a genuine effort to drag man out of the bog of savagery in which he had floundered for centuries. . . .

It was only one of the first of such efforts in the life of the Hebrew people, and was quickly followed by a second. Another history was compiled a generation or two later, this time by the prophets of the north, of the Kingdom of Israel. And it differed in many striking ways from the earlier document drawn up in the south. Its description of Yahveh was less childlike, and its moral ideas were less crude. Its code of commandments was more elaborate and more humane.* Every seventh day was to be given to the servants and the beasts of burden as a holiday, and the crops every seventh year left for the poor to harvest. It even commanded that kindness be shown to one's enemy!

Of course, it is hardly credible that the thinking of the masses in Israel and Judah was mirrored in this second history. Or even in the first. Both

* The law code belonging to the first, the "Yahvist," history is to be found in Exodus xxxiv. That of the second, the "Elohist," (called so because in it the deity is known by the name of *El*, or *Elohim*) is to be found in Exodus xx, 22, to xxiii, 19.

documents must have been esteemed wildly radical by the ordinary people of the day. And naturally so—for both documents were the work of those superb radicals, the neviim.

5

But not until the eighth century, with the coming of Amos, do we see the neviim at what is almost their highest. Now there is no longer any telling of tales in order to win over the people, nor any resort to tawdry miracles or fortune-telling in order to awe them. The prophet is now neither a magician nor a medium, but simply a preacher who sees the evil that is abroad in the land, and dares to arise and denounce it openly in the name of god. His tremendous earnestness alone is relied on to win him a hearing. If he prophesies at all in his talk of the future, he refers usually to the *immediate* future. His keen insight into the life of his time tells him what must soon happen. If he ever ventures to speak of the distant future, he is evidently giving utterance to a hope, a glowing dream, rather than to a cold and reasoned conviction.

Amos is one of the most dramatic figures in all this story of a most dramatic people. He was a simple sheep-herder and lumberjack from Judah who was driven by some quite unexplainable urge to go north into Israel and denounce it for its sins. His sermons form a little book in the Bible, and to this day they are among the eternal wonders of literature. For simplicity, for power, for beauty of word they are altogether amazing. How any humble laborer was ever able to conceive them, or ever made the resolve or mustered the courage to utter them, must ever remain to us a bewildering mystery.

Israel just at that time was enjoying its last gay flare before the endless night of its destruction. The Arameans had been defeated, and the Assyrians were still only half awake. The land was flush with sudden prosperity, and evil was rampant everywhere. A few rich and powerful nobles and landowners were grinding the poor into the dust, thinking to atone for all their misdeeds by bringing fat offerings to the altars of Yahveh. At the high festivals these wealthy ones gathered in their temples amid great hilarity and drunkenness to rejoice in their good fortune. It seemed to them that Yahveh was pleased with them at last, for not in centuries had there been so much spoil in the land. They thought that they were living in "God's country," and that ill-fortune could not possibly touch them.

And at one of those riotous festivals in the bedizened temple at Beth-El, while the rich Israelites were carousing and dancing around the altar, suddenly a strange voice was heard rising above the din. It was the voice of an ill-clad, wild-eyed peasant who somehow had forced his way into the sanctuary and was now drowning out the festive songs with a piercing cry of lamentation. He was singing a funeral dirge!

> "Fallen is the virgin which is Israel,
> Nevermore shall she rise;
> Forsaken is she upon her land,
> There is none to raise her up."

Thus did the stranger cry mournfully in the midst of the merriment. And then in a voice terrible to hear he began to denounce the drunken throng. Death was almost on them! All Israel was about to be destroyed! None would escape, for Yahveh, the God of Justice, would mete out ruthless justice to the wayward people. Even as he had wiped out other nations for their sins, so also would he wipe out Israel. He would not be lenient simply because he had once chosen the Hebrews for his own. Rather he would punish them the more. Sacrifices by the thousand could not stay the judgment, neither would festive offerings by the myriad bribe the judge.

"I hate, I despise your feasts; and I will take no delight in your sacred assemblies," cried the ragged stranger in the name of Yahveh. "Even though you offer me your burnt-offerings and grain offerings, I will not accept them; neither will I regard the peace-offerings of your fat beasts. Take away from me the noise of your songs; for I will not hearken to the melody of your viols. BUT LET JUSTICE ROLL DOWN AS THE WATERS, AND RIGHTEOUSNESS AS A MIGHTY STREAM!"

So there was no escape, for in Israel there was corruption, not justice, and evil, not righteousness. The rich lolled on couches of ivory, smearing themselves with precious perfumes and cosmetics, and drinking costly wines. They were lewd and low and rotten to the heart. They cheated and robbed and enslaved the poor. So "Prepare to meet thy God, O Israel!" the prophet cried to them with awful voice. A fearsome enemy would sweep down on the land, conquering and destroying, plundering and burning. The rich and the mighty of the nation would all be taken captive to a far place, and the women would there be put to shame and the children would be cut down. "Woe, for the end of my people, Israel, is at hand. I can no longer forgive."

Thus did Amos, that simple sheep-herder and lumberjack from Judah, dare to address the drunken lords and ladies in their temple at Beth-El.

But they would not harken.

And forty years later, Assyria came ravaging through the land, and Israel was utterly destroyed! The words of Amos had come true. . . .

CHAPTER IX

THE IDEALS OF THE PROPHETS

Amos was but one of that grand array of prophets whose life-work imparts the richest color to the history of the Hebrew people. Sixteen whom we know by name have their words preserved in our Bible, but there must have been scores of others whose utterances were written down and lost, or were never written down at all. Were there but space, I would write at length of all those whom we know, for even the least of them played a dramatic part in our story. Altogether there were forty kings who sat on the thrones of Israel and Judah, yet hardly even the mightiest of them so deserves to be remembered as does the humblest of these heroic preachers.

Every nation of old had its kings and priests—but perhaps only the Hebrews had such prophets.

2

Some twenty-five years after the coming of Amos, there suddenly appeared in Israel another prophet, one named Hosea. He was a gentle, cultured man, however, and the burthen of his preaching was far less bitter to the taste than that of Amos. He too could see the certainty of Israel's doom if it persisted in its evil course; but with it he could see the possibility of repentance and forgiveness. For to this prophet Yahveh was not only a God of Justice, but also a God of Love! . . .

And by the utterance of that thought, Hosea blazed the path for all high religious thinking from then on. Yahveh, who had been a cruel, capricious despot to the bedraggled wanderer in the wilderness, and a jealous little tribal deity to Elijah, and altogether a stern, ruthless, avenging Judge to Amos—this Yahveh became wondrously changed into a Loving Father and a God of Mercy to Hosea!

The span from the Yahveh of the nomad to the Yahveh of Hosea is the whole distance between barbarism and civilization. . . .

Very probably the people who heard Hosea, laughed at him. It is easy to picture him as a mild little man who had a way of mumbling to himself. Ordinary people probably called him queer, and a bit "cracked." They could not understand what he meant. Even eight hundred years later, when another Jewish prophet gave utterance to just such thoughts as did Hosea, the people still could not understand. And that other prophet they crucified.

Even to-day, twenty-six hundred years later, there are still exceeding few who understand.

3

Hosea was the last to preach in Israel, for in a little while that kingdom was destroyed. The next prophet, Isaiah, belonged to Judah—or perhaps it might be truer to say that Judah belonged to him. For he it was who saved his land from being engulfed soon after the disappearance of Israel. It was his statesmanship, his hawk-like watch over Judah's movements as it scurried about between the feet of the lions, that made all the rest of this story possible. For had Judah gone down with Israel, then not ten but all twelve tribes would have perished. And our story would have ended with this paragraph.

Isaiah's sermons constitute most of the first thirty-nine chapters of the book that goes by his name; and for splendor of language they are perhaps unsurpassed in all the rest of the Bible. But to-day they somehow have less meaning for us than, for instance, the sermons of Hosea.

The trouble is that Isaiah's great interest in the political life of his little native country, his tremendous excitement about its material future, rather shortened his vision. He was perhaps too narrowly a patriot. Yahveh to him was still the god who ruled solely for the benefit of the Hebrews.

4

And Isaiah was an aristocrat. His greatest influence lay with kings and princes. He preached brilliantly, learnedly—but it is hardly possible that the plain people ever understood much of what he said. Not he, but another prophet, Micah, made the simple folk understand. Micah was one of them himself, for he came from a tiny village on the border of Judah. In that, and in the bitterness of his preaching, he was very like Amos, the sheepherder. He was the voice of the outraged masses, the flaming protestant against the wickedness of the rich and the hypocrisy of the priestly.

There was little originality in what Micah said, but there was genius in the way he said it. His ideas he got from all the prophets before him, and especially from Isaiah whom he may have known well; but he clothed those ideas with a simplicity and a charm that were altogether his own. For instance, see with what perfection he sums up the teachings of Amos, Hosea, and Isaiah, in the one verse:

> "It hath been shown thee, O man, what is good,
> And what Yahveh doth demand of thee:
> Only to do justice and to love mercy
> And to walk humbly with thy God."

Micah put things so that they could not but be understood and remembered. To this day men read with awe and wonder the words of that lowly champion of the oppressed in ancient Judah.

And with his searing eloquence Micah touched off a mighty train of reform. The temple in Jerusalem, which had long been given over to the filth of idolatry, was cleansed and rededicated to the service of Yahveh alone. A great Passover feast was held in the capital, and after it the people in great enthusiasm went away and tore down all the brazen images and stone pillars and other heathen symbols which had been worshiped on the hills and in the forests. All the idolatry that the Canaanite farmers and the Egyptian and Phœnician princesses had taught the Hebrews, was of a sudden swept out of the land. At last the "old-time religion" was supreme once more.

And in large part all this was the work of Micah, a peasant evangelist.

5

But the results of the sudden reform were soon undone again. Fifteen years passed, and then all the old idolatry came back. Indeed, things then became worse than ever. The religion of the Assyrians invaded Judah, and with it came all manner of lewd and coarse practices. Vile things were done to please the Phœnician god, Thammuz, and babies were sacrificed to the bloody god, Moloch. And all the reformers and the prophets of Yahveh were slaughtered or driven to cover.

From being almost too good the people suddenly relapsed into being unspeakably bad.

Perhaps that is the only way in which progress can be achieved: by leaps and falls. Perhaps man is a little like an infant in its struggle to climb a flight of steps. With desperate effort it manages to crawl up three steps; and then helplessly it slides back two. It tries again, climbing three more, and again falls down two. And so it goes on, straining and clambering, lunging forward and slipping back—but forever going on.

6

For almost half a century this spirit of heathenism was rampant in Judah, and then another wave of reform swept the country. Of course, this second reform did not come of itself, and without preparation. Indeed, during all the years of reaction the prophets were secretly girding their loins for the fresh assault on idolatry. Hidden high in the hills or far in the forests, they were intensely active. If they could not preach, at least they could write. They gathered and edited the sermons of Amos, Hosea, Isaiah, and Micah, preserving them on long parchment scrolls. They even dared to begin a whole new code of laws for Judah. It was a code based in part on their prophetic ideals, and they dreamed of putting it into effect so soon as they were once again in power. The earlier collections of laws had all been fragmentary, and had therefore been of little value. Now for the first time was there drawn up a code comprehensive enough to guide every act in the daily life of the Hebrews.

So did the prophets labor in secret, patiently preparing for the coming of the day of their deliverance.

CHAPTER X

MORE ABOUT THE IDEALS OF THE PROPHETS, AND THE STORY OF HOW THE PRIESTS TRIED TO MAKE THEM PRACTICABLE

At last the great day of the prophets dawned. A new king, Josiah, sat on the throne, a young man who from childhood had probably been under the influence of secret friends of the reformers. The prophets cautiously emerged from their hiding places and began to preach once more in the open. Zephaniah, a cousin of the king, and Jeremiah, a young man of an aristocratic family, were especially prominent as agitators for a new wave of reform. And strange to tell, the priests in Jerusalem were also active in the movement.

A terrifying chapter in Oriental history had just been written, and it served to hasten the coming of the reform. Of a sudden out of the dark forests of Europe, hordes of ravenous Scythians had poured forth. Across the Caucasus Mountains, through Asia Minor, down along the borders of Palestine the savages had plunged, pillaging right and left, and leaving a wide trail of blood and ashes behind them. They very nearly got Jerusalem in their claws, and even though the city escaped, the inhabitants were left weak with terror. It had been a frightfully narrow escape for them.

That gave the prophets their great chance. Up

and down the land they went, calling on the people to heed that dread warning. The awful Day of Yahveh's Judgment was at hand—"the day of wrath, of terror and distress, of wasting and desolation, of darkness and gloom." And there was but one means of escape, declared the prophets: *repentance!* "Return, O backsliding children!" they cried to the trembling people. "Return unto Yahveh or be destroyed!"

2

And the people did return. Led by the terrified young king, they forswore utterly their past wickedness. A mysterious code of laws was discovered in the temple at Jerusalem, a scroll supposed to have been written by Moses himself. In it was set down in harrowing detail the curses that would fall upon Judah if Yahveh's law was not scrupulously obeyed. And when Josiah, the young king, heard those curses, he rent his clothes in fear. Hastily he summoned all the free men of Judah to the temple in Jerusalem, and there he arose and read to them the whole book. And there and then the people vowed to make that new-found book the law of the land.

That book is still existent to-day, though in a greatly enlarged and altered form. Scholars say it is part of what we now call Deuteronomy, the fifth book in the Bible. Almost certainly it was none other than that self-same code of laws which the prophets had been secretly preparing all through the preceding half-century of heathenism. Parts of it—especially the repeated commands to worship Yahveh and Yahveh alone, and the laws favoring the unfortunate and the downtrodden—are unmistakably in the spirit of the zealous neviim.

But in that book there is also a spirit that is far more priestly than prophetic. A great to-do is made over the edict that in no sanctuary save the temple built by Solomon may Yahveh be worshiped. That meant that all the little village shrines of Yahveh must be destroyed. As one result, all their priests had to go to Jerusalem to find work as helpers in the Temple there. (For the first time now we must write the word with a capital T.)

Undoubtedly that was in one respect a wise ruling, for those village shrines had always been the starting points of corruption in the religious practices of the land. The village priests were an ignorant and superstitious lot, and seldom did they prevent their altars from becoming the centers of the crudest idolatry. With all religious observance centralized in the Temple at Jerusalem, the likelihood was greater that it could be guarded and kept uncorrupted.

3

But there was another side to this reform and one not so promising. The confinement of religious observance to one particular spot was destined to cause great distress and concern in the years to come. Perhaps the prophets foresaw this, but allowed the law to go into the code in order to win the support of the powerful Jerusalem priests. The whole code, indeed, appears a compromise between the high dreams of the prophets and the earthly desires of the priests. And as is usually the case with compromises, the earthly desires gained most by the deal. This code of laws made the religion of Yahveh a fixed and very rigid thing, a business of bringing proper sacrifices in a proper fashion at proper times, and of handing them over to very proper—but often low and greedy—priests. It took God, who is a wondrous yearning in the heart of all mankind, a hunger as wide as the world and a joy as high as the heavens, and tried to box Him up in a tiny little house of stone and mortar. It took that mighty spirit called Religion and tried to lock it in a stuffy feeble thing called the Church.

4

It was in the year 621 B. C. that the code of laws was "discovered" by one of the priests and shown to the king. No doubt the prophets greatly rejoiced over the acceptance of the code by all in the land, and thought perhaps their work of saving the soul of Judah was at last accomplished. But that code did not save the soul of the nation. Perhaps it helped save the body for a while—but only the hope preached by the greater prophets saved its soul. A code of laws is feared and obeyed; but a hope is loved and clung to. The Temple and its sacrifices were soon no more; but the hope voiced by the prophets that some day the oppressed and the lowly would find utter rest and peace—that hope lived on forever.

At least one of the prophets of the period, Jeremiah, shows that he felt this to be the case, for in his sermons there flames a spirit utterly opposed to the priestliness of the law book. Indeed, the whole burthen of his preaching was that Yahveh would Himself destroy the Temple, even though it had been built to His glory. For Jeremiah's insight told him that Yahveh did not demand this elaborate and messy business of sacrifice; He demanded only faith in the inward heart.

Jeremiah had the courage to utter that thought right inside the Temple at a time when the ideas set down in the new-found code were accepted by all the people. There were violent scenes in the Temple Courts, and a great clamor arose for the death of the daring prophet. Only with great difficulty did he manage to escape.

But soon he returned again, once more to utter what he felt was the word of the Lord. He was put into stocks, beaten, flung into prison, lowered into a miry pit and left to die—but still would he not halt in his high work of godly mischief.

There is something tremendously attractive about this man Jeremiah who forever spoke what was in his mind, no matter whom he offended. A scroll of his sermons was torn to pieces and burnt by King Jehoiakim; and the prophet himself was hounded from place to place. Nevertheless he did not falter. He lived through the most trying years in the history of Judah, years which saw it thrice invaded and despoiled by Babylonian armies. And all through that period he stood out for his own ideals against every one of the hysterical follies committed by the mob. When all the people were madly clamoring for war, he stood out alone for peace. There was in him nothing of that narrow patriotism that carried away many of the other prophets of his time. His

God was no possession of one little tribe, and did not dwell in one little shrine. He was Master of *all* the nations, Chieftain of *all* the tribes; and the roof of His temple was the sky that covered *all* the earth.

And when Jeremiah voiced these ideas, another revolution occurred in human thinking. Yahveh who once had been merely the equal of many other gods, and then merely one stronger than those other gods, became with Jeremiah the One and Only Master of all the Universe. He was no longer Yahveh at all—!

He was *God.*

5

But little joy ever came to him who wrought the revolution. When Jerusalem was destroyed by the Babylonian host, in 586 B. C. Jeremiah was left behind to keep peace among the rabble that had not been deported. But the mad desire to break away from the Babylonian Empire could not be allayed. A band of fanatics assassinated the noble Gedaliah who had been made ruler of the land, and then in terror lest the Babylonians march down again and avenge the murder, those fanatics arose and fled into Egypt. And when they fled they dragged Jeremiah with them.

But even in far-off Egypt the prophet would not be silent. Bitter quarreling arose among the refugees, and Jeremiah began once more to speak his mind. But this time he did not escape, for according to an old tradition an infuriated mob closed in on him and stoned him to death.

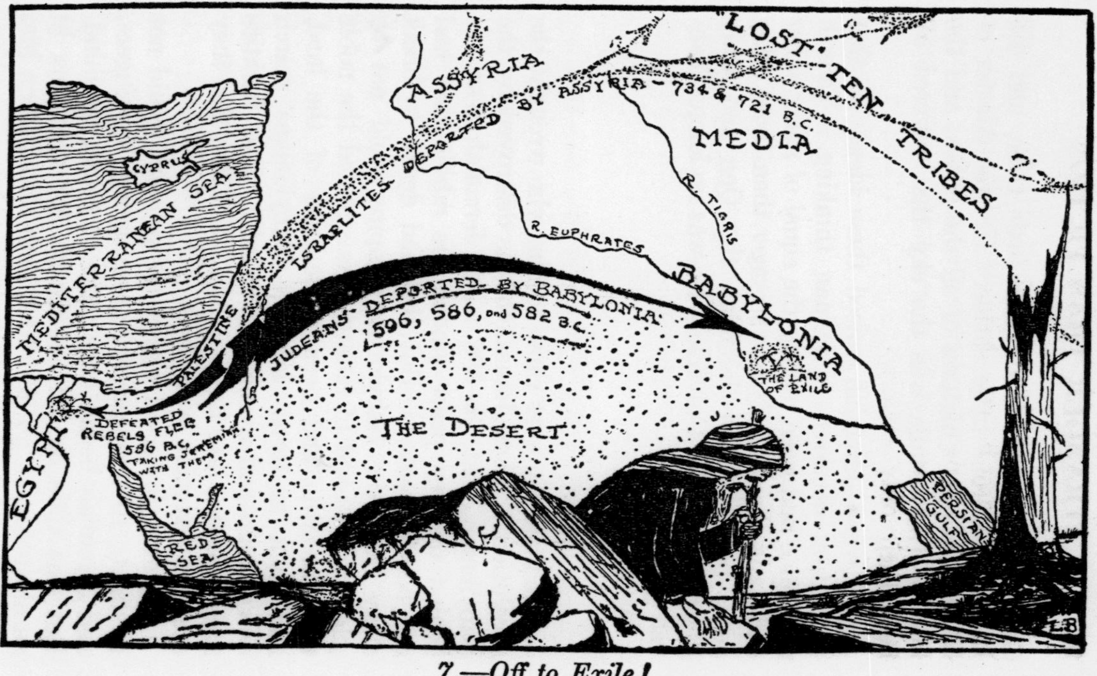

7.—*Off to Exile!*

That was the end of Jeremiah, a true Man of God. In his own day he was despised and loathed as the betrayer of his people; but we who now look back on his deeds and re-read his words know him to have been their only savior.

CHAPTER XI

HOW YAHVISM DIED AND JUDAISM WAS BORN IN THE BABYLONIAN EXILE

Most of the ten tribes of Israel deported by the Assyrians, probably merged in the course of time with the strange races in the lands of their exile; and their existence as a people ended forever.

One hundred and fifty years later, the two little tribes of Judah were deported by the Babylonians, but they, far from merging, became even more distinctively a separate people—and lived. And that seems to have been altogether due to the prophets of Judah who had preached and been persecuted for their preaching. In those one hundred and fifty years preceding the exile, they had managed to breathe into the tiny people of Judah a spirit which, unlike high walls and mighty fortresses, could never be burnt down or destroyed.

It is important to realize just how tiny a people this was, for then the miracle of its survival becomes even more impressive. After the catastrophe that occurred in 586, the tribes of Judah were torn apart into three main fragments. First, there was a dispirited remnant left behind in Palestine—poor, benighted peasants who were harried constantly by wild tribes from the desert. Then there were the fugitives who had congregated in scattered settlements in Egypt. Finally there was the community of exiles in Babylon. But all three groups together probably would not have sufficed to people an ordinary fair-sized American city like Paterson, New Jersey, or Des Moines, Iowa. Their total number could not have been much more than a hundred and twenty-five or a hundred and fifty thousand—about half as many Jews as there are to-day in Chicago alone.

And yet that little nation, dispersed over all the Orient, tossed about in the welter of empires like a cork in a furious whirlpool, managed to live on and come out triumphant!

2

The story of that survival is largely the story of the handful that was dragged off to Babylon. And not even of all that handful, for many of them deserted and took to the gods of the conquerors. Babylon was a mighty city whose outer wall was fifty miles in length, and so thick that four chariots could drive on it abreast. In it were mighty temples adorned with jewels and precious metals, and vast palaces brilliant with colored bricks and tiles. High almost to the heavens reached the towers and garden terraces; broad to the very horizon stretched its parks and meadow lands.

To the bedraggled Judeans, destitute wanderers from a backward little hill-country, the sight of all the magnificence of Babylonia must have been overwhelming. What was Judah compared with this? And who was the defeated Yahveh compared with the gods of *such* a land? How could one still believe Jerusalem the Holy City, or still worship

Yahveh as the mightiest of the gods? No, Babylon —*that* was the true Zion! And Bel, the sun god—*he* was the real Lord of Hosts!

So must many of the exiles have decided in their despair. And as swiftly as that decision spread, so swiftly did their old Yahveh die, and their old religion perish.

But in that same hour a new Yahveh—the One and Only Master of the Universe whom Jeremiah had championed—*He* came into His own. Yahvism, the old religion of the wild desert nomads who once had taken Canaan and then had been driven out again—that was no more. But now Judaism, a new religion, was born.

For not all the exiles were swept off their feet by the grandeur of Babylon and its gods. The majority went the way of all majorities, but an heroic minority stood its ground and refused to be stampeded. That minority turned now not to the living priests of Babylonia, but to the dead prophets of Judah.

And out of the teachings of those dead prophets the minority fashioned the newer and nobler faith.

3

There was prosperity and comfort for most of the exiles in their new home. They were untroubled by their conquerors, and allowed to manage their private affairs as they pleased. Opportunities aplenty were given to those who desired wealth and station, for King Nebuchadnezzar of Babylonia—who not undeservedly was called the Great—put no obstacle in their way. All he had wanted to do was to destroy the Kingdom of Judah, for its existence had made his hold on Palestine a highly uncertain one. And he needed Palestine desperately, for it was the bridge between his empire and the rest of the world. Now, however, that he held it securely, he wished the defeated and exiled men of Judah all the good in the world. And rapidly many of them began to get it. . . .

But always there were the few who could not be at ease in the strange land. Bread for their bellies meant nothing to them; they wanted food for their souls. So they sat by the waters of Babylon and wept. (They were indeed a strange people!) They hated the new land for it was not their own. It was "unclean" to them. And longingly they thought only of the little blue hills whence they had been taken. In their minds those hills became ineffably lovely, and the men who once trod them seemed immeasurably great. Like beggars around a fire, the exiles warmed their hearts with tales of past glories, with glowing stories which they elaborated about Moses, and David, and Solomon.

And for fear those stories—which to them seemed utterly true—might be forgotten in this foreign land, these homeless souls wrote them down on parchment scrolls. The two primitive histories written three hundred years earlier, the "Yahvist" and "Elohist" codes, were out of date. A crop of new legends had sprung up, and new interpretations of the old legends, and these were all set down in writing during the exile in Babylonia. All the stories in existence about their ancestors were written on scrolls by Hebrew scribes. They patched together the ancient traditions that had come down to them on old worn scraps of parchment or by word of mouth. And of them they made a new history.

That new history simply had to be written not only for its own sake but also to keep the weak among the exiles from drifting utterly away. Some reason had to be given why Yahveh's people had been crushed; and the only good reason was the old prophetic one that the people had been crushed because of their sins. Yahveh had not been defeated when Israel and Judah were destroyed. Of course not! On the contrary, it was Yahveh Himself who had brought about the destruction of His people to punish them for their idolatrous ways! Yahveh could not have been vanquished by other gods, for there were no other gods to vanquish Him. He alone was Lord of Heaven and all the Earth! He alone was God!

And it was to establish this belief that the unhappy souls in exile wrote the new history.

4

But the history was not the only work of the "scribes" among the exiles. They not only gathered together all the memories of their past; they also began to prepare for the future. Never for a moment would they admit they had reached the end of their story. No, their story was but beginning, they believed; for in a little while God would of course take pity on them once more and restore them to their own land. And then unheard-of glories would be theirs, they told themselves. No more would there be wicked kings to bring idolatrous princesses into the land, for God's "Anointed One" would Himself then be King. The Temple would be rebuilt and unnumbered priests would minister at its altars. In that day, joy and peace would reign throughout the land, and all would be well with God's children on earth forever!

It is curious to see how the dreams of the prophets and the hard sense of the priests are commingled in the air castles those exiles built. Perhaps it was because one of the leaders among the exiles was a prophet who happened to be the son of a priest. His name was Ezekiel, and like every other ancient prophet, exalted moments came to him when he seemed face to face with God. He had strange visions and afterward in frenzied words he told the people what he had seen. Like every other ancient prophet, he was what we call a mystic.

But with all his visions and almost insane enthusiasm, he was also a shrewd thinker. He knew the importance of organization, and many of the laws that were already being prepared for the future, were directly inspired by him. And those laws were altogether the laws of a priest.

It is not easy for us to feel any fondness for priests or priestly ways. Much easier is it to favor the prophets, who were in those days as leaven in the bread of life. But the fact is clear that leaven without grist would have made sorry bread indeed—and grist then was the gift of the priest. He was the organizer and the preserver; he was the man who saw to things and ran them. That is why Ezekiel must be counted one of the most important figures in this whole long story. His influence on the future of his people proved tremendous.

For the children of those exiles did not outlive Ezekiel's priestly ideas for at least four hundred years. Indeed, many have not outlived them to this day.

5

But long before those ideas could be put into effect, Ezekiel died and was buried. Then for a generation no prophet arose to take the vacant place in the little community. Many of the exiles grew rich and powerful at the court of Babylon, and forgot altogether the humble land whence they had come. And the rest plodded along in aching homesickness. They could not sacrifice to God, for sacrifice in Babylon would have been a violation of the Deuteronomic Code of Laws revealed to them fifty years before. Jerusalem was still considered the only proper place for sacrifice.

The best they could do was to devote one day of the week, the Sabbath, to undivided thought of their God. Perhaps they prayed and fasted on that day in little synagogues (the word really means "meeting-houses"), standing always with their faces turned yearningly toward Jerusalem. And piteously they begged there for the coming of the day of their redemption.

6

And at last that day seemed about to dawn. A new empire was arising in the East, the empire of Cyrus, a mighty Persian conqueror. Babylonia seemed certain to fall, for King Nebuchadnezzar was long dead and a weakling sat on the throne. Feverish whispering went on in the little settlement of the exiles, and then loud and heroic agitation. A great prophet arose, a man whose name we do not even know, but whose wondrous orations form the latter part of the Book of Isaiah. (That is why modern scholars usually speak of him as Deutero-Isaiah, which means the Second Isaiah.) In the mind of this Great Unknown, it seemed evident that Cyrus was the "Anointed of God," a conqueror divinely chosen to crush Babylonia and set the Judeans free.

So this herald went about in the market places and bazaars of the homesick exiles and cried, "Be comforted, ye people, be comforted!" The great day of deliverance was at hand, he assured them. Judah was about to be restored once more. But not as a pampered nation, sipping sweet favors from the fountain of God's grace. The Chosen People of God had a harder life than that in store for them. They were to be a light unto the heathen, suffering servants whose duty it was to bring the knowledge of God to all the nations of the earth! . . .

Perhaps our psychologists would call that idea a "compensation for an inferiority complex." The people among whom the Hebrews lived, talked constantly of their world conquests; and though the Hebrews themselves were only a handful of humiliated outcasts, they too wanted to talk in that way. They too wanted to feel the pride and self-respect felt by conquerors. But they knew only too well how feeble was their military strength, so they had to think up some new way of conquering. And that new way was of course the way of the spirit. The other nations might have chariots and battering rams, but they, the Hebrews—so they now told themselves—alone had Right.

Just what Right was, they hardly stopped to define—except perhaps that it meant the favor of the God who commanded fair play to equals and mercy to the weak. But whatever it was, they believed, that by the grace of the God of Heaven and Earth, they had it—and with it they believed they would conquer. With it Babylonia would be humbled and they themselves would be released. And with it some day they would be triumphant in all the earth: *their* spirit, *their* ideals, *their* God, would reign supreme. Jerusalem would become the center of the world, and the Temple would become a house of prayer for all the nations. They, the Jews, who were now scattered and broken, who were being spat upon and laughed at, they in the end would be the mightiest conquerors of all!

And in 538 B. C. Cyrus of Persia captured Babylon and set the exiles free. They were free now to conquer the world—with Right.

CHAPTER XII

THE TRIALS AND DISAPPOINTMENTS AFTER THE RETURN FROM BABYLONIA

The glorious conquest began most ingloriously. Of all the exiles in Babylon only a very few took advantage of Cyrus's decree. The rest found it too hard to tear themselves away from the shops and homes they had established in the "unclean" land, and remained behind. Perhaps some of them even resented the decree, considering it a reflection on their Babylonian citizenship. They refused to think of themselves any more as Judeans; their boast was that they were "one hundred per cent" Babylonians. Even most of those who still longed for the homeland, those who admitted freely that they felt themselves spiritual strangers in Babylonia—even they did not stir. Instead they gave money—and of course much free moral encouragement—to the few daring souls who did make ready to go back.

They were daring souls indeed. To get back to the old homeland they had to journey three months across the desert. And when they got back, only shambles greeted their gaze. Disappointments and hardships followed on each other's heels from the very start. Jerusalem was a heap of ruins, and the fields roundabout were choked with wild growths and weeds. Houses had to be put up and cisterns dug; the fields had to be cleared and tilled.

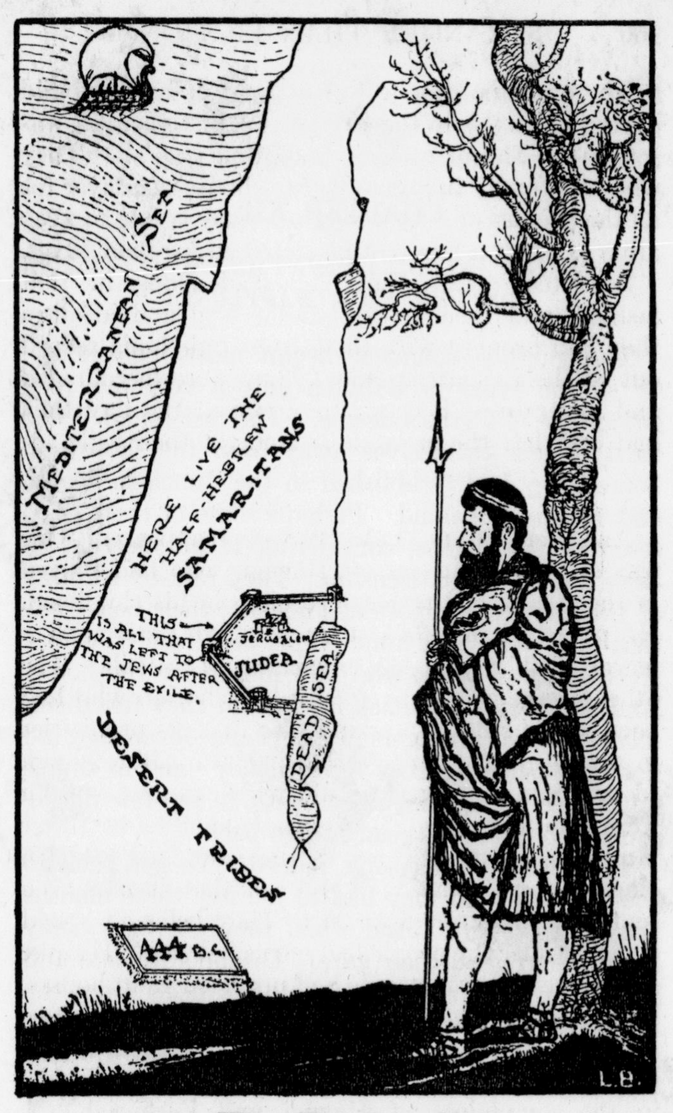

8.—When They Came Home

There was no time to dream great dreams or build glittering castles in the air. A rough stone altar was set up on Mount Moriah—and that was all. They who had fondly hoped to build a house of prayer for all the peoples on earth, were too busy trying to keep alive to make a house of prayer even for themselves.

Seventeen years they struggled along in that fashion, and then almost all the zeal and idealism they had brought with them from Babylonia seeped out of their wearied souls. They were discouraged and miserable. Perhaps they cursed the day they had ever left the prosperous lands of their exile.

2

And then once more the prophets reappeared. One was an aged man named Haggai, who had played in the streets of the old Jerusalem in his childhood. He preached in simple homely words, and with a fervor that recalls the preaching of Micah. The other was a young man named Zachariah who had been born in Babylonia and who cast his prophecies in a new and rather artificial pattern. But though so different in character and style, these two men were altogether at one in their thought. A bitter famine was sweeping across the land, and to both Haggai and Zachariah it seemed that it had been sent as a divine punishment. They believed it had come because the people had neglected God's Temple. For themselves the people had provided stout houses, but for God they had built naught save a rude altar.

(It is interesting to note how marked is the priestly spirit of the Deuteronomic Code and Ezekiel in the complaints of Haggai and Zachariah. A hundred years earlier, living prophets would have said that God's anger had been aroused because the people had not dealt justly or lived cleanly. But now the great crime was only that they had not built a sanctuary and sacrificed properly. Priestliness had become an all-important thing in the minds even of the prophets.)

Through all the streets of Jerusalem went those two men, Haggai and Zachariah, with their bitter complaints. They beseeched and cursed, they pleaded and reviled, until at last they drove the people into a frenzy of fear and agitation. Every imaginable joy and glory was promised them if only they rebuilt the Temple. The Jewish Messiah, the "Anointed of God," would surely be sent to rule over them, and all the nations of the earth would come to pay homage in Jerusalem. The dream of the Unknown Prophet of the Exile would immediately be realized—if only the Holy of Holies was once more erected.

3

So in a mad fever of anxiety the settlers now began work on the long-ruined sanctuary. The undeported Hebrew peasants who had stayed on in the land, offered to share in the labor; but they were spurned. The returned exiles looked down on them as an inferior lot. Those peasants, especially in the north, in what once was the realm of Israel, had intermarried with the heathens who had been settled there by the Assyrians two hundred years before; and they had become ignorant and debased. Even those who had been left behind in the south, in Judah, had intermarried and lost caste. The folk just returned from Babylonia acted very much like country folk who after many years in the big city, return to the village of their birth and snub the neighbors among whom they were reared.

Alone, therefore, the returned exiles labored at the rebuilding of the sanctuary, and with such tremendous earnestness that in less than five years their work was done. In size the new Temple was much like that of Solomon; but of course it lacked all decoration and ornament. The old, old men, who still hazily remembered the first Temple, wept with disappointment when they set eyes on the second. It was so plain, so crude!

But still it was a Temple. Perhaps it had less gold on its walls, fewer pillars in its courts, than the first; but nevertheless it was a House of God. And now that it was builded, the people sat back in happy exhaustion and waited. Anxiously they waited for the grand reward the prophets had promised them. Even those in far Babylonia caught the fever of hope, and in haste they sent a heavy golden crown to Jerusalem for the coronation of the Messiah. It seemed but a matter of days now before the whole world would be turned topsy-turvy. Cyrus had died, and his empire seemed about to crumble to pieces because of the wrangling among his successors. Anarchy reigned throughout the Orient. It seemed to them that to-morrow—the next day at the very latest—the triumph of Right (and Judah) would surely be realized. In a moment all the kings in the world would be swept away, and God's "Anointed One" alone would reign at last.

Of course, those poor Jews, worn out after their labors, were rather like the Jacobins after the first flare of the French Revolution, and the Bolsheviki after they first rode into power in Russia. They expected all the world to accept their new ideas immediately.

4

But the days passed—many days. Even years. And nothing happened. A new conqueror arose in Persia, a mighty man named Darius, who quickly set the empire in order once more. The world revolution which was to overturn all earthly kings and make the Messiah alone supreme—that did not occur.

And then the hearts of the exhausted Jews in Jerusalem turned to gall. They lost all faith in God and His prophets. God had fooled them, they thought. His prophets had promised all manner of glories if only His Temple were rebuilt—and He had not kept His word. His prophets were all liars, and God, therefore, was a fraud! The Messiah would never come! Never!

So did those Jews grieve bitterly as they struggled along in their wretched little land. Fifty years of neglect had made the place a wilderness, and now recurrent drought and famine made its redemption unspeakably difficult. Enemies from every side came raiding and plundering—Edomites from the south, Philistines from the west, and worst of all, those half-breed Israelite peasants, the Samaritans, from the north. (They were called Samaritans because their chief city was the old Israelite capital, Samaria.) The whole land of Judah was no larger than a little county, but twenty miles from end to end! And hatred and disgust filled the souls of its dejected inhabitants.

5

Only a tiny minority—there has always been that minority among the Wandering People—still clung to God and His promise. They were called the "Pious," and they refused to give up hope. While the rest went astray, intermarrying with the heathens around them, and breaking all the other laws that had been given them, those pious ones kept the faith. Even the priests became corrupt, sacrificing unclean things on the altars of God. Cruelty and injustice and vice were rampant throughout the little land. And only a very few of the people, the "Pious," dared to protest.

The chief protestant was a prophet whom we know as Malachi, and though priestly ideas had taken fast hold on him, there was still much of the old prophetic spirit ablaze in his preachment.

But in vain did he raise his voice, for the day had almost passed when a prophet could command the respect of the mob. The Word of God had lost its power in Judah and only the word of some earthly authority could carry any weight in the land now.

And just in time that word came.

CHAPTER XIII

THE PRIESTS COME INTO POWER

The word of authority came from Babylonia, and it was brought by a high official in the Persian court, a Jew named Nehemiah. Learning of the desperate plight of his brethren in Judah, this Nehemiah asked the king of Persia for permission to go back as governor of his people's homeland. The permission was quickly granted, for the king—like Cyrus long before him—well knew how important it was that the bridge called Palestine be held by a people who bore him good will.

So, armed with all the authority of the great Persian emperor, Nehemiah started out on the three months' journey to Jerusalem.

His first undertaking, once he arrived in the ruined city, was that of rebuilding the wall. He realized that until the city was protected from its enemies, the inhabitants could never be at rest. Accordingly he drafted all the able-bodied Jews in and around Jerusalem, and set them to work. It was a difficult undertaking, chiefly because the Samaritans would give the builders no rest. Two divisions had to be organized: one to build and another to fight. There was endless spying and conspiring and deception. Nehemiah hurried the work with all his might, for the Samaritans had carried their agitation against him as far as the court of

Babylon, and he feared he might suddenly be recalled.

Finally, though laboring most of the time under fire, Nehemiah's men completed the wall. It extended much further than the one it replaced, for it inclosed not merely Jerusalem but also several little nearby villages. It was high and thick and strong. In effect it was the foundation of the restored Jewish state.

2

The rebuilding of the city wall, however, was but the beginning of Nehemiah's work. Within the community the morale was at its lowest ebb, and to this the leader had to turn his attention next. The poor, who had had to neglect their farms while working on the wall, were now being crushed in the fists of the money lenders. The priests were lazy and dissolute; the laymen scoffed at God and His worship. The Sabbath, which had attained such importance in the Exile, was now neglected and forgotten. The taking of heathen and half-breed women as wives, was common in every family. Unless a complete and drastic reform was brought about immediately, it was clear that the career of the whole community would soon be ended.

Nehemiah and another leader, a scribe named Ezra, realized this and fell to work. The whole people was assembled in Jerusalem and there a new code of laws, one that had probably been drawn up in Babylonia on the basis of Ezekiel's ideas, was forced upon them. All those who had taken heathen wives into their homes were ordered to send them away. Outstanding debts were canceled; the priesthood was purged; the Sabbath laws were strictly enforced. From end to end the life of the community was swept clean by the two reformers. From a lawless, reckless, godless populace, the Jews were suddenly transformed into a band of puritans.

And the community was saved—for a while.

3

Now for the first time those who had remained in exile began to throng back to their homeland. From Babylonia they came in a steady stream; probably from Egypt and other lands too. Back they came to the blue hills of Judea, once more to take up life there. But it was a life far different from that which their ancestors had known two centuries earlier. The newcomers were filled with a thousand new ideas gleaned from the foreign peoples among whom they had sojourned. They were no longer simple tribesmen with crude "small-town" ideas. They had traveled and seen the world. They were "civilized."

Yet for all that they were "civilized"—perhaps because of it—their religion was hardly so vital, so dramatic, as it had been in the days of Micah or Jeremiah. It had become a religion of law rather than a free play of the spirit. It laid stress on showy externals, on essentially unimportant things—not eating certain foods—bringing regular gifts to the priest—observing certain festivals.

And the Exile was very largely to blame for this change. Even before the destruction of the old

Temple, the seeds of a religion of priestliness had taken root in Palestine. But it had been unable to flourish then because the greater prophets were most strenuously opposed to it, and the people themselves had only feebly been attracted by it. Now, however, that the Jews had seen the great temples and had witnessed the gorgeous ceremonies of priest-ridden peoples like the Babylonians, they took to the imitation of that sort of thing with alacrity. And gone were the rebels, the true prophets, who might have stemmed the tide in its favor.

The change was a tremendous one. Before the Exile the Jews had all transgressed their religion because that religion, the work of the prophets, had been too high for them. But now the Jews no longer transgressed it—because at the hands of the priests it had been brought low.

4

To what extent it had been brought low can be learned from a study of the prophecies of the day. There were still prophets in the land, but a tawdry, time-serving lot they were. The style of their preaching was stilted and forced. They did not cry out with the thundering directness of an Amos or a Jeremiah; they used strange symbols and spoke in twisted and far-fetched allegories. And for the most part the burthen of their preaching was a cheap jingo nationalism. These prophets declared the Jews were a pious and perfect people, all because they brought sacrifices to the priests at Jerusalem in a pious and perfect fashion. As for the other peoples on earth, they were all unspeakably wicked and sinful. Soon, these prophets declared, very soon, they would be cut down.

The old yearning for the coming of the Reign of Peace was despised now, and the new prophets looked forward instead to the day when plowshares would be turned into swords, and pruning-hooks would be made into spears. The old dream of a Messiah who would bring justice and freedom to all men, was perverted into an ache for a ruthless conqueror, a war lord, who would wade in the blood of every heathen who refused to bring sacrifices to Jerusalem three times a year! The Jews alone were considered blessed; the *goyim*, the Gentiles, were all accursed.

It was a mean and loathsome doctrine. It was very like the doctrine—only with the characters completely reversed—which is still uttered to-day by too many preachers in the world.

But it was a doctrine that did not go unchallenged in that early time. There were some in the land of Judea who did see the ugliness of it, and even though they dared not openly preach against it, they were not altogether silent. They voiced their protest not in sermons but in stories, in light bits of fiction which below the surface were freighted heavily with meaning. For instance, someone wrote the beautiful story which we call the Book of Ruth, and someone else wrote the powerful novel which we call the Book of Jonah.

5

The Book of Ruth is a veiled protest against the laws of Ezra and Nehemiah prohibiting intermarriage. It tries to show that even King David, who by this time was thought to be the greatest monarch that ever reigned, was himself descended from a noble Gentile woman, a Moabitess named Ruth.

The Book of Jonah in a like fashion was a veiled protest against the narrow nationalism of the new prophets. Its main character, Jonah, is just such a prophet: a man who thinks God cares only for the Hebrews. When the divine call comes to him to preach to the Gentile city of Nineveh, the age-old foe of Jerusalem, he is highly displeased. Why should he, a Hebrew prophet, trouble himself about the sinful heathens? Let them perish in their sin! . . . So instead of obeying the command, he tries to escape God's reach by sneaking off to a foreign land. But soon he learns that God's reach extends far beyond the borders of little Palestine, for the boat in which he hides is overtaken by a furious storm. He is cast into the sea and is saved from death only because God sends a whale to swallow him.

And then, when Jonah is once more on dry land and the call to go to Nineveh is repeated, he is overawed and obeys. He goes to that city, tells the inhabitants that within forty days they will all be destroyed, and then sits back righteously to see his prophecy fulfilled.

But to his vexation he is totally disappointed. Those *goyim* prove not nearly so wicked as he had thought them, for they take his words to heart and repent. And when Jonah bursts out in angry complaint because the city is spared, God reasons with him gently and explains His conduct. The picture drawn of God is almost that of an old and wise man

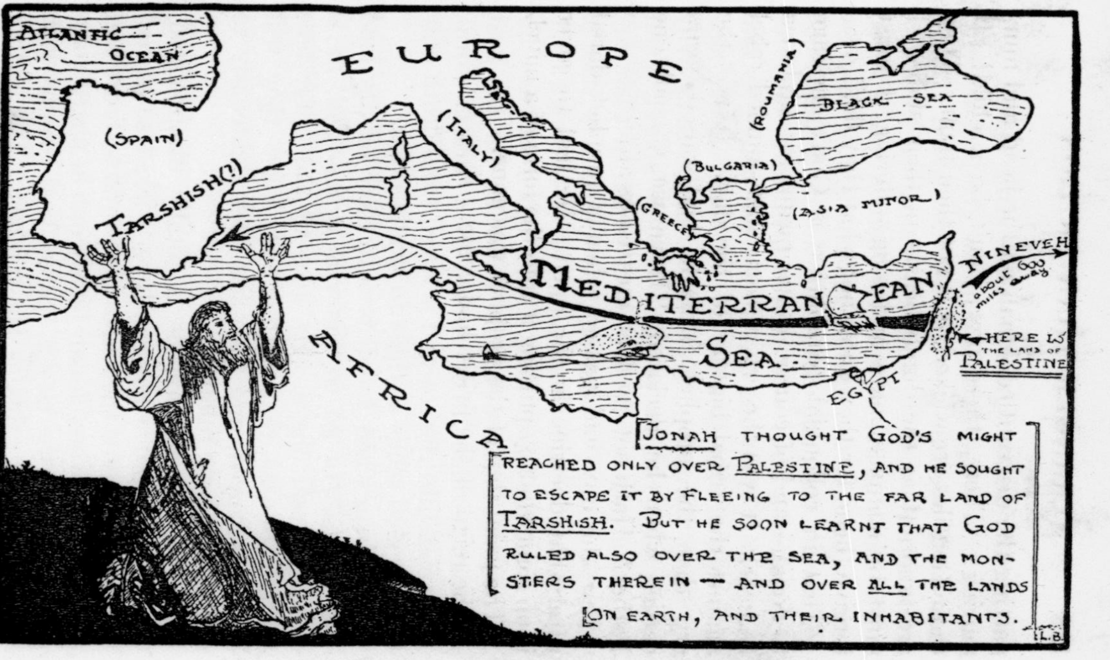

9.—The Meaning of the Book of Jonah

patting the disgruntled Jonah on the head and murmuring: "There, there now, don't be a child! If those Gentiles are wicked, it is not their fault. They are ignorant as the dumb beasts in their stalls. I must be compassionate and long-suffering; I must forgive them, for they know not what they do."

That in colloquial paraphrase is God's message to Jonah—and of course, it was meant for all Judea to hear. It was the cry of some high-minded rebel against the tribal bigotry of the day. It was the cry that the prophet Malachi had raised years earlier when he declared, "Have we not all one Father? Hath not one God created us all?"

But the day had passed when a prophet dared utter that doctrine in the open. He had to cover it up somewhat by putting it into the form of a novel.

The great day of the prophet was gone.

The reign of the priest had come.

CHAPTER XIV

THE GREEK INVASION BRINGS ON THE FIRST WAR FOR FREEDOM OF THOUGHT

Year by year the power of the priests grew mightier among the Jews. Wealth rapidly accumulated in their hands, for each season the plain people had to take them the choicest portions of their flocks and harvests. The old democratic ideal of the prophets that all Jews were priests, was forgotten. Now only those who were supposed to come of the tribe of Levi were allowed to minister in the Temple; and furthermore only those of the family of Aaron of the tribe of Levi were considered holy enough actually to perform the sacrifices; and still further, only one directly descended from Solomon's favorite priest, Zadok, could possibly become the High Priest.

The High Priest was virtually the king of the land, and the lesser priests were the princes. They were no better, of course, than lay kings and princes. They were forever conspiring among themselves, cheating and murdering their way from one office to another. But for all their corruption, they did succeed in doing one thing: they kept the Jews alive as a separate people. They walled them in with their little rules and regulations, keeping them rigorously segregated from all the other tribes and peoples. Even the half-Jewish Samaritans were cut off completely and had to start a temple of their own in northern Palestine.*

2

But, despite the efforts of the priests, foreign influences did seep into the life of the people. Gradually their language was corrupted from pure Hebrew to a jargon called Aramaic, so that after a few generations they could not understand even their own Scriptures. In their synagogues each Sabbath—for those "meeting-houses" they had created in the Exile had become common now throughout Judea—they had to read their Holy Writings through an Aramaic translation called the *Targum.*

And many of their religious ideas changed too. From the Persians they had learned of angels and devils, and also of Another World. For the first time in their history they began to believe in Satan, and in hell and heaven. Before this time God had seemed very near to the Jews; but now they began to think of Him as very far away—so far that he had to do His work through the agency of good or evil messengers. And at one time the Jews had thought that all life was lived in this world, and that after death both righteous and wicked simply descended to the "Pit," where they wandered about as lifeless ghosts. But now that this world held but little joy in store for them, they began vaguely to dream of a World to Come which only the righteous would inherit.

* The Samaritans are still to be found there to-day, but two hundred of them in all—the last remnant of an ever-rejected but never-daunted people. And still to-day they have their high priest and their ancient worship!

Outwardly no sign of this change in thought was evident. None was there to hail it, and so none could rise to decry it. With meek regularity the people brought their offerings to the priests, and with sanctimonious grace the priests accepted them. And seemingly nothing was happening.

But then came the Greek, and all was made open.

3

In the fateful year 333 B. C. Alexander the Great became master of the Persian Empire, and a year later, on his march toward Egypt, he took possession of Palestine. (The little land was still the one bridge used by the Empire builders. . . .) But this Alexander, a mere boy in years, was quite unlike the ordinary world-conqueror. His aim seems to have been not so much the gaining of power as the spreading of culture. He dreamed of scattering throughout the world the seeds of the high Greek civilization. In every land he entered he tried to create a center of Greek influence; and so well did he succeed that though he died at the age of thirty-three his Greek colonies dotted all of the then-known world.

Alexander's effect on the Jews and their religion was greater than that of any other non-Jew in history. He was generous to them and gave them every liberty; but at the same time he located peaceful settlements of his own people throughout Palestine. The result was a growing familiarity with all things Greek. Jews began to affect the use of Greek words in their conversation, and began to give their children Greek names. Just as nowadays little Samuel is called Seymour and little Sarah is named Thyra, so in those days little Jochanan became John and little Shalomtziyon became Salome. The young Jews began to frequent the gymnasiums and to idolize the Greek athletes. They became "sports."

Hellenism—the word comes from *Hellas,* meaning

10.—Alexander's Empire

Greece—began to make itself felt in every walk of Jewish life, especially in the many Jewish settlements outside of Palestine. Unfortunately, it was not the Hellenism of classic Greece, the Hellenism that flowered in the genius of Socrates, Plato, Sophocles, and Phidias. Rather it was that Hellenism debased and sullied through long-handling by Macedonians and other lesser tribes.

But debased as it was, it nevertheless proved attractive. Even the priests in Jerusalem began to take to it. Indeed, they were attracted to it even more than the plain people. The story goes that they actually left the sacrifices unburnt on the altars in the Temple, and hurried off to the arenas to watch the Greek athletes there. Greek manners—and vices—became the great fashion of the day, for the

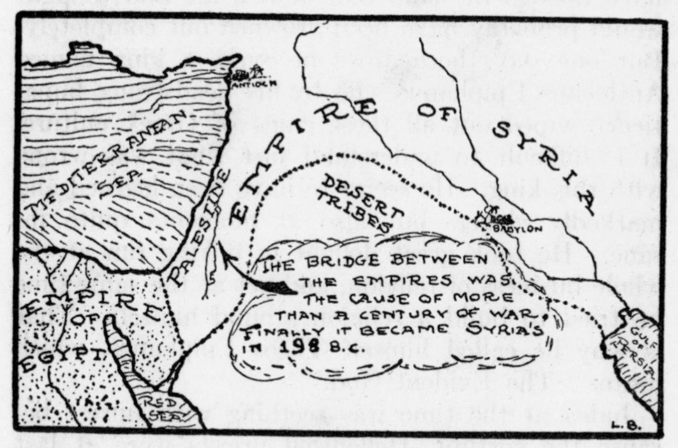

11.—After Alexander

more a Jew aped them the better seemed his chances of growing in power and station.

4

Of course, this change did not come about overnight, but took three or four generations. After Alexander died his empire was divided into three kingdoms; and Palestine being the bridge between two of them, it naturally became for over a hundred years the scene of constant warfare. But finally, in 198 B. C., it was definitely made a part of the kingdom of Syria, and for a while there was peace.

Perhaps because the Greeks made no attempt to force its progress, Hellenism had continued seeping steadily into Palestine during all that troublous century. In the course of time it would so have flooded the land that Jewish life and thought would probably have been drowned out completely. But one day there arose in Syria a king named Antiochus Epiphanus who by his headstrong impatience wiped out all these gains of Greek culture. It is difficult to understand just what was wrong with this king. He seems to have been learned and markedly clever—but also at moments quite insane. He took great delight in poking fun at the whole business of religion, and yet at the same time he tried to build a religion around himself. That is why he called himself Theos Epiphanes, which means "The Evident God."

Judea at the time was seething with unrest because the corrupt, Hellenized priests were at last being brought to book by a few of the pious Jews. It looked something like a political uprising to Antiochus, and on his way home from a campaign in Egypt he stopped in the middle of the "bridge" to attend to the trouble. He looted the Temple and then simply ordered Judaism to cease. Just that! Evidently he thought it would be quite easy for him to stamp out this obscure and, as he thought, very odd little religion. His orders were that never more should the Sabbath, or the rite of circumcision, or the difference between "clean" and "unclean" food, be observed. Anyone found with a

Hebrew book in his possession was immediately to be put to death. Henceforth if there was to be any sacrificing it must be of swine's flesh, and to Antiochus as god.

5

For a while starkest horror swept the land as the army of Antiochus began to put those orders into effect. There was looting and murder, wailing and shame. And then, like the breaking out of a mad fire, the people blazed into rebellion. A pious old priest named Mattathias began it when he ran his sword through one of the Syrian officers. Fleeing into the wilderness with his five sons, he there began to gather a band of desperate zealots. Then up and down the countryside they went, tipping over the hated altars set up by the foreigners, and putting to death the renegade Jews who had sacrificed on them.

It was magnificent, but it seemed insane. The tattered rebels were untrained, unequipped, unsupported—a tiny band of priests and peons fighting with little more than their bare fists. The great hosts of Syria, armed, disciplined, and led by the greatest generals of the day, outnumbered them ten to one. It seemed sheer suicide!

But it was not. Old Mattathias died soon after the beginning of the rebellion, but he was succeeded by one of his sons, Judas, who proved altogether a genius in warfare. Four tremendous armies were sent against him—one accompanied by dealers to buy the defeated Jews as slaves—and all four he utterly routed. Judas Maccabeus, Judas the "Hammerer," he was called by his elated followers—and deservedly. Stationing his little army in narrow passes, or rushing them by night marches to make sudden attacks at dawn, he harried and hacked and hammered the Syrians until at last they fled from before him.

There came a lull in the fighting. On December 25th, in the year 165 B. C. the Jews amid great rejoicings, cleansed the Temple of its swinish filth and rededicated it to God.*

6

And then they went on with the struggle. More than twenty years they went on with it, losing in the strife one after another of the five stalwart sons of old Mattathias. And finally in 143 B. C., they triumphed completely. The Syrian was driven utterly from the land, and Judea at last was free.

Almost for the first time in history a war had consciously been waged for a spiritual principle. Not because of grinding taxation or political domination had the Jews leapt to arms, but solely because of religious oppression. They had fought for that holiest of all causes, Freedom of Thought.

And they had triumphed.

* To this day the Jews celebrate that great victory with their annual Feast of Lights called Chanukah.

B.C.

JUDAH (South)

ISRAEL (North)

"Yahvist" History (Judah)

"Elohist" History (Israel)

800

AMOS
HOSEA

Israel deported to ASSYRIA 722 B.C.

700

ISAIAH
MICAH

§ Temporary reform
§ Reaction
§ Reform again

Deuteronomy (adopted 621 B.C.)

JEREMIAH

600

Judah deported to BABYLONIA 597–582 B.C.

Some flee to EGYPT

The return from exile 538 B.C.

500

HAGGAI and ZECHARIAH preach

Temple rebuilt

(Hard Times)

NEHEMIAH Govenor, 444 B.C.

Walls of Jerusalem rebuilt

Institution of the Priestly Law

"Five Books of "Moses" completed

400

(Reign of the Priests)

ALEXANDER introduces Greek culture

(Hellenism takes root)

300

(The "Pious Ones" war against Hellenism)

Chart B. The Adventures of the Jews, Part II

CHAPTER XV

THE ROMAN CONQUEST SETS THE HELPLESS LITTLE NATION YEARNING FOR A MESSIAH TO DELIVER IT

But the triumph of the Jews had been too complete. The war which had been waged at first only for religious freedom, ended in winning also political independence. And that added gain proved their undoing.

Simon, the last of the five sons of Mattathias, was succeeded on the throne by his son, the High Priest, John Hyrcanus; and with him the tragedy began. Drunk with his new-found power, he undertook cruel and costly wars against his neighbors. In pursuance of his dream of carving out a great empire for himself, he hacked down the Samaritans on the north and the Edomites on the south. And not content merely with making those lands subject to his rule, he even compelled their inhabitants to accept his religion. Forcibly he converted them to Judaism. The grandson of old Mattathias who gave his life for the right to worship his own God in his own way, was now spending all his days trying to wrest that very right from others.

But very soon a group of protestants began to make themselves heard in the land of Judea. They were called the Pharisees, the "Interpreters," probably because they were pious men who spent much of their time studying and interpreting the Holy Scriptures.* They cared not in the least for empire or dominion; their whole interest was in the Holy Law and its fulfillment.

Those who belonged to the party in power in

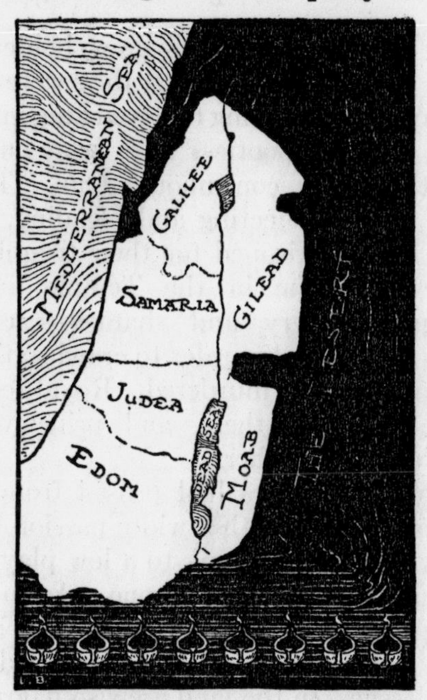

12.—The Realm of the Maccabees

the land were called the Sadducees, because they all sided with the supposed descendants of the ancient High Priest, Zadok. They were Hellenized aristo-

* Pharisees does not mean "Separatists" as scholars long thought. Probably it comes from the Hebrew word *pharash*, which means "to make clear."

crats, for the most part priests; but they showed but feeble interest in their religion. Essentially they were politicians. Sacramental ward-bosses, one might call them.

2

Day by day the Pharisees grew bolder in their attacks on these Sadducees; but they were powerless to effect any reforms. King followed king in troublous succession, and the bootless wars went on. Within the land there was continuous strife. The Pharisees went about, objecting and pleading, and were butchered and imprisoned for their trouble. There was endless intrigue in the Temple among the priests, open bribery and shameless corruption. Pretenders committed murder to crawl to the throne, and then in turn were murdered. Royal sons plotted against their own fathers, and princely brothers made war on one another.

Not a hundred years had passed from the time all Judea had blazed with a white passion for liberty —and now the fire had sunk to a low play of smoky flame around a petty little throne. As so often has since happened in the world's history, a glorious revolution failed only because it succeeded.

The lawlessness in the land grew so flagrant finally that the Pharisees could stand it no longer. In despair they appealed for help to Rome, the great world-power of the day. No doubt they realized they would have to pay with their political independence for Rome's help; but that did not deter them. What cared they who was master of their land, so long as they were left masters of their religion?

Pompey, the Roman general, answered the call of the Pharisees; and after his conquest of the land there was quiet for a while. Many of the Sadducees were sent as prisoners to Rome, and the Pharisees were left in peace to study their beloved law.

3

But soon trouble began again. Sadducee leaders escaped from Rome and returned to foment rebellion in Judea. One after another they appeared in the land, raising little armies, terrorizing the countryside, and then going down to quick and bloody defeat. Finally the Romans began to lose patience, and grew less tolerant toward the whole people. The Temple was looted and the land again and again pillaged by Roman armies. For more than twenty years virtual anarchy prevailed in Judea. Kings and pretenders, governors and high priests, generals and bandits all clawed and fought in the mad scramble for power.

For a while an Edomite half-Jew named Herod managed to get control of the land. By conniving with Rome he had himself made king of the Jews, and then with unspeakable cruelty he battered his people into submission. He murdered his own wife, three of his sons, and many others of his family, in striving to make his position firm. And then he built a magnificent new Temple in belated effort to win the favor of the Jews.

But it was to no avail. The splendor and prosperity which the king brought to the land meant nothing to the people. They hated and loathed him, and the moment he died they rebelled against the son who succeeded him. Three thousand Jews were slaughtered right in the Temple courtyard, and the rebellion was crushed. But in a little while another started and flamed up. Again there were massacres, and again the Temple was sacked. But the people would not stay under control. They utterly refused to be subject to the son of the hated Edomite, and Rome finally had to transfer him from the land.

The last vestige of independence was gone. Judea was now but a part of the Roman province of Syria.

Yet still no peace came to the unhappy little land. The Roman governors proved a cruel and rascally lot. They provoked the people in a thousand ways, and all Judea seethed with unrest. Violent patriots arose, and they spread a reign of terror against all who were supposed to sympathize with Rome. The Zealots they were called, and night after night they committed murders in the cities and villages of Judea. There were riots and lynchings; and in punishment, innumerable crucifixions. Judea was gory with its own blood as it writhed in the talons of Rome.

4

But dark as was the night—and never had it been darker—still a hope gleamed for the people. It was the old hope of the great prophets, the wild hope that soon, very soon, the Messiah would come. Through all those years—it was now fully four hundred years since Haggai and Zachariah had promised that the "Anointed One" would come if the Temple were rebuilt—the hope had been kept alive in Judea. It had been kept alive by many writers whose names we do not know, but whose books—called by us the Apocalypses—are still extant.

Most of those Apocalypses were written secretly and put in circulation as the works of various great men of the past. Some were claimed to be the work of Ezra, others of Jeremiah, of Solomon, of the Patriarchs, even of Noah. The real authors had to make such claims because otherwise their books would not have been read at all. People thought that only the great men of the *past* had known the Truth, had been inspired by God. Therefore only the very ancient writings seemed to them holy enough to be read in their synagogues, and these they called simply *seforim,* "Books." (The Greek for *seforim* is *biblia,* from which we get our word Bible.) So the latter-day author in order to get his own book included among these *seforim,* had to say that he had discovered an hitherto unknown production of some ancient worthy.

To us that may seem sheer dishonesty; but that is only because our standards are different. An author's first desire is to get his book in the hands of the people, and in those days, it was considered no harm to resort to this trick to secure publication.*

* Sometimes an author not merely palmed off his own ideas as the thought of some other and greater man; if he got the chance he even inserted them bodily in that other man's genuine writings. That is one of the main reasons why so many contradictions and bewildering inconsistencies deface most of the books of the Bible. Those who copied them on new scrolls year after year—for it was centuries before the invention of printing—not merely made mistakes and carelessly skipped words and lines, but also wrote in whole new chapters of their own devising.

5

In the horror of the Syrian and Roman persecutions, the land was flooded with these books bearing false titles. Almost all of them dealt with the coming of the Messiah, and described in detail just how and when this present world would be utterly destroyed and the new one miraculously ushered in. We can hardly understand most of them, now, for they are written in a queer and incoherent style. They are chock-full of strange visions and tortuous calculations attempting to prove all the old prophecies literally true. For instance, before the Exile Jeremiah had promised that after seventy years Judah would be restored to its own land to enjoy the blessings of the Messianic kingdom. Probably he had meant that to be taken as a round number. It was like saying that "before very long" or "in the lifetime of our children" these great wonders would happen.

But the later writers took the numbers in those prophecies *literally*, and since they knew that the seventy years had long passed and no Messiah had come, they began to juggle with the figures. At one time, they said seventy years meant really seventy weeks of years—in other words, four hundred and ninety. That particular calculation was made when about four hundred and eighty-eight of the four hundred and ninety years had already passed, and fierce terror and joy swept through the land at the nearness of the Great Day. . . . But the four hundred and ninetieth year soon passed, and no Messiah came—and more juggling had to be done.

The number seventy somehow fascinated the Jews of the time, and they twisted and tortured and dragged out of it the most far-fetched and ridiculous calculations. It was not that the people had lost their heads—though the times were cruel enough to make them do so. It was simply that these Jews, with their tremendous will to live, knew themselves to be on the verge of death. And they would not die. Anything—any wild promise or wilder distortion of a promise—anything was clutched at in that terrible hour. They would not die!

CHAPTER XVI

JOSHUA OF NAZARETH, A YOUNG PROPHET, IS HAILED AS THE MESSIAH BY THE JEWS, AND IS CRUCIFIED BY THE ROMANS

There is something intensely pathetic in the sight of tiny Judea bleeding to death in the claws of a great empire, yet always, always, dreaming on of release. But even more pathetic is the story of the hysteria and excitement which that constant dreaming stirred up in the land. The more horrible the persecutions and massacres, the nearer seemed the advent of the "Anointed One." Each day was thought to be the very last, and every hour the people pricked up their ears for the sound of the Messiah's trumpet. It was like being adrift at night in an open boat—none knew when the cries for help would be answered.

Frenzied mystics, many of them more than half-mad, went up and down the land and cried in shrill, hysterical voices: "Repent ye, for the kingdom of Heaven is at hand!" Most of them belonged to a secret fraternity of hermits called the Essenes, and they believed that strict piety, charity, and bathing in the streams—baptism as it was called in Greek—would alone prepare the people for the coming of the Messiah.

In some of these mystics the great spirit of the ancient prophets seemed reborn, and they attracted enormous followings. One of them, a Jew named John, was especially influential in those days. He was a wild-looking young man who took his stand by the River Jordan and called on the people to leap in and be cleansed of their sins. They called him John the Baptist, and hundreds flocked to him. But because he offended the cruel king Herod by his open denunciations of the ruler's wickedness, he was imprisoned and later put to death.

Many others, however, arose to take John's place: young wild-eyed men who flayed the people with bitter tongues and drove them to the verge of stark madness, and gentle souls who tried to bring them comfort, and only stirred them the more.

There was one preacher in particular, a youth named Joshua—he who is known to us as Jesus of Nazareth.

2

It is not easy to write of this man Joshua. To some he has become altogether a god, and to others—because so much evil has been done them in his name—he seems very like a fiend. But if we are to obtain any true knowledge or understanding of him, he must be to us neither god nor fiend, but simply an earnest young Jew who came to his people in their night of terror and sought to bring them light.

More has been said and written of this one man than of any other in all history—but still we know exceedingly little about him. All that is preserved of his own words was set down years after his death in a tongue he did not speak, and by men not nearly so great as to understand all he said. And even that little was copied and recopied by scribe after scribe until to-day much of it seems tortured out of all likeness to what may have been the true words. Save for what is set down in the New Testament, we know not a thing about this prophet Joshua. The Pharisees, who were writing whole volumes at about the same time, make no mention of him whatsoever. Nor have the Roman records any light to throw on his life or death. This lack of any reference to him in the writings of the day is very perplexing. Perhaps preachers and prophets were too common in the land then for extended comment to be made about any one of them. . . .

While he lived, hundreds came eagerly to hear him; but once he died he was soon forgotten—soon forgotten by all save a few. But those few remembered him well.

3

He was born in the north of Palestine, in Galilee, and his father was a humble carpenter. He, too, in his youth was a carpenter. He had little learning, for in that region and among such poor folk, learning was exceedingly rare. He spoke in Aramaic, the jargon of the day, and perhaps he could not even read Hebrew. But like most other Jewish lads even of his lowly station, he did know the words of the great prophets of old, and the prayers which the pious Pharisees were wont to recite in the synagogues. And what is far more important, the God-hungry spirit of the Jew was mighty in his bones. He saw the travail of his people and it so stirred him that he could not abide in peace in his village. He arose from among his tools, and taking staff in hand he went forth to make ready for the Day of the Messiah.

First he was one of them that followed that great Jew, John the Baptist. Then, when John was murdered by the king, young Joshua went forth and preached by himself.

He preached in the villages of Galilee, and the simple folk, the peasants and the fishermen with their wives and little children, flocked to hear his words. Sometimes he spoke in the synagogues, for it seems any Jew who so desired could arise in them and preach. But more often he preached on the dusty highways, on the beach of the Sea of Galilee, and in the fields.

Of what Joshua looked like, we know nothing. No doubt he was dark like all the other Jews then, and probably he was thin and not very strong in body.

He had no new gospel to bring to the people, but only sought to have them understand and love that which long before had been brought to them. He told them, as had so many prophets before him, that God was a Loving Father who would forgive them all if they but repented. Also he told them that soon, very soon, the Messiah would come, and that then the Kingdom of Heaven would be seen on earth.

He taught the people to recite simple and comforting prayers like the one beginning, "Our Father which art in Heaven"—prayers made up of verses which the Pharisees in Jerusalem were wont to recite. And he reminded the people of certain laws and commandments in the ancient *seforim,* the Holy Scriptures. Especially he reminded them of that highest law of all—that they should love one another. Even their enemies should they love if they would enter the Kingdom of Heaven.

4

But what must have attracted the people most was the manner of this young prophet. A spirit breathed through his preaching that rarely if ever before had been known in the land. There was an overwhelming warmth and kindliness, a tremendous love in it all. With the exception of Hosea, the other prophets seem to have been fierce and impatient men. Their words were like whetted swords that cut down the sinners, that bruised and stabbed and pierced them through. Or they were like knotted whips that flayed them.

But this Joshua, save at rare moments, was all tenderness and benignity. Not merely did he *tell* of God's great love; most earnestly he tried to *practice* it.

And that was a day when not love but hate was sovereign among men. The Romans crucified the Zealots, the Zealots murdered the Sadducees, the Sadducees loathed the Pharisees; and all of them together despised the wretched folk in the slums of the towns and on the farms of the land.

Perhaps that was why the young Galilean was so followed and so devotedly believed. To a people tired unto death of hate, he came with a word of love.

Especially to the cowed and broken, to the poor

and unlearned, he came with that word of love. He told them that in God's sight they were more precious even than the wealthiest and the most learned in all the land. He went down to the sinners in the places of shame, to the outcasts and the pariahs, and told them that if they would but repent they could not fail to enter the Kingdom of Heaven.

And they believed him. Desiring to believe, thirsting for the certainty that they too might enter the World to Come, the souls of the lowly went out to this Joshua and his words as the parched tongues of cattle reach out for the rain.

And they were grateful to him. They flung themselves to the ground and kissed his feet for his goodness toward them. Indeed, they were too grateful and praised him so that he had to chide them. Only the good God, he declared, deserved such praise.

But he could not stay them from it. Never before had so benign a prophet come among them; and their adoration would suffer no curtailing. And as the months passed and he continued preaching, lo, he began to seem in their eyes even more than a mortal being! They began to believe that he could work miracles, that he could heal the halt and blind—even that he could raise the dead. He seemed too near perfection, too wondrous to be just a man like themselves. He seemed the very Messiah! . . .

5

We cannot tell for certain whether Joshua himself ever became possessed of that idea. Perhaps he did. With a great multitude hailing and worshiping him as the "Anointed One," the thought must have been nigh impossible to resist. But though there is this uncertainty as to his own mind, there can be none as to the mind of the people. To them he was indeed the long-promised Messiah come at last to usher in the Kingdom of Heaven. And when after ministering three years in Galilee, the prophet went down to keep the Passover in Jerusalem, his fame preceded him and he was greeted there by ecstatic mobs as the awaited Deliverer.

But his triumphal entry into Jerusalem proved young Joshua's undoing. Before five days had passed, he knew his end was near. The Sadducees, whom he had flaunted the very first day, were feverishly busy, plotting evil against him. He had driven their money changers out of the Temple courts, and they could not forgive him for it. He tried to escape beyond the city walls, but he was pursued, betrayed, and taken prisoner to the house of a high priest. There hastily he was tried by a court of priests, and found guilty—though of what crime we cannot now tell. Perhaps his very condemners could not have told either. They wanted to put him out of the way, as centuries earlier they had wanted to put Jeremiah out of the way. He was their enemy, and they could have no thought of mercy.

From the high priests' house he was taken to the palace of the Roman governor, Pontius Pilate. Again was he questioned, this time by the governor alone. And then abruptly he was sentenced to die. . . .

There was no justice in it all. Pilate, a quick, choleric official, could have had no real understanding

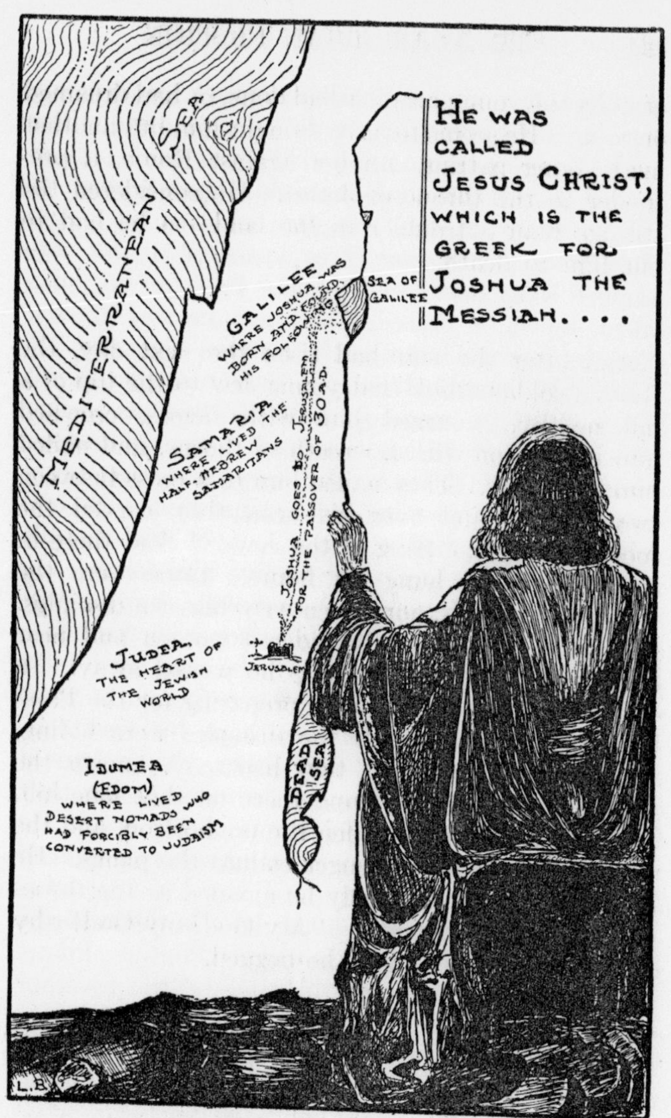

13.—The Story of Joshua of Nazareth

of what the young prophet had done, or had dreamed of doing. He seems to have thought him but another mad young patriot, a rebel against Rome, a pretender to the throne of Judea. He considered the strange man a troubler in the land—so he had to put him to death.

6

And after the sun had risen the next day, the Roman soldiers took that young Jew to the top of a hill nearby, scourged him with fagots, crowned him in derision with a wreath of thorns, and nailed him to a cross. They nailed him to a cross between two thieves, and over his head they carved the mocking words, "King of the Jews." And there in mortal pain he hung for hours. Gone were the huzzahing crowds; gone even were his own disciples. Only a little knot of bewildered women and near friends stood by to watch as he passed away. In the city the Jews were busy preparing for the Passover feast; in the fields the disciples were hiding, too terrified to confess they had even known the martyr. Deserted he hung there on that lone hill.

The sun began to redden the far horizon, and the man Joshua could no longer endure the pangs. He began to moan. Brokenly he moaned as the throes of death came over him. "My God! my God! why hast thou forsaken me?" he begged.

And then he died.

CHAPTER XVII

HOW A NEW RELIGION WAS CREATED AROUND THE STORY OF THE CRUCIFIED PROPHET

Joshua of Nazareth died, and as far as Pontius Pilate and the priests were concerned, that was the end of that matter.

But it was not. Rather it was but the beginning. The Jerusalem mob soon forgot the young man who had been killed for preaching war with Rome when he had only preached peace with God. They forgot him because other preachers, perhaps many others, came after him—and were also killed.

But among the fishermen and peasants of Galilee there was no forgetting him. His prophecies had become too much a part of their life for them ever to forget him who had uttered them. And when the bedraggled disciples came trudging home with the news of the prophet's death, great was the consternation among those poor people. They were utterly desolated. For if the Romans had been able to kill this Messiah, then he could not have been the real Messiah after all! He must have been a charlatan and a fraud!

But that they could not believe. They who had known the young man Joshua, they who had heard him and followed him, could not possibly believe he had deceived them. They could not even believe he was dead. To them it seemed incredible that a soul so wondrous and godlike as his could have been snuffed out on a cross hard by Jerusalem's gate.

And soon there began a furtive whispering among those scattered believers. It was said the body of the Master was no longer in the tomb where it had been buried. On the third day it had disappeared, so the rumor went. The body had gone up to heaven—straight up to God—just as the body of Elijah had gone up to God. People had seen it go up. Solemnly they swore they had seen it ascend into heaven.

And they that set those rumors afloat were not consciously telling falsehoods. They themselves believed them. They believed them because they could not bear to think that he whom they had looked on as their Messiah had perished. And they that heard the rumors—and eagerly passed them on—believed them for the same reason. Those unhappy folk, aching in every limb because of the travail of the world that then was, would not without a struggle give up their hope of the World to Come.

2

And thus was born a strange and obscure sect called the Nazarenes. Its members were all Jews, but Jews with a peculiar doctrine. They believed that the Messiah had already come, and that he was now in heaven watching over them with tender but troubled eyes. If they lived the life he had commanded them, if they loved one another and shared their wealth and held no slaves in bondage, and put away all lust and vain desire, then he would be able to return to them. Swiftly he would return to them and this time he would surely usher in the Kingdom of Heaven.

Perhaps there were five hundred in Galilee, perhaps a thousand, who held to that doctrine. The other Jews paid little or no attention to the sect, for they knew its members were simple peasant folk living in a region where new doctrines, and fanaticisms, and sects arose almost daily. The other Jews were too much occupied in their death struggle with Rome to concern themselves with the tiny movement.

3

And while the other Jews fought with governor after governor, complaining, petitioning, rebelling, and dying, that tiny movement grew. A certain man named Saul or Paul, a Jew of Roman citizenship, became its champion. He was not like the other Nazarenes, for he was a man of the world, a person of culture, a magnificent orator. Nor was his doctrine at all as simple as theirs. He took the one central thought, the belief in the Messiah—the Christ as he called him in Greek—who had died on the cross; but to it he added many other thoughts gleaned by him in the market places of Asia Minor and the isles of the sea.

Even in his day, however, the movement was not yet considered a new religion, but still esteemed a part of Judaism. And Paul preached it to Jews in their synagogues scattered throughout the Mediterranean lands. Jewish colonies had long been established in many of those foreign cities, but they were made up in large part of Gentiles who had been converted to Judaism. Such conversions had been common everywhere for so many years, that there were many more Jews outside of Judea than in it. But the Jerusalem Pharisees looked upon all those new Jewish converts as only half-Jews. Most of them were uncircumcised; and they did not keep all the laws set down in the *seforim*, the Holy Scriptures. They still clung to many of their old beliefs and superstitions.

It is difficult for us to understand just what was going on in the civilized world at that time. A great hunger seems to have taken possession of all the races, a hunger for faith, for religion. It was a tired, a dying world—a world that had lost its best blood in wasteful wars of conquests. And in its last hours it gulped thirstily from every cup of faith held to its lips, hoping wildly that some one of them might contain the elixir of life. In the lands around the Mediterranean there was almost an orgy of belief-making in those years. All sorts of gods belonging to all sorts of religions were fused together—even their names were combined!—and sacrifices were offered to them all at one time. Not having complete faith in any one God, the people tried to make use of them all.

For that reason, the strict orthodox Jews looked with suspicion on the converts they were winning day by day. The newcomers into the fold were too hectic, too feverish. And they came with too many of their old beliefs still strong in their hearts. So they were received with reservations—with severe reservations.

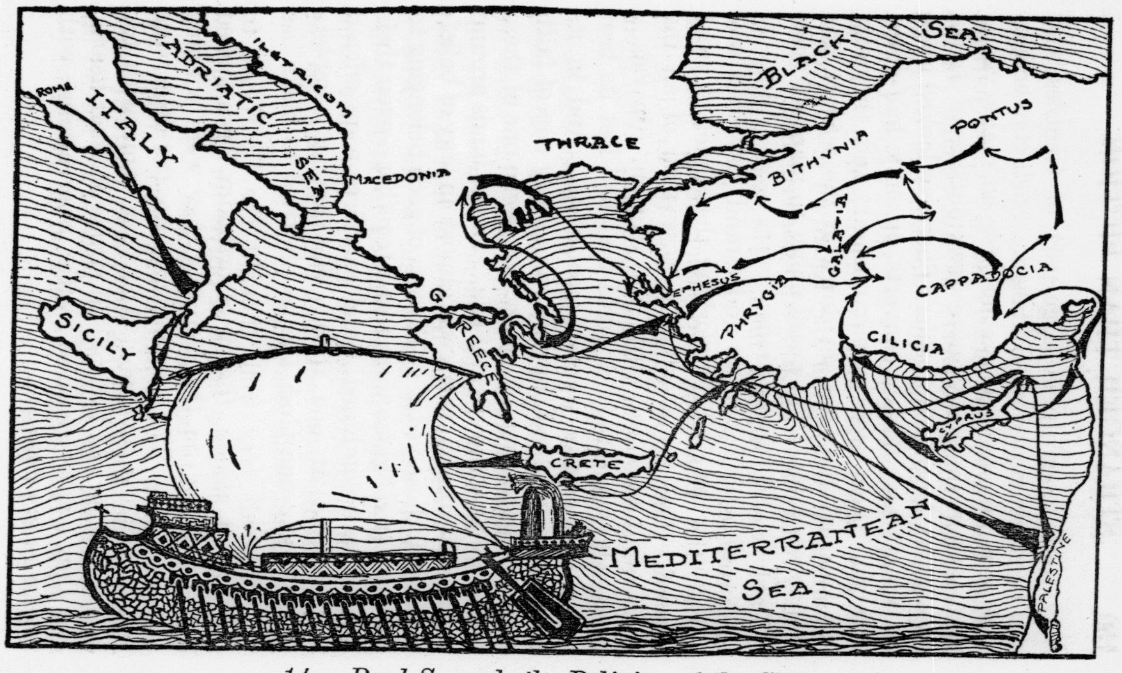

14.—*Paul Spreads the Religion of the Christ*

4

But Paul was not nearly so strict, so narrow. He treated those converts as his equals, for he claimed that now that the Messiah had come, all of the old laws were no longer valid. Now Gentile and Jew were one, and uncircumcised as well as circumcised could enter the Kingdom of Heaven—if they but believed in him who was crucified.

Paul was a shrewd man. He was willing to compromise.

But the Pharisees, the strict Jews, were less shrewd. They were willing to lose the world rather than annul one jot or tittle of their law. With them it was all or nothing.

Some say that was wrong of those Pharisees. They say they should have been less stiff-necked and uncompromising. Perhaps so. But when we see what came of Paul's leniency, how far his followers strayed from the religion of him they called their Christ, we can hardly censure the Pharisees. Perhaps they were indeed bigoted to withdraw behind their high stockade of Law. But they seem to have sensed the fact that the hour was not yet ripe for them to do otherwise.

It was all very well, thought the Pharisees, to make God's house a house of prayer for all people—but first it had to be *their* God's house.

And thus a new religion was born. While the Pharisees in their self-righteousness hoarded what was, after all, the religion of Jesus, Paul spread far and wide what became the religion of the Christ.

And so did Christianity begin.

CHAPTER XVIII

THE DESTRUCTION OF JERUSALEM BY THE ROMAN LEGIONS, AND THE "END" IT BROUGHT TO THE JEWISH NATION

In Judea the gory struggle between Roman and Jew dragged on. Only for a brief moment was there a respite when a grandson of Herod, a man favored by Rome yet beloved by the Jews, was made king of the land. But he died in the year 44 A. D. and from then on there was unbroken turmoil. Seven Roman governors followed each other in rapid succession, each one more cruel than the other. They drove the people to despair and madness by their wanton violations of religious feeling.

Perhaps those governors were not altogether to blame. They were at their wits' end. They had been able to handle all sorts of people in every part of the then-known world—but these Jews were altogether beyond them. They were the only people on earth who would rather die than offer sacrifices to the image of an emperor. They were willing to give up everything, their wealth, their homes, their land, their very lives—but they would not give up their God. To the Roman officials they seemed a spoiled, obstinate, half-demented people; and failing to win them over with kind words, they tried their swords. Thousands of Jews were put to death in those ghastly years. They were burned and crucified and massacred in droves.

Finally, in the year 66, matters reached a climax. The Jews could stand the tyranny no longer, and openly rebelled. Roman legions were sent down from Syria to quell the uprising, but to no avail. The Jews fought like maddened lions, and could not be subdued. Nero, the Roman emperor, realized this was no ordinary little outbreak, and quickly sent two of his ablest generals, Vespasian and Titus, to the scene. Down through Galilee they marched, fighting wildly a whole year before finally reducing it to subjection. Then west of Jerusalem they plowed a bloody furrow; then south; and then at last up to the walls of the city itself.

2

It is chiefly from the writings of a Jewish general named Josephus, a man who deserted his forces and then tried to do penance by recounting the heroism of those who stayed true, that we know what happened during the siege. Jerusalem became the scene of one of the most devastating contests in all history. The besieged within the city were divided into three camps, each wrangling with the others over who should be leader and how the war should be carried on. One held the lower city, another the upper, and a third the Temple area in between. Two of the factions began to quarrel over the possession of the town granaries, and after repeated raids and massacres, someone set fire to the whole vast store so that it was completely destroyed. There they were, a million or more Jews butchering each other in an ancient, dirty, high-walled city hardly a mile square in size; the food supplies gone; and the dread Roman already at the gates! . . .

And yet they would not surrender.

Vespasian had been called back to Rome to be crowned as emperor, and Titus, his son, began the siege. His artillery hurled great boulders a quarter of a mile into the heart of the city. Great mounds were built close against the north wall and on these huge battering rams were placed. (Every tree within ten miles of the city had been cut down to make those rams.) And then, day and night the thunder of the rams was to be heard.

Fifteen days the incessant pounding went on, and at last a breach was made in the outer wall. Nine days more, and the second wall fell.

At last the Romans were masters of the lower city.

But still the Jews would not surrender. In the upper city they huddled, starving and dying. There was murder among them over scraps of meat or bread. At night those who stole out to pick herbs and roots in the fields were crucified by the Romans who captured them—five hundred were crucified in one day—or were slain and robbed when they returned home.

Yet they would not surrender.

No, rather they became even more madly stubborn as their terrors increased. They undermined the Roman mounds so that the huge battering rams suddenly came crashing to the ground. Then out they stormed like ravenous demons, flinging themselves full tilt at the enemy, and clawing, slashing, biting their way through.

The great legions wavered—tottered—broke. And Titus retreated.

But then came even greater horrors for the besieged. Titus had a high wall of earth five miles in length thrown all around the city—and sat down to wait. The suffering of the Jews seemed beyond bearing. Even Titus, a hard Roman not unused to war, could not stand the sight of it. He begged the mad zealots to surrender and have done with it all.

But no. No surrender. Never!

A month passed. Two. The Romans returned to the attack. One wall fell, but a second had been raised by the Jews in the meantime. The second fell. But still the heroes fought on. They were taking their stand in the inner fortress now. The narrow streets ran with blood. Sickening was the stench of the dead bodies rotting in the hot summer sun. Jews fought each other in the streets over handfuls of the most loathsome food—filthy straw, bits of old leather, even offal. The wife of the high priest, who had been wont to have thick carpets laid from her house to the Temple so that her sandals might not be soiled, now staggered about in the alleyways in search of crusts. The daily offerings on the altars were no longer made because of the lack of animals. . . .

But still no surrender.

Titus again offered to make terms, but again the zealots refused to parley. They knew what terms with the enemy would mean—giving over the city. And they believed the city was God's, not theirs, to give. And so wondrous was their faith that at the sight of it some of the Roman soldiers even deserted their own legions and ran to throw in their lot with the besieged.

The fortress walls were scaled, and the zealots were forced to retreat to the Temple courts. For six days the battering rams savagely pounded the sacred walls, and then at last the inevitable end drew near. Titus ordered that the sanctuary be spared, but his infuriated soldiers refused to listen. A burning torch was hurled through the Golden Window, and immediately the wooden beams caught fire. Into the Temple courts the soldiers dashed, massacring the thousands who had taken refuge there.

And then there was quiet for a moment.

But again the resistance blazed forth. The zealots retreated to the upper city, to their last inch of ground, and once more defied the enemy. Almost a whole month they held out there before they crumpled for good. They were starved out and exhausted. Their strength was utterly spent.

The Romans came raging in, slaying until their arms were tired. Every alley, and room, and corner was choked with bleeding corpses. Then fire was set to everything—houses, buildings, walls—and the conquerors stood back to watch the flames.

And thus was old Jerusalem destroyed.

3

It is said that more than a million Jews died in that siege. Of those who survived, ninety-seven thousand were made slaves. They were deported to labor in the mines of Egypt, or were forced to fight wild beasts in the Roman arenas. Titus himself took the noblest of the zealots away to march in his triumphal procession through the broad streets of Rome. A great arch was built there to commemorate his ghastly triumph, an arch on which were carved figures of his young captives carrying the sacred vessels of the Temple.

The remains of that beauteous arch are still standing in old Rome. And the ruins of the blood-soaked wall still stand in old Jerusalem. Only there are no Romans now to look on that arch and rejoice in the triumph it commemorates. The Jews alone are left, and they come to pray at their old wall even to this day. The Romans have gone—gone the way of the Egyptians and Assyrians and Babylonians and Persians and Greeks. Only the Jews still live.

In the year 70, with Jerusalem destroyed, it seemed as if the Strange People, the Jews, had indeed reached their end.

But it was not their end.

It was but a new beginning.

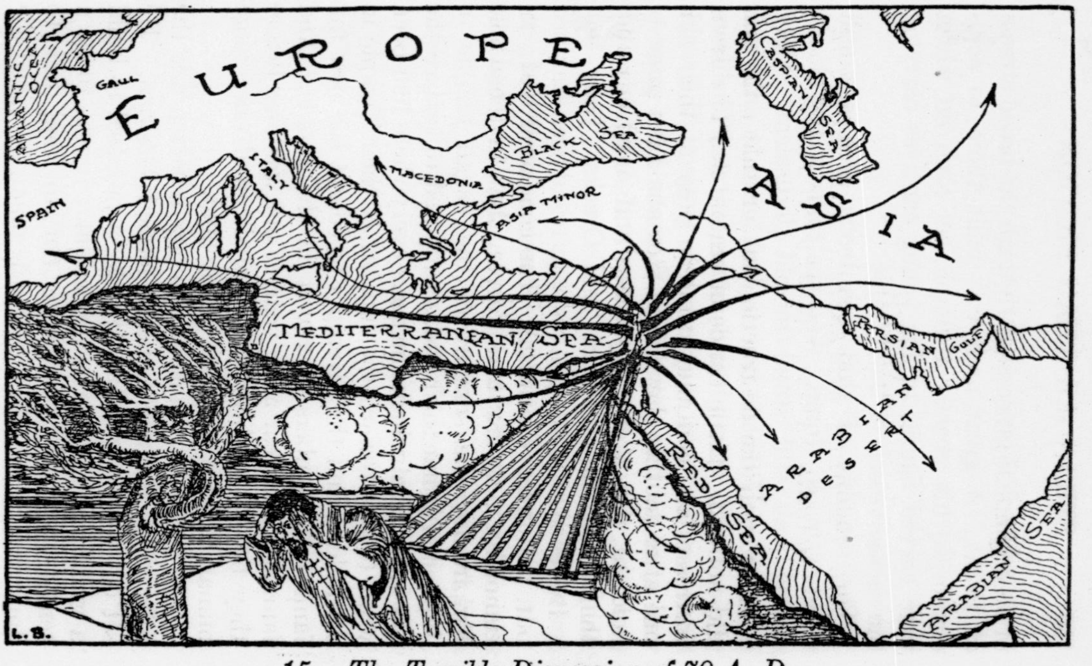

15.—*The Terrible Dispersion of 70 A. D.*

CHAPTER XIX

THE TERRIBLE DISPERSION, AND HOW THE RABBIS SAVED THE JEWISH FAITH

Even with the destruction of Jerusalem the war did not end. Little bands of zealots fled to distant fortresses and continued to defy Rome. And when one after another they found they could not possibly hold out, they preferred to destroy themselves rather than surrender.

But even after all open resistance had been stamped out, the unrest continued. The conqueror had proclaimed a new law taxing every Jew in the whole Empire for the support of the pagan temple of Jupiter in Rome. This was supposed to replace the old half-shekel which the Jews everywhere had been wont to pay toward the support of their Temple in Jerusalem; and the attempts to collect the new tax fanned the embers of revolt in the people. And fanning them year after year, it not was long before they burst into high flames again, and once more human blood was spilled in the land.

The immediate cause of the new rebellion was the folly of a Roman emperor named Hadrian. He set out to win over the Jews by a proposal to build a grand new temple in Jerusalem. It was to be a temple dedicated, however, not to God but to Jupiter! Hadrian in his Gentile mind, imagined the Jews would be delighted with *any* sort of a temple, so long as its location was Mount Moriah in Jerusalem. And he was greatly enraged when he learnt that they resented the very idea of his building such a sanctuary. He gave up all hope then of winning them over with kindness, and resorted to force. He determined to put an end to the fanatical faith of the Jews, no matter what the cost. He forbade the observance of the Sabbath and the rite of circumcision. The study of the Holy Law he made a capital crime.

2

But it was in vain. All that he accomplished was a repetition of what happened three hundred years earlier when Antiochus Epiphanes tried in a like manner to crush Judaism. The Jews leaped up in violent rebellion.

Their leader this time was a man who took the name of Bar Kochba, meaning "Son of the Star." Evidently he was but another of those individuals who were hailed as the Messiahs by the credulous people; and his following was a tremendous one. Even the great Rabbi Akiba, the most learned man of the time, supported him. Coins were struck, and on them Bar Kochba was described as "Prince of Israel."

Three years the rebellion continued before Rome's greatest general could stamp it out. And then there followed massacres even exceeding those following the triumph of Titus. Akiba and many other leaders were executed; thousands of other rebels were sold into slavery. Part of the land was distributed as loot to the Roman soldiers and the rest was auctioned off to the highest bidder. Jerusalem was renamed Ælia Capitolina, and over its gate was impaled a swine's head. All Jews were absolutely forbidden to enter the place "for all time to come."

Only on the ninth day of the month of Ab, the anniversary of the destruction of the temple, were the Jews permitted to approach Jerusalem. On that one day in the year might they come to the wall, and leaning against it, weep over its desolation. Even then they had to bribe the sentries not to molest them while they wept. They had to "buy their tears," as a great writer of the time puts it.

3

And thus, in the year 135, the contest between tiny Judea and mighty Rome was ended. The *Golus*, the great and dread Exile, had definitely begun. The Jews as a people never again took up arms in their own defense. Never in eighteen hundred years. They became pacifists, not from choice but from necessity. They did not dare again to rebel against any foe. They were too few and too scattered.

The scattering of the Jews through foreign lands—the Diaspora as it is usually called—had already been in process for many centuries before the fall of Jerusalem. Perhaps as early as the days of Solomon there were little colonies of Hebrew traders in strange lands. Certainly there were many after the destruction of the Northern Kingdom in 722 B. C., and still more after the destruction of the Southern Kingdom in 586 B. C. Indeed, some scholars say that from that last date on, there were always more Jews living outside the borders of Palestine than within them.

In Alexandria, that wondrous city founded in Egypt by Alexander the Great, there grew up a Jewish community so powerful that it could boast complete self-government. It lived in its own section of the city, had its own laws and officers, and produced its own very distinctive culture. One of the greatest writers of the Hellenistic world was an Alexandrian Jew named Philo, and his work influenced the thought of all early Christian scholars.

There were similar colonies in Rome, Antioch, Athens, Babylon—indeed throughout the known world of the time.

But until the fateful year 70, Jerusalem had been recognized as the center of all these settlements. It was in a way the capital of a vast spiritual empire. To it the scattered Jews made regular pilgrimage—much as the Mohammedans make pilgrimage to Mecca to-day. To it they paid the annual Temple tax of half a shekel. And to it they looked for their religious laws and regulations. It was a firm and solid anchor to the Jews who sailed on pagan seas.

But with the Fall of Jerusalem all that was ended. The anchor had parted, and all the scattered settlements seemed to be loose and adrift.

4

Had the Jews been simply a nation, certainly they would not have survived that hour. They would have disappeared as did the Phœnicians and the Arameans. And had they been devoted to an unchangeable priestly religion, certainly they could never again have flourished. A few devoted souls would have huddled around the ruined Temple, and there dwindled fast away.

But the Jews were more than a nation, and their religion was more than a priestly cult. Indeed for generations before the Destruction, it was neither politics nor sacrifice that had been at the heart of Jewish life, but a strange thing called the Holy Law.

The priests, as we have already seen, first came into power by inducing the people to impose certain laws upon themselves which they called the laws of Moses. But so soon as the priests took too great advantage of that power and became shamelessly corrupt, the people began to grow restless. The rebellious spirit of the old Prophets was awakened in them, and they began to protest. But they had to protest in a queer roundabout fashion. They did not dare say openly that the priests were a bad lot and ought to be driven from the land, for that would have meant flying in the face of the *Torah*, the "Law of Moses." Even by the third century before the Destruction, this Torah had become too well intrenched even to be covertly challenged. So the only thing left was to say that the Torah itself was perfect, but that the priests were not properly interpreting it.

In this way, as we have seen, the Pharisees arose—the "Interpreters" who made it their business to study the Law and discover just how far the priests might go.

In the beginning the Pharisees had very little

power, but as the years passed, the opposite became true. Indeed, by the time the Temple fell, the priesthood had come to occupy a position somewhat like that of the royalty in England to-day. It was all show. The real power had passed into the hands of the Pharisee leaders—the Rabbis, the "Teachers," as they were called. They controlled the Sanhedrin, or parliament, and they decided all the religious questions of the day.

5

It was that shift in power and leadership from the priests to the rabbis that saved Israel after the year 70. The Destruction of the Temple was a terrible blow—but not a mortal one. Although the priests and their sacrifices were no more, the Law which had ordained them still existed. And because that Law was intact—and learned rabbis survived to reinterpret it—Israel survived.

Most people love to read of the mad zealots who fought to death against Rome; but in the light of history the truly great men of that ghastly hour were those rabbis who did not fight. They were the true saviors of the people, for they alone saved the faith.

Their leader was a man named Jochanan *ben* (which means "the son of") Zakkai. He was a disciple of a great Pharisee named Hillel, a man in whose teaching there seemed to live anew all the grand spirit of the Prophets. (Hillel it was who said some thirty years before Joshua of Nazareth was born, that the whole of the Law was included in the one verse, "Do not unto thy neighbor that which is hateful unto thee.") Jochanan himself reminds us a little of the prophet Jeremiah, for he too realized the folly of warring with the sword against overwhelming odds. When Rome laid siege to Jerusalem he fled from the city to the village of Jabneh on the seacoast, and there he took charge of a little "house of learning." He was quite willing to let Rome have the capital and all the land—so long as he could have his little school in Jabneh.

And he was right.

When Jerusalem was at last destroyed, Jabneh was prepared to take its place. It became the new center of the great Jewish Diaspora, the one light of the Golus. There the rabbis gathered at the feet of Jochanan ben Zakkai, and there a new Sanhedrin was created. The house of learning and the synagogue became what the Temple had been, and study and prayer took the place of the old sacrifices.

The day of the priest was over. The great day of the rabbi had come.

CHAPTER XX

HOW THE RABBIS BUILT A WALL OF LAW AROUND THE JEWS

There is something intensely dramatic about the life and work of those rabbis of the early centuries. Usually we think of them as very ancient and feeble men with long white beards, and dreamy lack-luster eyes. But they were nothing of the sort. For the most part they were young or middle-aged men, brawny fellows who worked hard all day as craftsmen. They did not take to the study of the Law because they had nothing else to do with their time, for many of them had to earn a livelihood as tentmakers, or blacksmiths, or carpenters. They went to the house of learning only in their leisure hours, and it was to them what the lodge-room and the theater and the pool-hall are to the tired workingmen of our own day.

But they passed the time in those houses of learning in a quite extraordinary way. They talked! They argued and discoursed and quibbled at endless length. And not only about strictly religious matters, but about everything else connected with life. They discussed not merely what prayers should be recited in the synagogues, and what writings were holy enough to be read there, but also why Negroes have flat feet, how the stars move in the heavens, in what manner to set a broken bone, and just how beautiful a girl was Ruth.

All their free hours and days and years they spent in those houses of learning, gravely worrying about everything under the sun. Sport they frowned upon, for by very temperament they could not enjoy it. So instead of playing in the sun in their spare time, instead of running races or throwing javelins like the Romans, they withdrew into their dark little schools and talked.

And thus a new type of man became their idol—not the great athlete but the great scholar. And a new sort of aristocracy arose among them—an aristocracy not of birth or wealth but of learning.

2

Of course, in time this led to a marked evil. The learned began to grow proud and snobbish. They looked on the *am ha-aretz*, the ignorant man—especially if he spoke with a Galilean accent—as little better than a heathen. As early as the time of Joshua of Nazareth this snobbishness was already rampant among the Pharisee scholars, and that is why the young preacher so bitterly denounced them.

And with the passing of the years that snobbishness did not seem to decrease.

Among the learned themselves, however, there was complete democracy. Wealth or parentage made no difference among them, and legend has it that several of the greatest rabbis spent their boyhood in peasant huts. A learned man, even though he was the son of the lowest woman of the streets, was regarded as of nobler rank than an unlearned high priest.

Houses of learning had long existed in most of

the large Jewish settlements, and only the fame of Jochanan ben Zakkai made the one in Jabneh chief among them after the Destruction. Naturally the most brilliant students went there to study under Jochanan and thus made it possible for the Great Sanhedrin of seventy-one scholars to reorganize itself there.

But during the persecutions under Hadrian, when all study was forbidden, Jabneh lost its leadership. That, however, did not end the work that had begun there. Though all study of the law was prohibited on pain of death, study of it nevertheless continued. Rabbis were murdered day after day—but with their last breaths they appointed their successors. And these successors fled to the north of Palestine, to Galilee, where the Roman soldiers could not so easily catch them. And there in the city of Usha they organized a new academy and a new Sanhedrin.

The center of Jewish learning, however, did not long remain in Usha. It moved regularly to whatever town happened to be the home of the next in the line of the great scholars. The brightest pupils flocked there from all ends of the Diaspora; and there the Sanhedrin had to be set up anew. From Usha the center shifted to Shefaram; from Shefaram to Beth Shearim; from Beth Shearim to Sepphoris; from Sepphoris to Tiberius; and at last from Tiberius right out of Palestine into Babylonia. . . .

3

It was while the center was in Sepphoris that the learned Rabbi Judah compiled what was called the *Mishna*, the "Repetition."

This Mishna is a work in six volumes, and was intended to serve merely as a text-book of rabbinic law. The old legislation in the first five books in the Bible, the Torah, was no longer suited to the changed circumstances of the people. The Jews in the year 200 A. D. had outgrown it almost as much as we in modern times have outgrown the simple laws of the Middle Ages. Steadily the Jews had been outgrowing their old legislation, and just as steadily they had been re-interpreting and adjusting it. They had never conceded the old laws were wrong and should be forgotten, but merely that they needed a little "touching up." So all those years the scholars had been touching them up.

Thus did the Oral Law originate—the law handed down from teacher to disciple by word of mouth.

But a new difficulty arose. No two great teachers taught exactly the same Oral Law, and when the disciples from different houses of learning came together, often there were almost violent disagreements. One said, "My master taught thus and thus," and another declared, "But *my* master taught so and so." For that reason several great rabbis at different times tried to compile huge notebooks for the use of students everywhere.

On the basis of those earlier notebooks, Rabbi Judah some time before the year 200 compiled his Mishna. In it he gathered together about four thousand legal decisions (the Torah contained only six hundred and thirteen!) and these he divided into different groups and sections. It was not supposed to be a final code of law. It was merely another of those notebooks. It did not say "thus and thus

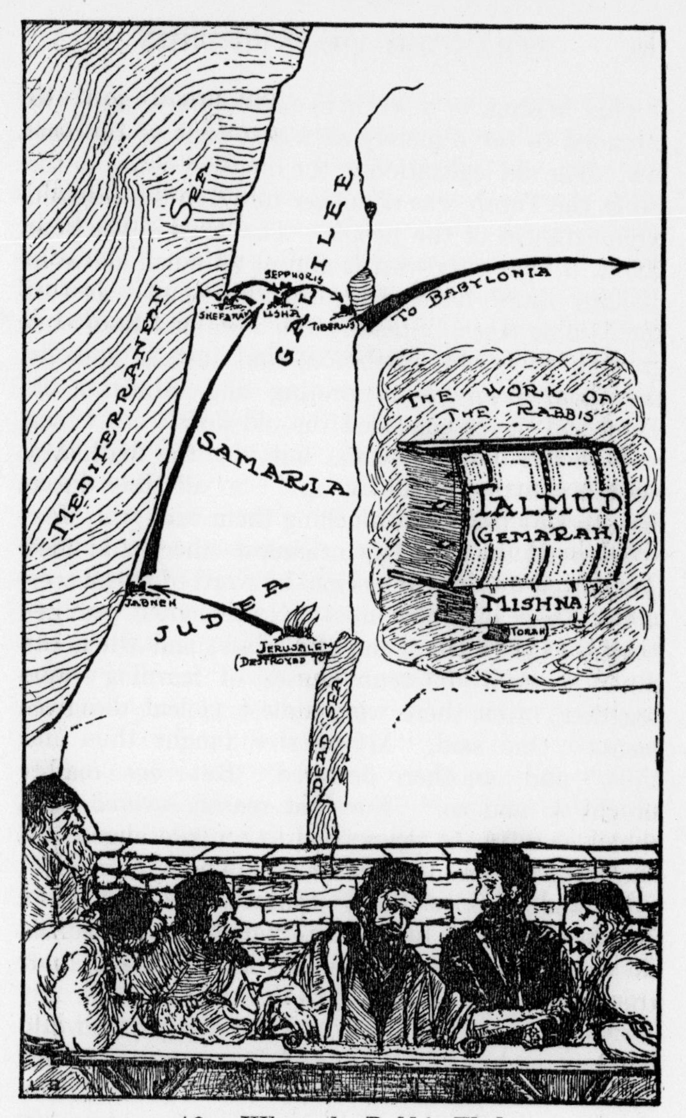

16.—*Where the Rabbis Fled*

is the law on this question," but usually gave the varying opinions of the leading rabbis of the past, together with Rabbi Judah's own opinions.

It was not long, however, before Rabbi Judah's pronouncements quoted in the Mishna came to be looked upon as absolutely authoritative. The passing suggestions and hesitant opinions of a learned but still imperfect mind, came to be regarded in a little while as divine commands.

4

It is not difficult to explain why the Mishna so soon became authoritative. It was probably due to the bewildering conditions under which the Jews lived in those centuries. Their country and their Temple, the things that once had united them, were gone. The Law was all that was left. And just then the preachers of the new religion called Christianity, were bitterly attacking that Law. They were saying it was an evil thing, for it kept the Jews from mingling with the rest of the world.

That was why the pious among the Jews so readily accepted Rabbi Judah's Mishna. It served as a direct rebuke to those Christian preachers. It showed the world that far from minimizing the Law, faithful Jews intended to magnify it. Tenfold, a hundredfold, they intended to magnify it. . . . And do so they would just *because* it kept them apart from the rest of the world. . . .

For the Jews could now see how the pagan world lived, and what manner of gods it worshiped. They could see the vice in the homes of the Romans, and the bestiality in their temples. They could see all the moral leprosy that was eating into the heart of the Empire and bringing it fast to its doom.

That explains why the Jews desired only to keep away from the *goyim*, to avoid them as they would loathsome lepers. Ever higher they built the wall of Law around themselves, barricading themselves on all sides. The simple command not to eat meat with non-Jews, was now extended to forbid them from eating *anything* with them. Even the bread prepared by non-Jews was considered "unclean."

5

Some people swing back and forth between incredulity and contempt when they read certain of the laws in the Mishna. They find it hard to believe that the rabbis who passed them could possibly have been sane. But they were very sane, those rabbis. They saw how near their people were to death, and they cast all scruples to the wind. Panic-stricken they clutched at every imaginable regulation that might keep Israel alive. They were like men who pile up boulders and bricks and even pebbles in frantic effort to build a dyke against a rapidly encroaching sea.

Curiously, the laws developed and accepted by those rabbis, dealt with and regulated not only the life of their own time; even more minutely did they deal with and re-order the chapters of Jewish life that had passed into history. At endless length they prescribed just how the ancient sacrifices should be offered, and how the tithes should be paid to the long-deposed priests. Perhaps three-quarters of the

Mishna deals thus with a ritual that was utterly destroyed a hundred and thirty years before the Mishna was compiled.

There was a reason. The rabbis believed that all that past life would be relived again in the future. The wild dream of the coming of the Messiah was still alive in their hearts. Despite all the evil that had come to them—rather, on account of all that evil—they still hoped for the Great Day of Redemption. Only now they no longer dreamed, as did the old prophets, of redemption for all mankind. No, now the dream was of redemption for themselves alone. The iron of persecution had gone too far into their souls for the Jews still to dream of saving the world. They must have hated and loathed the world. All they gave thought to, at any rate, was their own sorry selves—their desolated land, their ruined Temple, their scattered and broken nation.

It was not for lack of something better to do that the rabbis developed their innumerable laws; nor was it out of stupidity that the disciples accepted them. It was out of sheer need—fearful, desperate need.

Israel was being drowned in the sea of paganism. And the Law alone could stem and hold back the tide.

CHAPTER XXI

THE MAKING OF THE TALMUD

Another century dragged by, and life for the Jews grew to be no longer bearable in Palestine. The Christians had become all powerful in the land, and through their influence at Rome they caused the Jews to be plagued most cruelly. The Emperor Constantine himself became a Christian, and harsh

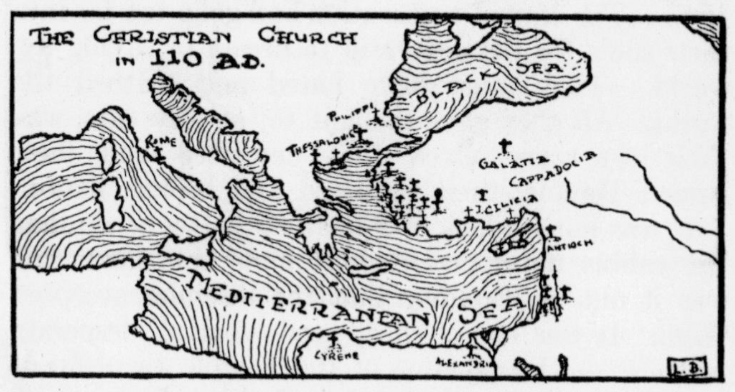

17.—The Church after Paul Died

indeed were the laws he passed against those who clung to the older faiths.

The Jews therefore began to flee to other lands. Chiefly they fled to the East, to Babylonia, which was outside the empire of Rome. The vast Jewish community which had flourished in that land from the time of the Exile in 586 B. C., had helped not a little in keeping Babylonia free from the Roman yoke. It had sent out regiment after regiment to fight off the dread conqueror of the West. And as a result it enjoyed almost complete freedom under the Parthians who ruled the land. The Jews had their synagogues and their primary schools and their houses of learning. And they had their own leader—*Resh Galutha*, "Prince of the Exile," he was called—who was recognized by the government.

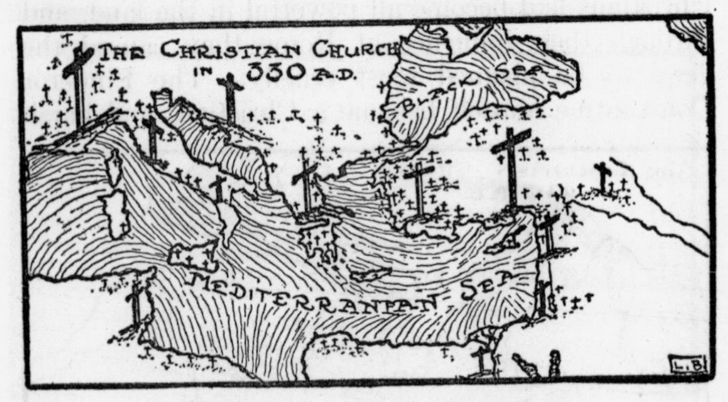

18.—The Church under Constantine

Until the Destruction of the Temple the Jews in Babylonia had, of course, looked to Palestine as their spiritual home. Even for two centuries after that calamitous event they still sent their best students to the rabbinical academies in Jabneh, Sepphoris, and Tiberius. But from the beginning of their exile, the Babylonian Jews had rather resented the position of leadership which the Palestinians enjoyed. Later generations of them somehow felt that even though they had never gone back to the homeland, they were nevertheless as good as, and perhaps even better than, those who had. Probably the Babylonian Jews regarded their brethren in Judea and Galilee much as American Jews now regard their brethren in Poland and Russia—as a more pious and orthodox, but a far less cultured lot.

2

But a time came when it was no longer necessary for the Babylonian Jews to look up to their brethren

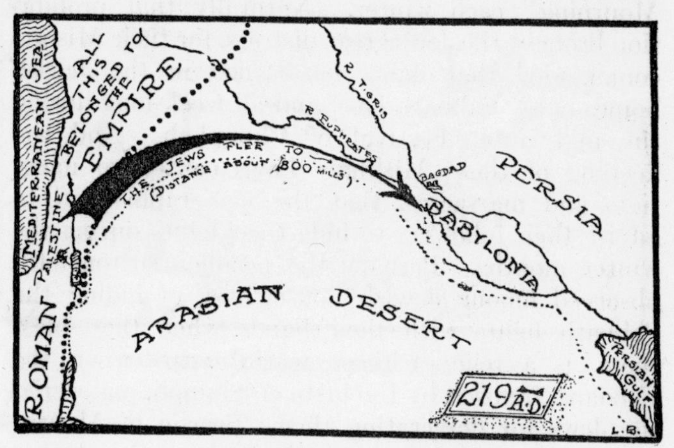

19.—*Off to Babylonia*

in Palestine. They began to develop great academies of their own, and thus attracted the finest Palestinian scholars. Just as in our own day the center of Jewish life and learning has begun to move from Eastern Europe to America, so seventeen hundred years ago it began to move from Palestine to Babylonia.

It moved to Babylonia because of the persecution in Palestine; but almost as soon as Babylonia became the center, persecutions began there also. The fanatical Persians who had been driven from power by the Parthians, succeeded in the year 226 in regaining that power. And immediately the Jews began to suffer. Those Persians, in the first flush of their triumph, started to celebrate by butchering all whom they considered "foreigners."

The Persians were fire-worshipers, and forbade the burning of the lights during their "Season of Mourning" each winter. Naturally that prohibition brought the Jews great distress, for their Mishna commanded that lights be burned in the Jewish homes every Sabbath Eve, and all week long during the mid-winter Festival of Chanukah. And the keeping of these Mishnaic Laws caused so many riots and massacres, that the new rabbis had to advise their followers to hide their lights during the winter months. Perhaps the peculiar custom still observed among Jewish housewives, of hiding the Sabbath lights with their hands when they bless them, is a relic of those fearful years when the Persians, frenzied by the taste of triumph, massacred the Jews for desecrating their "Season of Mourning."

Of course, compared with the horrors which Jews were suffering in Palestine and the rest of the Roman Empire, these massacres in Babylonia were hardly deserving of mention. I have spoken of them only to show how they influenced the rabbis of the time to modify the Mishnaic laws slightly. Such modifications were being made constantly, as day by day new problems arose. And naturally that meant in time the need for a new notebook—one far completer and more up-to-date than the Mishna.

And when that new notebook was compiled (it was a little before the year 500 A. D.) it was called the *Talmud*, the "Teaching."

3

There are two Talmuds: one that was developed by the rabbis who struggled on in Palestine, and the other developed by those who flourished in Babylonia. Much of the Palestinian Talmud has long been lost, but the fragments that still exist make it obvious that it was far the inferior work. So when we speak of the Talmud we usually mean the one produced in Babylonia.

The Talmud is not a book; rather it is a vast, rambling, loose-jointed encyclopedia. It is a great wilderness of words in which can be read the whole history of the Jewish mind during many centuries. Everything the Jew thought about anything—religion, philosophy, astronomy, art, law, biology, history, botany, medicine, politics—is included in that one great work.

Probably it set out to be merely another and larger Mishna—a sixty-three volume index to the innumerable new laws that had been proposed, discussed, and accepted after Rabbi Judah finished his modest six-volume index. But before it was complete it became very much more. It gave not merely the laws, but also great chunks of the rambling discussion that preceded the acceptance of those laws. The Mishna was a little like a well-swept lumber yard in which trimmed logs had been neatly arranged in six great stacks. But the Talmud was more like a clearing in which whole trees with all their branches and foliage, their nettles and ivy-growths, had been piled up in sixty-three wild and sprawling heaps. If there was any order at all in the whole big area, it was because down at the bottom of each of the heaps lay some of the trimmed logs of the Mishna.

4

There was a reason for the unkempt way in which the trees had been left lying around in the Talmudic clearing. In Rabbi Judah's day the learned men in Israel had been confident that the trimmed logs alone would suffice to keep the fires of their religion burning, and so they had not been afraid to lop off the branches and throw them away. But that confidence was largely gone three hundred years later in Babylonia. The new rabbis had seen how quickly these fires could burn low in the fierce wind of persecution, and they were afraid to throw away even the least scrap of their fuel.

How those rabbis ever had the patience to assemble all those mountains of words, is bewildering indeed. It all seems to have been done under the supervision of two scholars named Rab Ashe and Rabina; but any number of other scholars must have assisted them. In our printed editions the Talmud fills almost six thousand pages! The bare task of gathering the material and writing it down must have been a stupendous one.

But somehow it was done, and with it another compromise was effected between the dreams of the prophets and the common sense of the priests.

For though these rabbis had set out as heroic protestants against the priests, they had after all these centuries become very like priests themselves. Their thought had come to run in what are essentially priestly grooves. Laws, little rules and regulations, had become everything to them.

Perhaps it was necessary for this to happen if the Jews were to continue as a separate people. *The dreams of the prophets may have given the Jews a reason for living—but it was the little laws of the priest-rabbis that kept the Jews alive.*

Naturally, there was great risk that those little laws might smother the very dreams they were supposed to keep aflame—that in the strain of just keeping alive, the Jews might forget all good reason for living. And that danger became very real as the years passed by.

Indeed, half of the rest of this story of the Jews is just the story of the struggle against that danger.

B.C.

JUDEA

(Hellenism grows)

200

ANTIOCHUS tries to end JUDAISM

168 MACCABEAN REVOLT

Judea is Free

JOHN HYRCANUS forcibly converts IDOMITES

Pharisees vs. Sadducees

100

63 ROMANS CAPTURE JERUSALEM

Wild Hunger for the 'Messiah'

A.D.

JOSHVA OF NAZARETH

PAUL — Begining of CHRISTIANITY

70 DESTRUCTION OF JERUSALEM

SANHEDRIN meets in JABNEH

100

THE DISPERSION (Golus)

132-135 BAR KOCHBA rebellion

RABBINICAL Academies moved to

GALILEE

Mishna Compiled

200

RABBINICAL Academies moved to

BABYLONIA

The Wall of Law is Built

JEWS persecuted by PERSIANS

300

JEWS persecuted by CHRISTIANS

Palestinian Talmud compiled

Chart C. The Adventures of the Jews, Part III

CHAPTER XXII

THE CONTENTS OF THE TALMUD

So little is the Talmud known by most people, and so much nonsense is therefore uttered about it, that at least one more chapter ought to be devoted to it here.

Perhaps a passage or two taken from the work itself will throw most light on its character. For instance, here is a bit picked almost at random from the volume on the Sabbath laws:

A commandment in the Torah declares: "Ye shall kindle no fire throughout your habitations upon the Sabbath day." Now for centuries this was understood and followed literally, and probably the Jews all sat in the cold and dark from sunset on Friday to sunset on Saturday. But then came the early Pharisees with one of their new interpretations. They said it was perfectly proper—and indeed legally necessary—to have lights on the Sabbath, so long as they were kindled *before* the Sabbath began. But those lights must not be touched again until *after* the Sabbath closed, otherwise the commandment would be transgressed. And thereafter, all sorts of new little regulations had to be made to guard the people against accidentally touching those lights.

For instance, the Mishna contains the regulation that "one shall not read by the lamplight,"—

presumably because one might be tempted to snuff the wick if the flame burnt low. In the *Gemara,* which is the Talmudic law based on the Mishna, this regulation is discussed at great length.

But let me quote for a moment—though with many explanatory insertions, for the Talmud is almost unreadably concise:

"Rabbah (a Babylonian scholar) said (that one should not read by the lamp) even if it be placed (far out of reach—say,) the height from the ground of two men, or two stories, or even on top of ten houses, one above the other.

"(That is) '*one* may not read.' But it does not say *two* may not read together, (for then one can guard the other against snuffing the wick). Against this supposition, however, there is a tradition that 'neither one nor two together' (may read).

"Said Rabbi Elazar: 'There is no contradiction here. The Mishna allows (two people to read together) so long as they read the same subject. But the tradition (forbids it only if) they are reading *different* subjects.' . . ."

And in that manner the discussion is continued on and on. . . .

One rabbi declares that a prominent teacher *may* read by the lamplight, for such a person would hardly be so careless as to snuff the wick. To which someone answers that Rabbi Ishmael ben Elisha, who was a great person indeed, once read on Friday night and actually caught himself in the act of snuffing the wick. As proof of this fact, Rabbi Ishmael's diary is quoted, for there he confessed the crime and vowed to bring a fat sin-offering to the Temple the moment it was rebuilt. (No doubt that vow was made in all earnestness. The coming of the Messiah and the rebuilding of the Temple were still momentarily expected!) But some one else counters that the case of Rabbi Ishmael is not a fair one, for though that scholar was great at teaching laws, he was notoriously lax in observing them!

Next the question arises as to whether a servant may examine the cups and dishes by the Sabbath lamplight, to see if they are clean. Here too there is a dispute. One rabbi says yes and another says no. Then a third tries to compromise by saying that a regular servant may *not* examine the dishes, for he, in his eagerness to hold his job, might be tempted to snuff the wick in order to see better. But a servant called in merely for the day, *may* examine the dishes, for he would probably not care whether they were clean or not, and therefore would not dream of snuffing the wick. That compromise, however, is not found acceptable, and a fourth rabbi suggests that even a regular servant *may* examine the dishes by the Sabbath lamp so long as it burns naphtha and not oil. For naphtha smells badly and the fellow would hardly be tempted to come too near it. And than a fifth rabbi offers still another suggestion. . . .

And so it goes on. . . .

2

This example is not at all extreme. Passages might be cited from the Talmud which would seem infinitely more ridiculous. There is, for instance, a thrilling debate on whether an egg laid on the

Sabbath may be eaten by a Jew, since the hen probably broke the Sabbath rest in laying it!

Into every line of the Biblical law, into every word, every letter, even every part of a letter, some strange and far-fetched meaning was read by the Talmud-makers. The priestly law declared that in sacrificing a kid on the Temple altar it may not be boiled in its own mother's milk. Probably the passing of that law was due to the superstitious dread that the udders of the mother animal would dry up if such an act were committed. (There are savage tribes in Africa to-day whose diet is still regulated by that dread.) But the rabbis did not dream of such an explanation. No, they believed the law was of divine origin and had some divine though mysterious reason back of it. And they elaborated it so that it forbade the mixing of *any* meat and *any* milk (or butter, or cheese) in *any* Jewish household. What was more, even the plates used for meat might not be mixed with plates used for milk, and the water and cloths used for cleansing the meat plates might not be also used for cleasing the milk plates!

Nor was that the end of the matter, for the length of time one should wait after eating meat before being allowed to drink milk—and vice versa—had to be thoroughly discussed and determined!

3

But it is important to remember that such little laws, irrational as they may seem to us, nevertheless all had a purpose. That purpose, however, was not, as some people nowadays imagine—to preserve the physical health of the Jews. (Whatever hygienic value there may have been in the laws, was altogether accidental.) No, their purpose was the preservation of the *spiritual* health of the Jews. They helped to wall in the Jew. They were part of the impregnable dyke raised by him against the non-Jewish tide.

Moreover, it is also important to realize that not all the laws in the Talmud were of so narrowly ritualistic a sort. Many of them were of a high ethical nature. The Jews had gone far since the days when the laws in the Torah had been written. Their whole outlook on life had grown less primitive. As a natural result, their laws had to be changed so that they were less primitive too. The law code is the clock that tells what time it is in the civilization of a people; and in the Talmud we see that the hands of the clock had moved a great ways since the time of Deuteronomy. Old laws had been tempered, modified, and robbed of their cruelty. For instance, the barbaric command, "An eye for an eye, and a tooth for a tooth," had by re-interpretation come to mean that the assailant must pay for his crime not with his own eye or tooth, but with a heavy fine fixed by law. Provision was made to administer an extreme penalty like flogging in a humane manner unknown to European law courts only a century ago. And capital punishment was made practically illegal. A court that had pronounced one sentence of death in seventy years deserved, it was declared, to be called a "court of murderers!"

4

It is altogether vain to try to pass judgment on the Talmud, to try to declare whether it is good or bad, wise or foolish. It is like life—a higgledy-piggledy mingling of both good and bad, of both wisdom and folly. For it came directly out of life, directly out of the hateful, exciting, hopeful, despairing, heroic life of the Jewish people. It is rather like a moving-picture film that has been mutilated and broken in ten thousand places and then has been blindly patched together again. It reveals everything that came to hurt and heal the Jews in a thousand years of incessant hurt and healing. And so it contains very nearly everything.

There are in it myths and vagaries, idiotic superstitions and unhappy thoughts, things that are not merely irrational but sometimes even quite offensive. But there is also much profound wisdom buried in it, and much lofty and generous thinking. Not all the rabbis were bitter and hateful—though, Heaven knows, they all had reason enough to be. And not all of them were small-minded and bigoted. Indeed, a strain of almost prophetic nobility runs through much of the Talmud, and a clear note of protest against the clannishness choking the people behind the dyke.

For instance: "All men who do not worship idols may be called Jews." Or again: "All who accept merely the Ten Commandments may be considered as though accepting the whole of the Law." Or still again: "The good men of all the Gentile races will inherit the World to Come."

Or in another vein: "Be thou the cursed, not he who curses." "Even the birds in the air despise the miser." "Honor the sons of the poor, for it is they who advance science." "Charity saves one from death." "When the thief cannot steal he thinks himself an honest man." "The soldiers fight and the kings are called the heroes." "When the ox is down, many are the butchers." "The passions are not all evil, for were it not for them, no one would build a house, marry a wife, beget children, or do any work." "Drink not, and thou wilt not sin." "Even if the bull have his head deep in his trough, hasten upon the roof, and drag up the ladder after thee." "Commit a sin twice, and thou wilt think it quite allowable." . . .

All the rest of this book could easily be filled with just such bits of Talmudic wisdom and irony and high prophetic preachment. Not all of the voluminous work is given over to dry legal discussion. Indeed fully a third of it consists of clever fables and quaint legends and amusing proverbs. Granted there is much chaff in the work, there are also kernels of richest wheat.

And the fact that in bulk the chaff far exceeds the wheat, should not be at all surprising. After all, the Talmud is the product of an age when a peculiar type of mind alone could thrive. Israel was exhausted. The little dormouse in the cage of mad lions seemed to be piteously breathing its last feeble breath. It was too broken, too clawed and mauled and wet with its own blood, to arise and cry with the might of the prophets. It was too near death to worry about *why* it should go on living; it merely wanted to know *how*.

And the *how* it could learn only from the mouths of the new priests, the rabbis. The *how* it could discover only in such a work as the Talmud.

CHAPTER XXIII

HOW MOHAMMED BUILT A NEW RELIGION AROUND THE JEWISH IDEA OF GOD

When the Jews fled from Palestine their whole aim was to get as far as possible away from the talons of Christian Rome. Many of them fled to Babylonia, as we have already seen. Some ran off to Gaul and the Teutonic lands, because the people there were still barbarians, and had not yet learnt the Christian hatred of Jews. Others fled to India, and perhaps to China. And still others retreated into the heart of Arabia, that barren land from which their own ancestors had escaped more than a thousand years earlier.

The fate that befell those Jews who fled to Arabia is in certain ways much like that which befell their brethren in all the rest of the Diaspora. Outwardly they became just like the people among whom they settled. They turned nomad, and formed themselves into warring desert tribes. In a little while sheiks of their own led them in battle, and fortresses of their own served them in retreat. Poets of their own wrote them songs in Arabic, and minstrels of their own sang to them. They took Arab names and wore Arab garb. Just as certain butterflies protect themselves by folding their wings so that they look exactly like the leaves of the trees among which they flit—"protective coloration" the scientists call it—

so these Jews preserved themselves by looking and speaking and acting exactly like the people among whom they dwelt.

Inwardly, however, they persisted in remaining a separate folk. They cherished the Bible—that was why their Arab neighbors called them *Ahl ul Kitab*, the "People of the Book"—and they kept what rabbinic laws they knew. Earnestly they tried to remain faithful to their One True God.

2

With the passing of the years that inward difference began to be copied by some of the Arabs. Their own desert religion was a low form of idolatry rather like that which the ancestors of the Jews had believed in before they struck out for the Fertile Crescent. Those Arabs had some three hundred little gods to worship, and one big one. (The idol of the big one was a mysterious black stone called the Kaaba, which rested in a shrine in the town of Mecca and attracted pilgrims from all corners of Arabia.) So it was not difficult for the Jews to make converts among the more intelligent of the Arabs. Indeed, we are told that whole tribes came over in a body into the Jewish fold, and that a smattering of Judaism was known throughout the Arab settlements.

3

Now in the town of Mecca there lived an Arab merchant named Mohammed, a strange black-bearded fellow given to epileptic fits, who began to tell people that he had been sent to preach a new religion.

That religion turned out to be in many respects remarkably like Judaism, for it proclaimed the existence of but One God, and taught that the memory of all the great Jewish leaders from Abraham to Jesus of Nazareth should be revered. Just where Mohammed had chanced upon this or that particular element of his new faith we do not know. Probably it was in the many market places in Arabia and Syria to which he had journeyed as a trader.

Evidently Mohammed talked with intense conviction of his new faith, for soon he won over certain of his relatives and friends. Indeed his following grew so large that the leading citizens of Mecca began to get worried. This new-fangled religion with its One God threatened to destroy the supreme position of their city as possessor of that great idol, the Kaaba. So they plotted to murder Mohammed, and he had to flee to the rival town of Medina to escape them. Now, in and around Medina there lived several tribes of Jews, and for that reason the populace there was better able to understand Mohammed's new religion. For years previously they had been hearing something like his ideas from the mouths of the Jews in their midst.

When Mohammed fled to Medina—it was in the year 622—one of his dearest desires was to make followers of the Jews there. With that end in view he eagerly took over many of their customs—just as Paul had taken over many of the customs of the pagans whom he tried to win for Christianity. Thus Mohammed accepted the Jewish Day of Atonement as a fast day, and ordered his followers to turn their faces toward Jerusalem when they prayed. He made friends of the rabbis in Medina, and not being able to read or write, he employed a Jew as his scribe.

20.—Where Mohammedanism was Born

The Jews showed some interest at first in the movement, for Mohammed claimed he had been sent by their God, and they thought he might be the Messiah. (Oh yes, the Jews were still eagerly awaiting the coming of the Messiah!) But when they came to know Mohammed better and found out how ignorant he was, and how much fonder he seemed of pretty women than of what the Jews considered godly ways, they refused to have anything more to do with him. Their minstrels ridiculed him in sarcastic poems, and tried to make him the laughing-stock of Medina.

The result was that as soon as enough Arabs had gathered under his banner, Mohammed turned on the Jews and butchered them without mercy. He had made up his mind that the stubborn "People of the Book" could not possibly be converted, and after decimating their ranks, he turned back to the more promising task of converting the rest of his own brethren. Particularly he wanted to win over his blood kin in the stronghold of the old Kaaba worship. With that end in view, he ordered his followers to turn their faces toward Mecca and no longer toward Jerusalem when they prayed. (Mohammed, you see, was quite a shrewd man.) Also he changed the time of the annual feast to the ancient Arabic season of Ramadhan instead of the Jewish Day of Atonement. (Yes, Mohammed was a *very* shrewd man. . . .)

4

And in time he won over his brethren not merely in Mecca but in all the rest of Arabia also. The triumph was not the product of gentle preaching, however, but of bloody persecution. Mohammed issued a declaration of Holy War against all who refused to accept his faith. He told his followers that the surest way for them to enter Heaven was by dying, sword in hand, in the act of waging that "Holy War." And his followers believed him.

It would be foolish to revile Mohammed's memory for adopting this programme. It must be remembered that after all he belonged to a people and a time still largely barbaric. Indeed, when one con-

21.—Mohammedanism Triumphs—750 A. D.

siders from what low spiritual ancestry and environment this Mohammed sprang, one cannot but acknowledge him, despite all his vices, a true genius and a stupendously great man.

But though good temper counsels us to spare Mohammed our ugly words, we cannot help deploring the evil he set on foot. Though he himself died, his doctrine lived on after him. Always thirsty for war and blood, the Arabs now suddenly found themselves with a holy excuse for slaking that thirst. To fight was now the godliest work they could engage in.

So they fought. Against the whole world they fought, for they were determined to win it all for their One God, Allah, and for his One Prophet, Mohammed. And they almost succeeded.

5

The tale of the great Mohammedan Conquests is one that cannot be told here. It is a bewildering, almost an incredible story. Twenty-five years after Mohammed died, his wild Arab followers were masters of Egypt, Palestine, Syria, Babylonia, and Persia. Another half-century, and all the northern coast of Africa and almost all of Spain had been added to their empire. Another decade saw them marching up into France. All the Christian world trembled as the terrible Arabs came sweeping on.

And thus a new chapter began in the history of the Jews.

CHAPTER XXIV

THE REVOLT AGAINST THE TALMUD

From the fifth to the seventh century the Jews were at rest in hardly a land in the world. In Christian countries—especially in Spain—they were hounded out of town after town, or were penned in like lepers in a single foul little alley. Christian kings and noblemen robbed them, Christian bishops wrote books against them, and Christian ruffians murdered them.

Conditions in Babylonia or Persia were not much better. In those countries, also, the Jews were harried and massacred. One "Prince of the Exile" was hung, and another was crucified.

Early in the eighth century, however, the dawn of a new day began to break. As the Mohammedans drove the armies of Persia and the Christian nations before them, the Jews began slowly to lift themselves out of the dust. For the Mohammedans were now strangely tolerant to the Jews. Mohammed himself had long been dead, and with him had died his chagrin because the "People of the Book" would not accept his Koran. His successors only knew the Jews as a people who by race and religion were somewhat like themselves. Perhaps they realized also that without Jews to serve as scouts, they themselves would have been almost helpless. For they could trust the Jews alone to show them their way about in the vast world beyond the Desert. The Jews had traveled everywhere, and seemed to know every language. Without their aid the Arab invaders would have utterly lost their bearings as they swept on through the great countries to the right on the east and to the left in the Mediterranean basin.

2

And under the tolerant rule of the Mohammedans, the Jews began to prosper. They who had been poor and bedraggled pedlars for centuries, now became wealthy and powerful traders. They traveled everywhere, from England to India, from Bohemia to Egypt.

Their commonest merchandise in those days was slaves. On every highroad and on every great river and sea, these Jewish traders were to be found with their gangs of shackled prisoners in convoy. Slave-dealing seems irredeemably vile and hateful to us to-day, but we must remember here again that standards have changed. Only seventy-five years ago it was considered altogether proper for the very "best" people in our own land to buy and sell human beings. In ancient times only the rarest of souls—the "cranks," as they must have been called—saw any great wickedness in such a traffic. And in the light of the customs of those times, the slave-traffickers were actually doing almost a moral work. They alone were keeping the conquering armies from slaughtering every one of their defeated foes after each battle.

And with the coming of prosperity to the Jews,

came also new life and vigor. Babylonia was still the heart of the Diaspora, and the "Princes of the Exile" now became powerful officials at the court of Bagdad. The bearer of this title after the Arabs conquered the land was actually given a daughter of the defeated Persian king as his wife.

And the rabbinical academies began to flourish once more. The president of the leading academy in Babylonia was called the *Gaon*, the "Illustrious One," and to him were submitted the religious problems of the Jews throughout the Diaspora. He decided what prayers should be recited in the synagogues, and he licensed the rabbis—they were really judges—to preside over the Jewish civil courts. For in Babylonia and most other lands the Jews still took their disputes and accusations to their own Talmudic courts for settlement.

3

But despite the prosperity and outer freedom that had come to the Jews, their inner life was becoming dry and choked. That high wall, the Talmud, that had been built to lock out the non-Jewish world, served also to lock in the Jewish soul. Its frowning shadow was cast over every path in Jewish life. It was no longer a means to the end of self-preservation; it had become an end in itself. It was no longer a thing to live *by* but to live *for*—yes, and even to die for. The Jews lifted it to a place of importance above the very Bible, and they studied it far more diligently. They memorized it from end to end—every one of its sixty-three enormous divisions!

All the Talmud was accepted literally. From end to end it was universally assumed to be a true and perfect development of the commandments which Moses had taught the Hebrews at the Holy Mountain of Yahveh. The new rabbis commented on its every line and word, striving to make clear its many muddy passages, and succeeding only in making them muddier. And on these commentaries, later rabbis wrote further commentaries, making the already muddy passages still muddier. So they went on, pathetically caressing their hoard of laws as a miser caresses his coins. The Talmud was no longer their servant; they had become its slaves.

And then came the protest.

It had been brewing for a long time, but not until now had it been able to get itself heeded. The Jews had been living in a sort of war-time hysteria during all those centuries, and the few protestants that spoke out had been given very little sympathy. They had been gruffly told to "fall in or get out!" And many of them, refusing to "fall in," had indeed gotten out.

But the protest had made itself felt nevertheless. The stern spirit of the Essene hermits—that spirit which had produced John the Baptist and also, in a measure, Joshua of Nazareth—still lived in the souls of some professing Jews. Prophets still appeared from time to time in remote corners of the Diaspora. Frenzied young Jews they were, and they cried to their brethren to cease entangling themselves in all the petty rules of the rabbis, and concentrate their thinking on the great commands of God. (They were usually the sort of men who objected to slave-dealing and the various other "business" activities which the Jews were being tempted to take up.) Generation after generation, new self-made Messiahs appeared, rising and falling like so many flaring rockets. Small Jewish sects leapt up and died down again in wild and rampant confusion.

Now, most of these obscure preachers and their sects, though traveling along paths quite unintelligible to each other, were headed toward essentially one goal. They were striving to get back to the basic truths of the "old-time religion." They were trying with all their might to get back to God.

That was why they were all opposed to that tremendous wall of Law which the rabbis had erected. They felt it was in their way. It had been built to shut in the religion and preserve it, but these preachers seemed to realize—though ever so vaguely—that true religion never *could* stay shut in. So they cried out at the top of their voices for an end to the wall.

But the vast majority of their brethren, entangled in their little rules and regulations, deafened as it were by the clatter of their meat dishes and milk dishes, did not heed that cry. Not until the coming of Anan ben David did they heed it. . . .

4

Anan ben David was a learned Jew of high station in Babylonia. Indeed he was the heir of the Prince of the Exile. But about the year 762, when it came his turn to succeed to that office, the rabbis of the day elected his younger brother in his stead. (Probably Anan had already let it be known that he belonged to those who were not altogether satisfied with the Talmud.) And when Anan found he had been cheated out of what he considered his birthright, the commotion raised by him rocked the whole Jewish world.

A new sect, almost a new religion, was founded by him. Anan declared war on the Talmudic Law, taxing it with being all false and ridiculous. And hundreds flocked to support him. They joined him on his march to Jerusalem, there to set up what they considered a *truly* Jewish community—one governed solely by Biblical Law.

But it did not take long for the followers of Anan to discover how impossible of success was their task. The ancient Biblical Law, well enough developed for the work it had to do in its own day, was not adapted, by itself, to govern a more civilized community in a later age. To make it at all adequate, the Biblical Law had to be completely revised. Just as the first rabbis, when they rebelled against the tyranny of the priests, had to begin "interpreting" the Law, so these later rebels found that they had to begin "interpreting" also. In fine, the followers of Anan ended by doing just what they had set out to undo.

And that of course meant the beginning of the decline and fall. Anan ben David's sect lived on, but its high spirit of protest against legalism sickened and rapidly died out. The new legalism of its own that it developed was in many respects even more rigid and unreasonable than that of the Talmud. The heroic little band of rebels that had set out to cast down the high wall of the rabbis, succeeded only in building a higher wall of their own.

But despite this, the movement lived and grew. Though its declaration of principles was only a crazy quilt of queer doctrines and practices, it continued to win converts from among the orthodox Jews. Especially was this true in the century after Anan died, for then it produced several distinguished scholars who tried their best to correct many of Anan's mistakes.

The movement, which at first had been known as Ananism, was now called Karaism, the "Religion of the Bible." Unfortunately our sources of information are very undependable, for most of our reports come to us from the pens of its bitterest opponents. At its height Karaism may have been a valiant and earnest effort to establish a rather generous creed—a Judaism that could accept both Jesus and Mohammed as great teachers without sacrificing its right to go seeking still greater ones.

But Karaism quickly toppled from that height. It failed, as perhaps every such effort must fail, in a world still choked with fears and stupidities.

CHAPTER XXV

THE DAWN OF INTELLIGENCE IN BABYLONIA AND SPAIN

But Karaism failed only in spirit. In body it lived on and flourished. In the ninth century, indeed, it bade fair to become dominant throughout the Jewish world. The rabbis of the time were a weak and slavish lot. They tried to ignore the movement, largely perhaps because they lacked spirit enough to wrestle with it. The Karaite missionaries based all their work of conversion on arguments from the Bible, and the rabbis of the day hardly knew the Bible. All they knew was the Talmud, and the pathetic trickery, the twisting of phrases and wringing of words, by which it had been foisted onto the Bible. So for over a century those rabbis continued to bury their heads in their dry and dusty commentaries, and tried to make themselves believe that nothing was happening.

But then Saadya came on the scene, a rabbi of a new type—alert, intelligent, and unafraid. He was born in Egypt, but so great was his learning and fame that he was called at the early age of thirty-six to be Gaon of the foremost academy in Babylonia. Fourteen years later he was already dying, his health broken by his intense labors and struggles. Nevertheless, in those few years of life he managed to breathe a new spirit into Jewish learning.

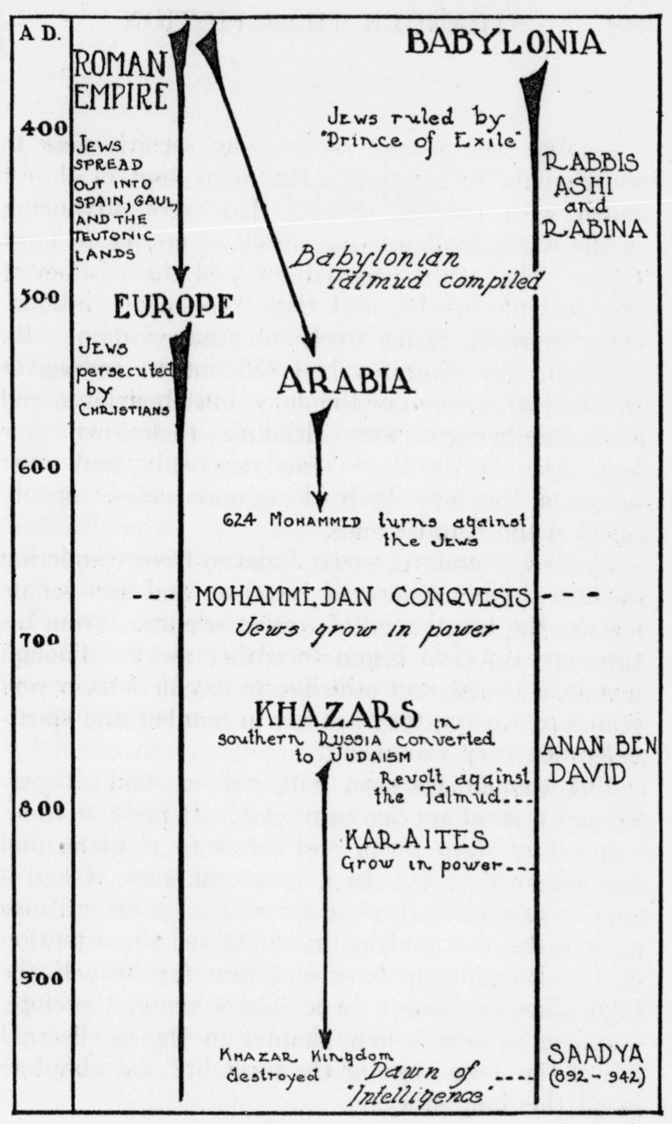

Chart D. *The Adventures of the Jews, Part IV*

2

Saadya was a man of amazing sensitiveness to the thought of his time. His mind kept in closest touch with the movements that were advancing in the world, and was not afraid to go out to meet them. The Arabs had rediscovered the wisdom of the ancient Greeks, and their keen eager intelligences were drinking freely of that wisdom. By contrast, the Karaites had set out to rediscover the ancient wisdom of the Jews, but their loose and slow intelligences were drinking their own new legal brew instead. So Saadya openly took over many of the new Arab ideas, and just as openly rejected the Karaite ones.

Saadya, therefore, saved Judaism from wandering off into the blind alley of Karaism, and first set its feet on the broad road of Arabic science. From his time on, Karaism began to wither away. Though members of the sect still live to-day in Turkey and Southern Russia, they are few in number and spiritually not very significant.

But though Karaism withered so soon, it performed a great service in its day. It pricked Judaism out of deep sleep, and set it to thinking and moving once more. In a very real sense it had a part in producing Saadya, for it was by his writings against the sect that he first attracted the attention of the Babylonian Jews and won for himself the high office of Gaon. In as real a sense, therefore, Karaism opened a new chapter in the intellectual life of the Jews—one of the most brilliant chapters in all this long story.

Only the first paragraph of that new chapter was written in Babylonia. A spirit of intolerance had grown up among the Mohammedans there, and it became impossible for the Jews to remain in the land. Rapidly, therefore, they began to flock along the caravan routes westward to Spain, taking with them their scholars and their scrolls. The revival of Jewish learning which Saadya had started, was like the last flare before the guttering-out of a candle-flame as far as Babylonia was concerned. Of the Gaonim who succeeded Saadya, two were thrown into prison by the Mohammedans, and the last was executed.

And with that last Gaon the flame died down completely—in Babylonia.

But a new flame was already alight and burning —in Spain. And it was far stronger and brighter than any Babylonia ever had known. Jews in Spain had possessed wealth and power almost from the time, three centuries earlier, when the Mohammedan invaders drove the Christians from the land. And with the passing of the years, that wealth and power had materially increased. Even after the Christians, hidden all this time in the mountains, began warily to creep down again and reoccupy the land, the position of the Jews did not greatly change. Those Christians were still too uncertain of their strength to dare antagonize the powerful friends of the Moors.

Those were wondrous days for the Jews. They wielded influence in every walk of life. Some were active in the armies—so active, indeed, that in at least one instance, both the Mohammedan and

Christian generals are said to have declared a truce for a day so that Jews on both sides might enjoy their Sabbath rest! Others taught in the great universities, and managed the royal treasuries. They were the leading physicians and bankers and merchants and diplomats of the time.

And that growth of Jewish wealth and influence was accompanied by the growth of Jewish literature and learning. For the first time since most of the Psalms were written in the period of the Maccabees, Hebrew poetry began once more to flourish. Much of it, of course, was quite inferior stuff, for Hebrew had ceased to be a living tongue. Prayers formed part of this new poetry—*piyyutim* they were called—which often were so stilted and involved in style that perhaps not even their own authors could puzzle out their meaning. On the other hand, there were hymns and epics, even love-songs and drinking songs, of amazing charm and beauty.

Every educated Spanish Jew at that time seems to have tried his hand at poetizing, for it was the fashionable thing to do. Letters of friendship, books on grammar and astronomy and religion, prayers, even business notes, were often written in verse. A mere list of the men who distinguished themselves in the art would fill the rest of this chapter. We will only mention one here, the greatest of the age, Judah Halevi.

3

Judah Halevi, born in Old Castile in 1086, began writing poetry while still a youth. But to us there is something almost alarming about that early

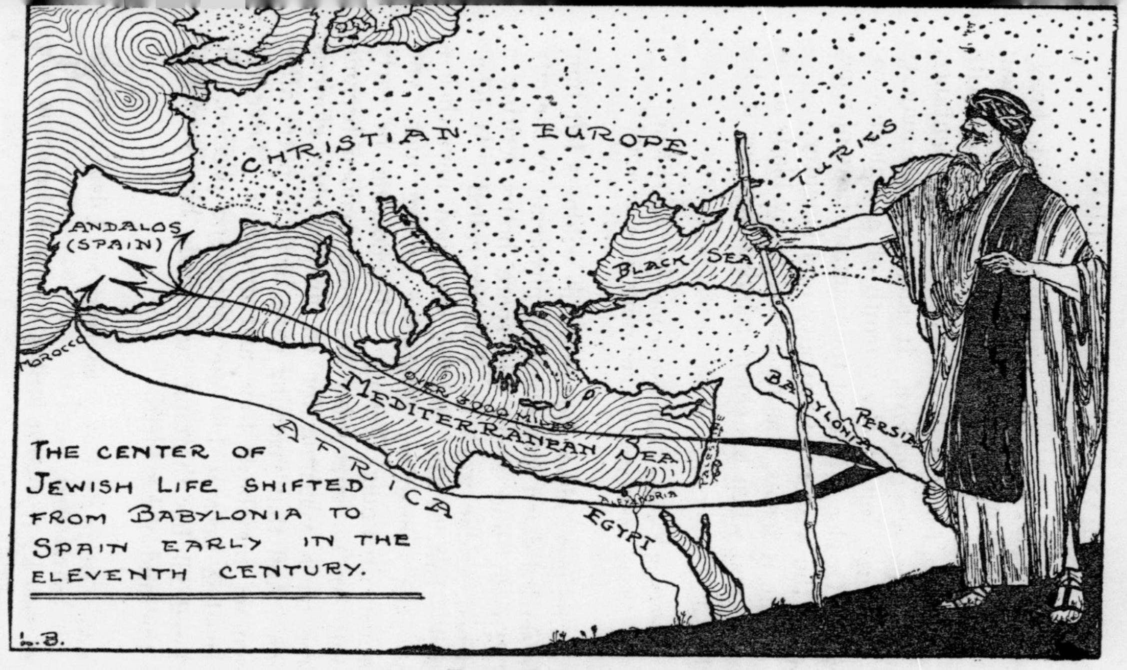

22.—From Babylon to Spain

poetry of his. It was written in limpid, lovely Hebrew; in a measure it had the ring of the ancient Psalms. But that was all it had in common with the Psalms, for it dealt not with sin and repentance, but with passion and love. It sang not of the majesty of the Lord, but of the warmth of a maiden's caresses. Or else it sang of the fragrant taste of wine, and of the wisdom of frivolity and laughter.

Judah, it seems, was no end of a gay blade in his youth; and when his elders rebuked him for it, his retort was:

> "Shall I whose years scarce number twenty-four
> Turn foe to pleasure and drink wine no more?"

As he grew older, however, his wildness left him. He settled down into a sedate physician in the city of Toledo, and spent his spare hours writing a learned Arabic work on Judaism called "Al Khazari." But to the end he remained nevertheless the poet: sensitive, ill-at-ease among men, and forever dreaming dreams. His craving in early youth for an impossibly beautiful maiden became later on a yearning for an unspeakably glorious Zion. And that yearning gave birth to poem after poem of matchless tone and grandeur. Love for Jerusalem became his one controlling passion. It colored all his thinking, and made him wretched in the land of his birth.

> "In the East, in the East, is my heart, and I dwell at the end of the West;
> How shall I join in your feasting, how shall I share in your jest?"

So did he mourn, and mourning so he died. Even though in his last years he did go to Jerusalem, still was he unable to join in feast or jest. For the Jerusalem he found waiting for him was not the Holy City he had imagined. Rather it was a dirty, ill-smelling heap of débris wherein Crusader and Mohammedan hacked at each other in unholy madness. And legend has it that as the despondent man stood by the ruined wall and wept, an Arab horseman galloping out of the gate, stumbled over him, and crushed him to death. . . .

4

In Judah Halevi is revealed, perhaps as well as in any other man of his time, the new spirit that had entered Jewish learning. The Talmud was no longer considered the beginning and end of all wisdom; nor was the writing of dry and spiritless commentaries still looked on as the only proper pursuit for Jewish scholars.

At last the sun shone once more. At last the gloomy shadows cast by the wall of Law, lifted for a moment. At last there was Jewish laughter as well as Jewish weeping on the earth—real relaxation once more.

CHAPTER XXVI

THE "GOLDEN AGE" OF JEWISH LEARNING IN SPAIN

It must not be imagined, however, that the scholars of this brighter age did not do their share of burrowing in the Talmud. They too wrote commentaries and long-winded interpretations. But to their credit be it said, they did other things as well. They wrote poetry, as we have already seen; and they studied the science of the day.

The field that seemed to attract and interest them most was the science of medicine, and for centuries all great sultans and kings had their Jewish physicians. Even the popes sometimes used them.

The science of grammar was another favorite subject. That study enlisted their zeal because it helped them to understand the Bible; and the Bible had to be understood if the Karaites were to be refuted. As a consequence, there were many great Hebrew grammarians during the "Golden Age" in Spain, most of them supported by wealthy patrons in the larger cities. The foremost of them all was one, Abraham *ibn* (the Arabic for *ben*) Ezra, who, however, did his best work beyond the borders of Spain. He was a man of great wit and wisdom and poverty. He was always meeting with ill-fortune, and used to say that if he were to turn shroud-maker, immediately mankind would cease

23.—The Wanderings of Ibn Ezra

to die. He was Spanish by birth, but before he died he had wandered to Africa, Egypt, Palestine, Babylonia, Italy, France, and England. In each he stayed as long as his welcome or his patience lasted, living off the bounty of some patron, lecturing to students, and writing on any one of a dozen or more subjects.

His most important work was a commentary on the Bible, and the spirit in which it was written may be said to mark the birth of an epoch. For Ibn Ezra approached the Scriptures almost with our modern critical attitude. He took no traditional reading for granted, but tried on the basis of his hard and fast rules of grammar to ferret out for himself the meaning of each verse. And when he came across passages in the Torah, the "Five Books of Moses," which flatly contradicted each other, he did not do the orthodox thing, and try desperately to darn and patch them together. No, instead he let them stand side by side in all their glaring contradiction, and wrote with perhaps a sly wink: "And the wise man will no doubt have his explanation for this puzzle."

Now that was a high and holy act of scientific daring. Even though Ibn Ezra did not enlarge upon all he suspected, at least he *did* suspect. He may not have said so openly what we to-day no longer question—that the "Five Books of Moses" are not really all the work of Moses, but a collection of traditions and codes belonging to varied localities and ages. But at least he seems to have thought it. And the bare harboring of such a thought in that early day, marks a tremendous advance.

2

Advances were also made by other Jewish scholars in that age. As I have already said, Arabs had stumbled upon buried scrolls of the ancient Greeks, and being a quick and eager lot, they had not rested until they had deciphered many of the old writings. As a result, a whole vast world of learning was re-opened. Mathematics, astronomy, chemistry, medicine, and philosophy began to flourish again for the first time in perhaps a dozen centuries. It meant the beginning of the end of the Dark Ages.

Naturally enough, the Jews, who were by long training an intellectual folk, eagerly took to this new world of wisdom. From Saadya's time on, they investigated its every corner, returning home to their own Jewish studies with heads crammed full of new ideas.

And thus, among other things, Jewish philosophy was reborn.

3

Philosophy is the attempt to discover *why* things have happened or are happening—just as science is the attempt to discover *how*. Jewish philosophy, therefore, attempted to discover the real reason why Jews believe what they do—why they believe in God and the Bible—indeed, why they remain Jews.

Many Jews of the "Golden Age" devoted themselves to this study, and curiously enough, for centuries afterwards even the Christian scholars pored over the books written by those Jews. That was possible because the books were written in so inclusive a spirit that often the followers of Christianity could find nothing in them with which to disagree. Indeed, one such book called in Latin "Fons Vitæ," the "Living Fountain," written by a Jew named Solomon ibn Gabirol, was always regarded in the European universities as the work of a Christian scholar named Avicebron. The true identity of the author was not discovered until about seventy-five years ago!

Ibn Gabirol reminds one somewhat of Philo, the great Jewish philosopher who lived in Alexandria more than a thousand years earlier. Both of them were ardent Jews, and yet both exercised their greatest influence on the Christian mind. Philo helped lay the philosophic foundation for primitive Christianity, just as Ibn Gabirol helped lay it for mediæval Christianity.

4

But the greatest Jewish thinker of this period was Moses ben Maimon. He is usually referred to as Maimonides, for the Latin suffix *ides* means "son of." (Had he lived in Germany he would have been called Maimonsohn, in Poland, Maimonski, and in Russia, Maimonovitch.) In his day—the second half of the twelfth century—he was the leading rabbi in the world. Officially he was merely the physician to the Sultan of Egypt; but unofficially he was King of the Jews. For Jews everywhere looked up to him as their supreme authority. The misfortune and ill-health that dogged his steps all his life, failed to prevent his working on almost without interruption. He wrote voluminously on any number of subjects: mathematics, astronomy, medicine, law, as well as philosophy.

In particular, he wrote a great book on the Talmud —not a mere commentary, but a monumental rearrangement that set all the stray and conflicting laws in order. For seven hundred years the scholars had crept and clambered in and out and over the piles of lumber and underbrush in the Talmudic yard; but not until the coming of Maimonides was any attempt made to clean up the whole place.

And when that tremendous task was done, Maimonides undertook another even more difficult. He tried to set down in clear and logical fashion sound reasons for all the Jewish beliefs. The final product was a volume entitled in Hebrew "Moreh Nevuchim," the "Guide for the Perplexed"—one of the most significant books in all of Jewish literature. Casting aside the Talmudic arguments, which were all based on dogma and authority— ("This is so because Rabbi Judah, or Ezra, or Moses, or God, said so")—he substituted new ones based on what he considered pure and scientific reasoning.

Of course, a great deal of what Maimonides considered pure reasoning seems to us decidedly impure. But it was utterly impossible for a man in the twelfth century to use only common sense and scientific truth as the basis for all his arguments. The time was not yet ripe for it.

Yet, as was true of Ibn Ezra's work, its great glory was that at least it made the attempt.

To try to show that science proves what faith accepts without proof, is what we call Rationalism. Essentially it is of little use, because faith always comes out on top. If science will not agree with it, then science is doctored so that it shall. As Prof.

James Harvey Robinson puts it in his book, "Mind in the Making": if *real* reasons do not prove the dogmas, then "*good*" reasons are manufactured and used.

But Rationalism nevertheless represents an advance over the stupid and unquestioning acceptance of dogma. At least it removes the dogmatic shackles upon thinking.

Until the time of Saadya there had been exceedingly little of such unshackled thinking among the Jews. In the years between Saadya and Maimonides it flamed with amazing brilliance. And after Maimonides it began to die down once more.

After Maimonides the "Golden Age" began fast to turn to iron.

CHAPTER XXVII

TWILIGHT IN THE CHRISTIAN LANDS IN EUROPE

Very little of the ease and freedom which the Jews enjoyed in Mohammedan Spain was shared by their brethren in the other lands of Europe. Those other lands were Christian, and they boiled with bigotry. The rulers themselves were more or less tolerant, for they depended upon Jews as their financiers. But the lower classes had no use for them, and butchered them whenever a righteous excuse could be found.

And righteous excuses were never wanting. If a plague broke out, of course the Jews had poisoned the wells. If a war was lost, of course the Jews had aided the enemy. If a boy mysteriously disappeared, of course the Jews had murdered him to procure blood for their Passover drink. . . . And always there was the standing excuse for persecution, that the Jews were not Christians. . . .

That standing excuse was responsible for the ghastliest massacres, especially during and after the year 1096. In that year the First Crusade was launched, and Europe went utterly out of its senses. The thirst for the blood of the Mohammedans was whetted first with the blood of Jews. Godfrey de Bouillon and many of his fellow Crusaders swore holy oaths that they would leave none of the hated infidels alive in the land, and although Godfrey was bought off with heavy bribes, the other Crusaders almost made their oaths good.

In Worms, eight hundred Jews—almost all in the city—were butchered. Amid jeers the rabbi and all his family were buried alive. One young Jewess, Minna, daughter of the wealthiest of the martyrs, was offered her freedom by friendly noblemen if she would but turn Christian. Indignantly she refused, and she too was put to death.

In Mayence, over a thousand Jews were massacred, and many were forcibly baptized. Among these unwilling converts were a father and two daughters who soon after their baptism seem to have gone mad with penitence. The father killed the two girls in his own house, set fire to it, then set fire to the nearby synagogue, and finally threw himself into the flames. Almost all the city of Mayence was destroyed before that fire could be put out!

In Cologne, the Jews escaped by the aid of a merciful bishop and many of the burghers. After three weeks of hiding in the nearby villages, however, the mob of Crusaders discovered them and were without pity. Many Jews took their own lives, drowning themselves in the lakes and bogs roundabout. The pious Samuel ben Yechiel, standing in the water and uttering a prayer, slew his own son at his side. And as the victim moaned "Amen" to the old man's prayer, all those looking on cried, "Hear, O Israel, the Lord is One," and let themselves drown in the waters. . . . Three hundred Jews trapped in one of the villages, selected five of their number to slay the rest and then to slay themselves!

24.—*Here go the Crusaders!*

So matters went in Regensburg, in Treves, in Prague—blood and fire, murder and shame.

These events all happened while the hordes of the First Crusade were marching their bloody way through Europe in 1096. And when at last they reached Jerusalem and captured it three years later, they drove all the Jews into one of the synagogues and burnt them alive!

2

And then there was the Second Crusade. . . .

And the Third. . . .

3

No laughter was left on the lips of the Jews who survived. Throughout Germany they went about in sackcloth and ashes, mourning for the *kedoshim*, the saints, who had perished. And throughout Christendom the Jews turned gray with fear and terror. Their only relief was their study; their only refuge was their house of learning. But among them there was none of that daring which marked the study of their brethren who had been reared in Spain. Philosophy and science were closed worlds to them; only the Talmud was open.

Moreover, even in their wanderings through the wilderness of the Talmud they were cautious and timorous. The courageous and independent thinking of an Ibn Ezra or a Maimonides was altogether foreign to them. The famous Rashi, their greatest writer of commentaries, based his interpretations not on the strict laws of grammar, but on the loose fancy of tradition. He darned and patched all the breaks in the text with the scarlet wool of myth and legend. (That is why simple folk among the Jews to this day prefer Rashi's commentary to Ibn Ezra's.) And their most diligent students of the Talmud, the French "Tosafists," made no attempt to overhaul the whole work and set it in something like order. Rather did they add to its disorder by scribbling worthless notes on its margins.

It was for all the world the same as it had been in the darkest days in Babylonia. Jews everywhere in England, France, and Germany, were in a panic. They dared not cast away a single twig of all the underbrush which their fathers had stored up for them, lest the fires of their faith die out for lack of fuel.

And what was still more tragic, they turned in rage on those who dared do otherwise. They bitterly attacked Maimonides for presuming to revise all the Talmud, and assailed him even more for writing his philosophic "Guide for the Perplexed." For years they reviled and cursed that free-thinking "Guide," even going so far as to appeal finally to the Catholic Church to have it burned. And it *was* burned. Stupid priests joined with stupefied rabbis to destroy the noblest product of the "Golden Age."

And as always happens when freedom of thought is suppressed, a new interest in magic and mysticism sprang up. Cabala, "Tradition," it was called, because its secrets were supposed to have been handed down from the most ancient times. It was a pathetically earnest attempt to get at the basic truths about God and the universe. But it sought to get at them not by the straight and stony path of reason and science, but through the thick, sprawling, tropical forest of imagination and mystery. It talked of demons and angels, of strange words and incantations, of hoary secrets hidden in unknown books, and other such stuff and nonsense. The little light there was in it was like the light of fireflies skimming over a stagnant pool. . . .

4

Only in the south of France, in Provence, did a gleam of reason and freedom still live on. A little light from the learning of Moorish Spain had seeped in there to dispel the fog. Jews taught in the universities of Provence, and served in the courts of the barons. One great family of scholars, the Kimchis, wrote grammars and dictionaries; and another, the Tibbonides, translated Judeo-Arabic works of philosophy.

But soon that solitary gleam of light was also snuffed out. A new pope, Innocent III, began to rule, and seeing the free spirit that reigned in Provence, his little soul was dismayed. Provence was the seat of a powerful sect of heretical Christians called the Albigenses, a sect of rationalists who protested courageously against the riot of darkness and corruption in the Catholic Church. If the truth were fully known, probably it would be found that the learned Jews in Provence were in large part responsible for the existence of this free-thinking sect. The doctrines which the Jews had been spreading throughout the land for years could not but have helped to undermine the Church's power.

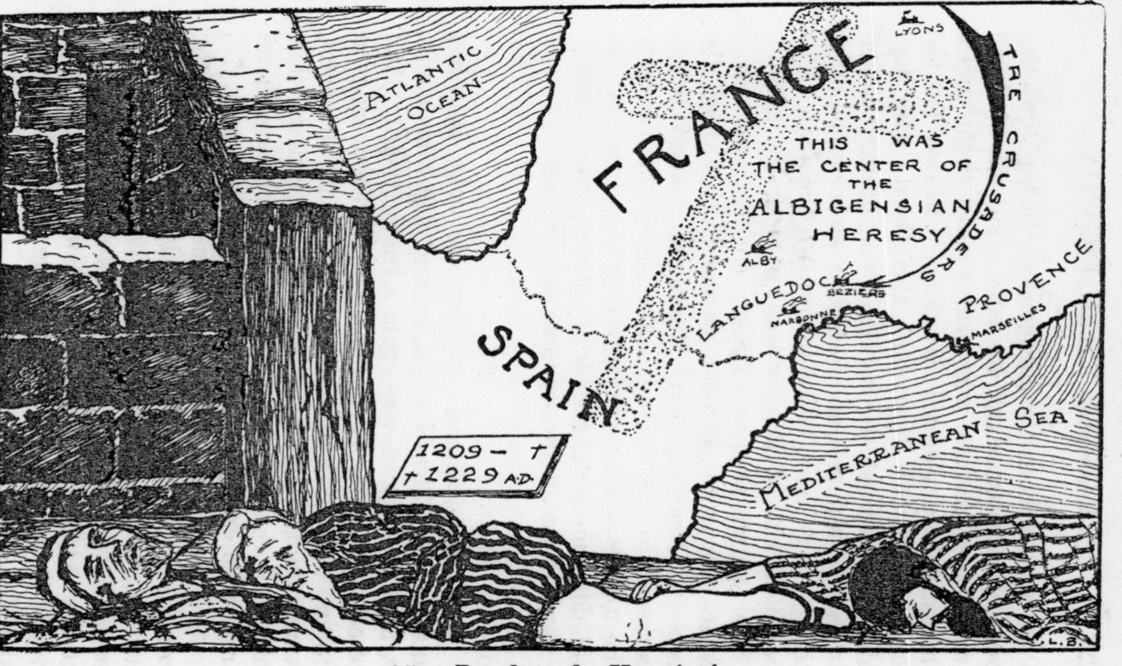

25.—*Death to the Heretics!*

So against both the Albigenses and the Jews this pope now directed all his fury. He issued a call in the year 1207 for a crusade against them; and a fanatical monk named Arnold of Citeaux, led the assault. Count Raymond the Good, who had always protected the heretics, was dragged naked to church, whipped, and forced to swear among other things never again to be tolerant to the Jews. The beautiful city of Béziers was razed to the ground. "We spared neither dignity, nor sex, nor age," writes the monk, Arnold, to his Holy Father, the pope. "Nearly twenty thousand human beings perished by the sword. And after the massacre the town was plundered and burnt, and the revenge of God seemed to rage over it in a wonderful manner."

And so ended the freedom in Provence.

5

Next came Spain. A crusade was launched against the infidel Moors there, and that same monk, Arnold of Citeaux, was again a leading spirit. And of course, the Jews suffered. The Christian kings in Spain, until now markedly tolerant to the Jews, were rapidly taught the error of that course. The plight of the Wandering People in Christian Spain from then on grew more terrible year by year.

And the Moors, who were crowded back by the crusaders until they held only little Granada in the far south of the peninsula, also gave the Jews no rest. They had long ago ceased to exhibit the generosity which had marked them when in the heydey of their power. Already in the time of Maimonides they had become a fanatical lot, and the great philosopher had been forced to flee from his birthplace while a boy. And with the shrinking of their realms, the Moors had grown even more intolerant.

So now there was no corner left in all Europe for the Jews. The last gleam of day was gone.

It was Night. . . .

CHAPTER XXVIII

THE TERRIBLE NIGHT OF PERSECUTION

A slow, senseless, pitiless crucifying of a people—that is the whole tale of the night that now fell. The Crusades had beaten the Jew to the ground, and now for five hundred years Christian serfs and priests, Christian kings and popes, took turns in kicking his prostrate body.

Christianity was not to blame for that, but only those sorry Christians. They did what they did only because they were still brutes—poor, lustful, stupid beasts just come up out of savagery. They knew no better.

Even their leaders knew no better. There was no conscious lie in their hearts when Christian priests declared it was for the sake of the loving Jesus that they crushed the skulls of gray-bearded old Jews. They really believed it! Of course, *we* know it was not at all for the sake of Jesus that they committed those horrors. *We* know it was simply to ease their own savage resentment at the sight of strangers in their midst. But *they* knew nothing of the sort. If they lied at all, it was only to themselves.

It is not difficult to see why the Jew was so steadily preyed upon. In the eyes of the provincial-minded Christians of mediæval Europe, the Jew was guilty of that most flagrant of all crimes: he was different. And what was even worse, he seemed to *want* to be different. No matter what pressure was brought to bear on him, the Jew obstinately refused to conform.

Now differentness is to stupid man what a red rag is to a bull! Always he charges down on it madly, determined to tear it to shreds. And if he cannot tear and destroy it, he tries at least to stamp it in the dust. For by so doing he assures his own wretched little self that the person flaunting that differentness is far, far inferior.

But the trouble with the Jew was that though he was different, he yet did not admit himself—nor seem—inferior. At least, not sufficiently so. And therefore the whole aim of the Christian world focused itself on the task of finding ways and means of demeaning the Jew more thoroughly.

That was the real intent back of the invention of the Jew-badge. A law was passed in 1215 by the Catholic Church forbidding all Jews on pain of death to appear on the streets without a colored badge of a certain shape sewn to their clothing. It was meant to be a brand of shame, an ever-present, visible sign of inferiority.

2

The Jew-badge only too well realized the evil intent of the Christians. Almost literally it broke the back of the Jew. Cringing, and drooping his shoulders, he went about the streets, a marked man, a constant target for the stones and oaths of ruffians. He lost his pride. Spat upon by everyone, pelted with offal no matter where he turned, he soon learnt to trudge about in the foulest of ill-smelling rags. His very speech ceased to be a language and became a jargon; his lyric gift in prayer degenerated into a pitiable whine. Even in his own eyes he almost became what the Churchmen tried their hardest to make him—a despicable and loathsome wretch.

Not unjustly do historians mark the year 1215 as the beginning of the Night.

But even though the Jew-badge broke his spirit, yet it did not end his life. The Jew still lived, and financially often had the name of prospering. He had wealth—tremendous, uncounted wealth, so the Christians believed. At least, when they had to have money, the Jew was often ready to be the money lender.

3

The Jews had become the money lenders of Europe for quite evident reasons. The Church sternly forbade all Christians to engage in the pursuit. And since money lending—or banking, as we now call it—was indispensable to the well-being of commerce and government, the Jews simply *had* to take it up. There was no one else in Europe free to do it.

And with great eagerness did the Jews take to money lending, for the occupation exactly suited their circumstances. Living in constant dread of riots, not knowing when they might have to flee, the Jews had to engage in a business requiring no bulky stock-in-trade. Farming would not do, for fields and haystacks could hardly be thrown into a chest and hidden in the ground, or carried off in the night. Coins and jewels and deeds were much better.

So the Jews became the money lenders of Europe. They developed a great shrewdness and cunning in the one and only field of opportunity left open to them. And with their shrewdness and cunning they developed a certain cruelty and greed. That was natural. The world was cruel to them, so when the chance was theirs, they were cruel in return. Their high "overhead" drove them to become usurers, and they charged all the interest on their loans that they could possibly get. There was no other way for them to survive. So many borrowers never repaid their loans, that those who did had to make up for those who did not.

And by shrewdness and cunning, by usury and thrift, the Jews managed to crawl and wriggle their way through to wealth. So the Christian world decided that its next task, now that the Jew had been robbed of his pride, was to rob him also of his pelf.

4

Robbing the Jew was not a difficult task, for he was altogether friendless in the Christian world. He would not consent to be a member of the Church, and therefore he was not allowed to be a member of the State. Occasionally, for an adequate bribe, a pope would protest against the more extravagant tortures inflicted upon the Jews by minor princes of the Church; but usually his protest was made after those tortures had already been inflicted. It is not unjust to say that the Catholic Church with all its prelates and priests and friars was from first to last the Jew's most implacable foe. Only on one condition would it spare him—if he forsook the faith of his fathers and turned Christian.

Nor was the State and its kings and princes much better. If the secular rulers spared the Jew at all, it was only because they could not easily get along without him. Somehow or other, the Jew always seemed able to get money. Even though he was robbed of his wealth one year, he seemed to find a way to get at least part of it back the next. And for that reason the rulers spared the Jew somewhat. He was a never-failing source of revenue.

To extort this revenue became almost an art with the rulers of mediæval Europe. The simplest and quickest method, of course, was to murder the money lender. But this method had its drawback, for it killed the goose that laid the golden eggs. So more usually the king had his own officers rob the money lender's house, and if the treasure had been removed and hidden where the robbers could not find it, the money lender was tortured to reveal the hiding place. King John of England is said to have ordered a tooth drawn every day from the mouth of one of "his" Jews in order to learn the whereabouts of such a hiding place.

But even this practice was not always satisfactory, for the size of the haul secured from a reputedly wealthy Jew was often far less than had been anticipated. So it was found more profitable to rob whole communities of Jews at one time. And this was frequently done. Charges of one sort or another were trumped up against the Jews of a particular town or country, their property was confiscated,

26.—*The Terrible Night in Germany*

and then they themselves were ordered out. And in a few years, after they were permitted back again, the devilish game was repeated.

In that manner the Jews were expelled from France in 1182, and then permitted to return in 1198. They were expelled a second time in 1306, and a second time permitted to return in 1315.

And so it went. Year after year without rest, the hunted Jews had to drag their weary feet from pillar to post. They were ordered out of Vienna, Cologne, Wittenberg, Hamburg, Bruenn, and Olmuetz. And out of Trent, Nuremberg, Ulm, and Magdeburg. From one town after another they were hounded without mercy, finding rest only in the grave.

Yet they would not surrender. Stubbornly they carried on, true to the faith of their fathers. Obstinately they persisted, still a strange, a different people.

5

Finally signs multiplied that the Jews were beginning to exhaust the patience of their persecutors. Expulsions grew more frequent, and permits to return more rare. The Catholic Church yielded at last—though only unofficially—to the demand for Christian usurers, and the Jews gradually became no longer indispensable. Good Catholics who were friends of the pope, were permitted to loan money to the kings of Europe; and thus the Jews in Europe lost the one function that so long had saved them from expulsion. In previous years a king sometimes arrested them merely to keep them from leaving his country; or he invited them back soon after they had been robbed or expelled. He had not been able to get along without them then.

27.—The Expulsion from England—1290 A. D.

But now all that was changed, and it became far more usual for him to drive out the Jews and tell them to stay out.

In the year 1290 every professing Jew in all

England was ordered out of the country "forever." Between sixteen and seventeen thousand of them had to flee, and none dared to return until almost four hundred years afterward. William Shakespeare wrote his "Merchant of Venice" probably without ever having seen a real Jew. . . .

In the year 1394 the Jews of France were also expelled—this time in earnest. To prevent their return, a law was passed making it a capital crime for any Christian to shield or even converse with a Jew.

A similar fate befell many of the Jews of Germany, though it was not the land as a unit, but certain individual towns that expelled them.

6

And finally it came Spain's turn. Persecution had occurred there on and off for over a century, and, after 1391, became almost incessant. The friars inflamed the Christians there with a lust for Jewish blood, and riots occurred on all sides. For the Jews it was simply a choice between baptism and death, and many of them submitted to baptism. One friar, Vincente Ferrer, is reported to have converted no less than thirty-five thousand of them.

But almost always conversion on these terms was only outward and false. Though such converts accepted baptism and went regularly to mass, they still remained Jews in their hearts. They were called Maranos, "Accursed Ones," and there were perhaps a hundred thousand of them in the land. Often they possessed enormous wealth. Their daughters married into the noblest families, even into the blood royal; and their sons sometimes entered the Church and rose to the highest offices. It is said that even one of the popes was of this Marano stock.

Fanatical churchmen were frantic with pent-up rage. Throughout Spain they saw men and women who called themselves Christians, enjoyed all the privileges of Christians, and yet still remained Jews. The monks who had labored so frenziedly to convert them, felt that they had been fooled and cheated. And in their anger they instituted the unspeakable Inquisition.

7

The Inquisition was a court to try, condemn, and punish those suspected of religious heresies. It was established in 1480 and continued its murderous work for many hundreds of years. Its broadsides at first were not directed against professing Jews—they were left to the mercies of the mob—but against professing Christians who secretly or openly doubted any of the Church dogmas. For many years the vast majority of its victims, of course, were the Maranos. The Church was determined to get rid of them, for they were like a canker eating at its very heart. And incidentally, Ferdinand and Isabella, the King and Queen of Spain, desired to kill them off in order to get hold of their enormous wealth.

Three years after the establishment of the Inquisition a fiend named Torquemada was put at its head. On the slightest fragment of gossip dropped by a Christian servant-girl in confessional, her Marano master and mistress were dragged before the Inquisition, tortured till they confessed their secret Jewishness, and then burnt at the stake. An auto-da-fé, an "act of faith," such a public burning was called; and it was a great sporting event for the Christians. They attended it in all their gayest raiment, and witnessed the death agonies of the condemned with songs and jeers.

But the Inquisition soon found itself incapable of handling all the suspects. There proved to be too many of them. The blame for this naturally fell on the Jews who had remained openly loyal to their faith even in name. It was common knowledge that they held secret prayer meetings to bolster the faith in the Maranos, and used other ways to keep the old religion alive among them. There was no help for it, therefore, but to turn on those unconverted Jews. For it was now plain that *they* were the real menace to the Church.

And so it happened that in the year 1492 all the unconverted Jews in the realm of Spain were driven out. They were more than two hundred thousand in number, and they were compelled to leave all their gold and silver and jewels behind them. A single word—just one gesture—to show they were willing to surrender their faith, and any one of them would have been spared.

But no. Rather would they all sacrifice their homes and their wealth, than forsake their religion. So off into the night they went, outcasts and fugitives. Off they wandered in utter bewilderment to seek a new home.

CHAPTER XXIX

HOW THE JEWS FLED FROM WESTERN EUROPE TO POLAND AND TURKEY

So once more we find the Jews cast out and wandering in search of a new resting place. Further west it was impossible for them to go, for the New World had not yet been discovered. Of necessity, therefore, they had to go back east again.

And by now things had changed for the better in the East, and they found a ready welcome there. Jews from the northern half of Western Europe—the "Ashkenazim" as they were called, because the Hebrew for Germany is *Ashkenaz*—wandered off to Poland. Probably there already were scattered communities of Jews in Poland to welcome the refugees from the west. We are told of a large tribe of Tartars called the Khazars, who in the eighth century were converted to Judaism and established a Jewish kingdom in southern Russia.* Although that kingdom was destroyed by the Russians in the tenth century, no doubt many of the descendants of the Khazars were still living in the region.

* Judah Halevi, the poet of the "Golden Age," made this conversion the central incident in his famous book called "Al Khazari." In it he gives the arguments used by the rabbi who won over the king of the Khazars. But Halevi wrote the book four hundred years after the event, and was of course drawing altogether on his imagination. Just how the Khazars really came to accept Judaism we do not at all know.

And no doubt they readily greeted their brethren as they came flocking in from Germany.

The kings of Poland did not at all oppose the vast immigration of Jews. Their land was still sparsely settled, and almost barbaric. There was little commerce in it, for there were exceedingly few towns or villages. So the Jews, who were now

28.—The Home of the Khazars

known to be primarily a commercial people, were welcomed by the shrewd kings. Wherever a Jew settled, there a store and a market place arose; and wherever a store and market place arose, there the Polish peasants began to stake out farms and build their hovels. Thus gradually many villages and towns began to appear in the land.

But many years had to pass before the Jews began to feel at home in the new environment.

29.—*The Flight Eastward*

The unrefined life of the barbaric serfs around them made them look back with longing to the civilized land from which they had been driven. They still spoke German—though with the passing of the generations that German changed to the speech now known to us as Yiddish. And they still called each other by the names of the German cities from which they had been expelled.

2

Exactly the same thing happened to the Jews who were driven from Spain—the "Sephardim," as they were called, because the Hebrew word for Spain is *Sepharad.* They wandered off to Turkey and to other Mohammedan lands; and the sultans received them with no little delight. But those Jews, too, felt themselves in a lower grade environment, and they never gave up their old speech. Just as the Ashkenazim in the north developed Yiddish, so the Sephardim in the south developed Ladino, a dialect also written in Hebrew characters, but made up principally of sixteenth-century Spanish interspersed with many Hebrew words.

3

Not all the Jews wandered off to Poland and Turkey, however. The many hundreds of thousands not courageous enough to uproot themselves and leave their old homes and the graves of their forefathers, remained behind. In Germany, Italy, and Austria they managed to drag out a pitiable existence in the comparatively few towns which had not absolutely expelled their race; and in Spain and Portugal they lived on, despite the Inquisition, as Maranos.

In each of those German and Italian towns they were forced to live in what was called a Ghetto. The first of them in Italy was created in Venice, and was located in a foul corner of the town near the "Gietto," the gun factory. And probably that is how we get the word.

From the very beginning of the Exile the Jews had been inclined to live together in little groups. Even before the Talmud became their law they preferred to keep to themselves, for after all, they *were* a "different" people. And the Talmud, with its innumerable minute regulations, only intensified that preference. No matter where the town, the Jews almost instinctively drifted toward one particular street or section in it. Thus in London before their expulsion most of them lived on a narrow lane which to this day is know as Old Jewry.

But in those earlier years it was always a matter of desire, not of duress. There was no law forbidding them to live wherever they pleased in a city. Only in the towns of early Spain, before the Mohammedans conquered the land, was any attempt made to restrict Jewish dwellings to certain streets.

But in the twelfth and thirteenth centuries such restrictions began to be made and enforced also in the German cities, and in the fourteenth century in the Sicilian cities. And gradually the evil custom spread to other parts of Europe. By the sixteenth century few indeed were the West-European Jews who were not forced to live in these segregated districts.

4

Almost always the ghetto was situated in the foulest part of the town. In Rome, for instance, a few vile alleys down in the lower end of the city sheltered the Jews. Year after year the River Tiber in flood sent its ill-smelling waters through those alleys, leaving behind thick layers of oozy mud that steamed with malaria and other diseases.

Almost always, too, the ghettos grew fearfully overcrowded. Though the Jews rapidly increased in numbers, bearing children and children's children, the ghettos were rarely if ever enlarged. In Frankfort-on-the-Main, for instance, four thousand souls were packed into fewer than two hundred houses in a gloomy street too narrow for a wagon to turn in! Two and three families had to live in one and the same room. Even the cemeteries became so choked that the tombstones were often piled almost on top of each other.

It was impossible to keep the ghettos clean. Refuse was littered everywhere, and huge rats scuttled about in the cellars and walls. If a fever broke out, hardly a family escaped; if a fire was started, not a house could be saved.

Nor was this all. High walls surrounded the ghettos, and their gates could be closed and locked. At first this was looked on as an advantage by the Jews, for their thought was that the walls would protect them from the murderous mobs. Every night they locked the gate in the belief that it safeguarded them from attack. But later they discovered that the gate shut them in far more effectively than it shut the Christians out. The ghetto became a prison yard, and when lustful mobs wanted their Jews, they knew just where to find them. Once the gate was battered down, the Jews were trapped in their narrow alleys and were lost.

And there was still another evil. Life in the ghetto with its imprisoning walls, its dilapidated houses, its open sewers in every street, came to affect the Jew for evil much the same as did the badge he was forced to wear. It not merely stunted his body, but it also warped his soul. It condemned him to skulk like a criminal or a leper behind bars. All his social life had to be lived in its close air. If he was caught outside the ghetto gates after dark, he was arrested and perhaps put to death.

Even during the day, when he was free to roam through the city, he could seldom make friends. The Jew-badge sewn to his ragged clothing, marked him off as low and despicable. Very rarely, now, was he able to carry on the business of money lending save on a petty scale. He could not be a craftsman of any sort because the guilds, the trade unions of mediæval times, rigidly excluded him from membership. Even as a trader he was restricted, for in many lands a law forbade him to sell any but second-hand goods. He had to eke out a livelihood as a rag-peddler or a haggling pawnbroker. Deeper and deeper he was ground into the dust.

5

But there was still one place left on earth where he was noble and free—and that place was his home. Even though it may have been but a corner of some foul cellar, still he was king there. All the love in his being, dammed in by the outside world, was lavished on his wife and children. The home became his temple, and the family table his holy altar. As often as the Sabbath came, he would throw off his rags, bathe, dress in his finest raiment, and feel himself once more the Chosen of God. The Sabbath table would be spread with its white linen, its bright lamps, its mountainous twisted loaves. The little wine cup would be drained to the glory of God and the Holy Days. Prayers would be offered and even merry songs would be sung. All the thousand woes of daily life would be utterly forgotten. And with that old hope that had never quite been crushed, the Jew would dream again of his Messiah.

That is the miracle of the Ghetto—and the miracle of the Jew. All the hideous degradations that a stupidly hostile world could heap on him, could not rob him of that solace. The frenzied words of the Prophets of ancient Judea still lived on in his heart. Through the week they flickered low in the wind of hatred, but on the Sabbath day in his own home they burst into triumphant flame. He would *still* be redeemed, he believed! Some day, some day, the God he had served all through that terrible night, would bring on the dawn again! Some day his Messiah would come! . . .

CHAPTER XXX

HOW THE JEWS HELPED TO BRING ABOUT THE PROTESTANT REFORMATION

The hostility of the Catholic Church to Judaism is simply explained. The foundation of that Church was the naïve claim that it alone knew and treasured the whole Truth. It would not admit that there might be "my" belief and "yours," but insisted that there could only be the "true" belief and the "false." All who belonged to the Church enjoyed the safety of the "true" belief; while all who were so foolish as to remain outside the Church, shared in the unvarying deadly harm of the "false."

It was an altogether absurd, a pathetically stupid claim—but nevertheless it was insisted on. And because the Synagogue frankly refused to accept it, the Church was as frankly relentless in its persecution. For no matter how battered and crippled and small it may have been, the Synagogue still constituted a living challenge. It was the one unmistakable, ever-flaming protest against the presumption of the Church. It was more than a thorn. Scattered as it was throughout the lands of Christendom, the Synagogue operated on every side rather like a network of tiny rapiers that bled the sense of self-sufficiency in the Church.

That explains why the Church would give the Jew no rest. He was its most dangerous enemy, for wherever he migrated he encouraged heresies. He did not do it by active agitation; he did not have to. His very presence in a community was enough. For his very presence proved it was possible to remain outside the Church, to be unorthodox, and still live and face death peacefully.

One cannot doubt, therefore, that it was this presence of the Jew in Christian Europe, and the spirit of protest which he kept alive, that helped bring on the great Protestant Reformation.

2

It is significant that the first skirmish in that Reformation sprang out of an attack on the Jews. A certain baptized Jew named Pfefferkorn, eager to show how good a Christian he had become, persuaded the Emperor of Germany in 1509 to order the burning of all the Hebrew books in the hands of the Jews of Frankfort and Cologne. Such burnings, especially of copies of the Talmud, had already occurred several times before in Europe; for it was charged that those books contained wicked attacks on Christianity. The Jews had always protested, but never with success.

This time, however, they had better fortune. The Emperor, desiring to be just, called in a famous Christian named Reuchlin to give an opinion on the case. Like many other great scholars of that day—the Humanists, as they were called—Reuchlin was well versed in Hebrew literature. He had studied in Rome under Jews, and had written on Hebrew grammar and Cabala. His report was favorable to the Jews, declaring that their books were useful for theology and science, and contained no heresy whatsoever. And as a result of that report the Emperor rescinded his order.

Immediately Pfefforkorn, with the aid of the Dominican friars whose tool he was, launched an attack on Reuchlin. But the humanist was a man of courage as well as learning, and he fought back. And the conflict that ensued helped to clear the way for Martin Luther and his Reformation. It opened the eyes of the more intelligent Christians to the corruption and the ignorance of the Church.

3

A new spirit had already gathered momentum in Europe—a spirit that came to be called the Renaissance, the "Rebirth." For the first time in centuries man dared to give his mind freer play, and dared again to ask questions. This generation was no longer content to accept all that the churchmen told it, but began to go back to the Hebrew and Greek writings from which those churchmen claimed to have derived their authority. Those writings were only available because of the activity of the Jews and the Arabs during the "Golden Age." It was Jews and Arabs who had translated and interpreted the Holy Scriptures of the ancient Hebrews, and the scientific works of the ancient Greeks, so that Christian scholars—now that they were interested—at last could see what those books contained.

Of course, the result was devastating to the prestige of the Church. Its religion was discovered to be grossly unlike the religion of the Hebrews and

Jesus; and its science, when compared with the science of the Greeks, was found to be altogether false.

Martin Luther, although himself a priest at the time, was one of those who saw how extreme was the difference between the religion of the Church and the religion of the Scriptures. He had studied Hebrew under Reuchlin and was able to read those Scriptures in the original tongue. And having read them diligently, he finally made public what he had discovered. On Hallowe'en Day in the year 1517, he nailed a statement of certain of his beliefs to the door of his little church in Wittenberg, in Germany. And with that courageous act, Protestantism was born.

Luther insisted that not the Pope but the Holy Scriptures were the final religious authority to which every man should bow. For that reason he made it one of his first tasks to translate the Bible into German, so that every man might be able to consult it for and by himself. In making that translation, he relied considerably on the commentary written by the Jewish scholar named Rashi who lived in France in the eleventh century. But save in that indirect fashion, Jews exercised little influence on the development of the new movement. By their long and heroic struggle against the Church they had pointed the way for Protestantism. By their very presence in Europe they had helped to bring the heresy into being. But once it was born, they let it severely alone.

4

It is curious how Luther acted toward the Jews. At first they were highly in favor with him, and he had nothing but praise for their age-old resistance to the Church. In an essay entitled "Jesus Was Born a Jew," he wrote: "They (the Jews) are blood-relations of our Lord; and if it were proper to boast of flesh and blood, the Jews belong to Christ more than we. . . . Therefore it is my advice that we treat them kindly. . . . We must exercise not the law of the Pope, but that of Christian love, and show them a friendly spirit. . . ."

But later it became evident that Luther had not written those words out of a desire to be fair to the Jews, but out of a desire to convert them. For as he grew older and saw that the Jews could not be converted, his whole attitude changed. With a rancor and bitterness hard to account for, he suddenly began condemning the Jews. He accused them now of all those fictitious crimes which had made Europe such a hell for them. He, too, now claimed that they poisoned the wells used by Christians, assassinated their Christian patients, and murdered Christian children to procure blood for the Passover. He called on the princes and rulers to persecute them mercilessly, and commanded the preachers to set the mobs on them. He declared that if the power were his, he would take all the leaders of the Jews and tear their tongues out by the roots!

5

The story of the earlier and later attitude of Luther toward the Jews of Germany strangely parallels that of Mohammed toward the Jews of Arabia. And just as Mohammedanism in the beginning brought the unconvertible folk exceedingly little benefit, just so Protestantism brought them no good. On the contrary, Luther's movement in those years caused the Jews even more distress—if that was possible—than they had known while in the talons of the undivided Church. For soon a reaction set in, and the Church with mad desperation tried to win back its old power. The laxity that had crept into its government, and that had made it possible for the Jews to live at all, was now suddenly checked.

All the harshest canons and regulations were now put in force again. The Talmud and other Hebrew works were ordered to be destroyed in the Papal States—and now no Reuchlin was permitted to intercede. Jews were compelled to support schools for their own conversion. They were not allowed to own real estate. Wherever they went, the men had to wear green caps, and the women green veils. The physicians among them were absolutely forbidden to attend Christian patients. . . . The Jews were expelled from Lower Austria, and twice within twenty years from Bohemia. . . . Even in Poland, where they had been left at peace until now, the Jesuit missionaries of the Church brought misery and death to the Jews.

Dawn had come to the Christian world, and the darkness that had reigned for thirteen hundred years, was at last being dispelled.

But for the Jews there was still no dawn. For them it was still unbroken Night.

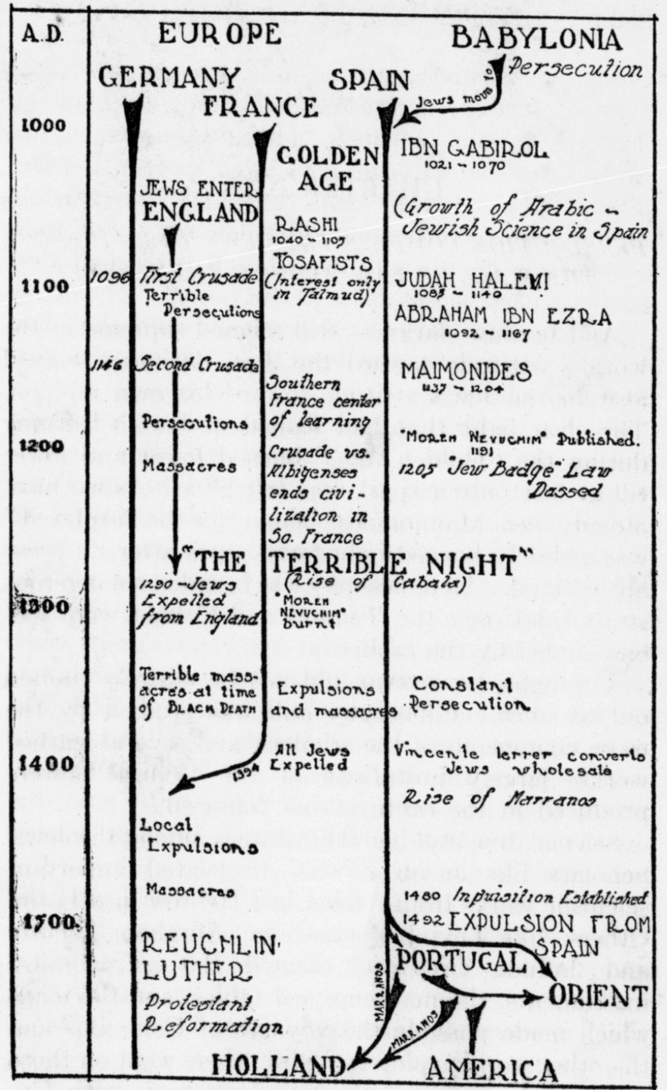

Chart E. *The Adventures of the Jews, Part V*

CHAPTER XXXI

PERSECUTION COMPELS THE JEWS TO RE-INFORCE THE WALL OF LAW AROUND THEMSELVES

And because darkness still reigned supreme in the world's attitude toward the Jew, darkness reigned also in the Jew's attitude toward his own religion. The clear light that had flamed in Jewish learning during the "Golden Age," burned lower and lower till at last only a spark was left alive. As we have already seen, Maimonides' "Guide for the Perplexed" was publicly burned only forty years after its great author died. All philosophy was branded a dangerous study, and only the Talmud and Cabala were recommended by the rabbis.

The light, however, could not be entirely snuffed out at once. Philosophy still was studied by the more courageous of the scholars, and several learned works—largely imitations of the "Guide"—were produced in the century that followed.

Science, too, still had its devotees among the Jews. Scholars like Jacob Anatoli translated important scientific works from Arabic and Hebrew into Latin. Others, like Levi ben Gershom, Abraham Zacuto, and Jaffuda Cresques, created the astronomical instruments, the mathematical tables, and the maps which made possible the voyages of Columbus and the other world explorers. Still others went on those voyages themselves. Several Jews were with Columbus on his expeditions to America, and the first white man to set foot on the continent was his interpreter, a Jew named Luis de Torres.*

2

Neither did the lively Hebrew literature of the "Golden Age" disappear all at once. Immanuel of Rome, a friend of Dante, wrote clever poetry that was rather shocking. And another, Kalonymus ben Kalonymus, dared to produce and circulate an amusing "take-off" on the Talmud.

The ferment of new ideas in Christian Europe which is called the Renaissance, did not pass by and leave the Jews unaffected. They themselves had helped to give the ferment a start, for Jews had been foremost among the teachers of the Humanists. Naturally, therefore, they themselves were influenced by its rise.

For instance, a Jew named Elijah Levita, who had taught Hebrew to many famous Christians, made at least one bold discovery concerning the text of the Scriptures. He became convinced that the vowel points in the Hebrew Bible had not been put in by Moses or Ezra, as people firmly believed, but by certain unknown scholars living long after the Talmud had been completed. His announcement bewildered the Jews and then aroused them to great anger. Levita's discovery meant that the text of the Bible in use among them was of relatively late origin!

Then there was a frail and withered scholar named

* This same Luis de Torres is reputed to have been the man who first discovered the use of tobacco.

Azariah dei Rossi, one of those amazing Jews who had wandered everywhere and seemed to know everything. He wrote voluminously on Jewish history and science, and always with fine daring. Whenever a real contradiction arose between reason and a time-honored belief, he sided completely with reason. And he was the first Jewish scholar with sufficient daring to declare openly that on matters of science the whole Talmud was unreliable!

But such scholars received no sympathy or encouragement from the run of their fellow Jews. On the contrary, their works were reviled and their lives were plagued. The poetry of Immanuel of Rome was rabbinically condemned. Elijah Levita found his brethren so hostile, that most of his life was spent solely with Christian associates. And Azariah dei Rossi narrowly escaped excommunication.

So it went with all the other scholars who dared to display independence and courage in their thinking. In the eyes of the orthodox rabbis of the day, they were "destructive critics." And in the judgment of those rabbis all destructive criticism—indeed, criticism of any sort—seemed fearful and dangerous. They insisted that there be no prying or doubting, but only dumb belief. Very much like the priests of the Church, the rabbis of the Synagogue could only tolerate unqualified orthodoxy.

For they were frightened. They knew that once more Israel stood in danger of destruction. It had been all very well in the "Golden Age" to lower the wall around the Jew and let in a little light. In the "Golden Age" the sea outside the wall had been calm and still. But now that the sea again raged with fury, even those breaches that had already been made, needed to be quickly closed against the flood.

3

So in the very century when light was streaming into the Church, the breaches in the walls of the Synagogue were being filled and all light was being shut out. The very age that saw the rise of prophetic reformers in Christendom, saw the rise of priestly rabbis in Israel.

The laws of the Talmud recovered their old importance, and along with them, myriads of new little laws that had been devised by later rabbis. New notebooks or digests were compiled to make those laws better known to the people. As early as the eleventh century one of these digests was compiled by a rabbi named Alfasi. In the fourteenth century, Asher ben Yechiel made another. His son, Jacob ben Asher, followed with a third. And there were also many others of lesser importance.

But not until the sixteenth century were the Jews ready to make a new gospel of such a law code, and then a rabbi named Joseph Karo compiled a work called the *Shulchan Aruch*.

4

Joseph Karo was a Spanish Jew who settled in Safed, in Galilee, and became chief rabbi there. (The rule of the Turks had grown tolerant again, and Palestine had once more become an important Jewish center.) He was one of those scholars who thought all worldly wisdom was confined to the Talmud, and he pored over it till he knew it almost by heart. He seems to have been a true product of his surroundings: a gadgrind with a marvelous memory but no originality, a vast capacity for work but no genius. His imagination was of the sort that trailed its wings in the stagnant waters of magic and superstition. And his courage was of the sort that essayed huge tasks rather than adventurous ones. His whole intelligence was typically that of the ultra-priest—slow, safe, and soggy.

Practically all his life was devoted to the one monumental undertaking, the compiling of his Shulchan Aruch. The book was an exhaustive digest of the laws and customs regulating the life of the Jew; and it covered everything, from a ruling as to which shoe should be put on first when dressing, to how love should be made, and how children should be reared. It clamped the Jew in an iron mold, and forced all his life and thought to become rigid and unchangeable. And soon after it was first printed (1564), the Shulchan Aruch was accepted as the highest authority in the legal literature of Israel. It gained acceptance in all the lands of the Diaspora, for although Karo himself had included in it only the regulations honored by the Sephardic Jews, a Polish Talmudist named Moses Isserles hastily added the many other regulations honored by the Ashkenazim. From then on succeeding scholars began to write commentaries on it as their predecessors had written commentaries on the Bible and the Talmud. They are still writing commentaries on it to this day, in Eastern Europe. . . .

And thus did the Jews take unto themselves a veritable "printed pope."

It was inevitable, of course, that this should happen. Persecution forced the Jews to build up their wall of law or else drown in the sea of oppression. It was but a repetition of what had happened in Palestine after the Destruction of Jersualem, and in Babylonia after the Dispersion, and in Northern Europe during the Crusades. Death had the Jews almost in its talons—and they would not die.

Even among the Jews themselves, there are many to-day who look on the triumph of the priestly Shulchan Aruch as one of the tragic incidents in this history. But perhaps there would not have been a to-day for the Jews if in the sixteenth century there had been no Shulchan Aruch. . . .

This code may have condemned them to imprisonment for life, but at least it saved them from death.

CHAPTER XXXII

THE GLOOM BEHIND THE WALL OF LAW GIVES RISE TO THE CABALA AND THE FALSE MESSIAHS

If there was any light behind the gloomy wall of Law which the Jews had built around themselves, it was but the phosphorescent glow cast by the Cabala. As far back as Bible times there had been a trace of that glow in Jewish life. It increased somewhat in Talmudic times, probably through association with the Persians. In Gaonic times it grew brighter still. Rabbis bored to desperation with sifting the dead ashes of the Law, eagerly took to playing with the flame of magic. It died down again while the sun of reason shone among the philosophers of the "Golden Age." But as soon as that sun set, the eerie gleam of the Cabala appeared again.

And then the real age of the Cabala followed. It received its first impetus from a book called the *Zohar* (the "Splendor"), late in the thirteenth century. This Zohar contained a Cabalistic explanation of the Torah that purported to reveal all the "secret meanings" underlying the peculiar phrases and words of the holy text. A Spanish Jew named Moses de Leon, who sponsored the book, claimed it had been conceived and written by a wonder-working rabbi eleven hundred years earlier, and that the manuscript had lain hidden away all the intervening years in a mysterious cave. In all probability, however, he had compiled it himself from stolen material lifted by him from Hindu, Persian, and Hebrew writings.

The popularity of the book in the Jewish world was amazing. Though it had set out to be merely a commentary on the Torah, it soon became, indeed, a Torah in itself. In every corner of every land of the Diaspora Jews pored over it and wrote commentaries on it. Contemporary Jewish philosophers and scientists attacked it to no avail, for its hold on the imagination of the people was too firm. For five hundred years stunted souls reveled in its mysteries with all the abandon of rickety slum-children playing in a mud puddle.

2

It is difficult for a modern mind to extract much sense from the Zohar or any of the other Cabalistic works. They all seem filled to the brim with diseased and pathetic nonsense. We can well understand and, indeed, admire the underlying hunger behind them, the sweeping sense of wonder at the unutterable mystery of all life. But our minds are offended by the way in which those works seek to allay the hunger.

Nothing is more reasonable than the conviction that veiled powers throng the universe; and nothing is more honorable than the desire to unveil them. But there are varied ways of attempting to satisfy that desire. There is the way of the scientist who by experimentation and invention tries courageously to tear the veils apart. There is the way of the religious mystic who by piety and meditation tries humbly to pray them apart. There is the way of the artist who by yielding to inspiration somehow stares them apart. Then there is the way of the Cabalist, who by mumbling incantations and boiling magic broths, tries almost treacherously to sneak them apart.

And of all four ways, the most popular has ever been that of the Cabalist.

Especially was it popular among the Jews between the thirteenth and the eighteenth centuries—and for a very valid reason. To the sorry creatures languishing behind the physical wall of the Ghetto and the spiritual wall of the Law, it came as a boon from Heaven. The Ghetto bound their feet, and the Law shackled their hands; but the Cabala let their minds run loose and wild.

That explains the rapid spread of the Cabala in the Jewish world. The Law was still studied and observed, more out of duty, however, than love. The Cabala alone was wooed with free-hearted passion. For the Law, though it did keep the Jews alive, yet did not make their life worth living. The Cabala alone seemed able to do that for them. For the Cabala put heart into them by its assurance that their individual souls were all-important and holy—that the whole universe revolved about them. The Cabala taught every man not merely that he was created in the image of God, but that he was actually a *part* of Him. All could taste the ecstasy of union with God, of meeting, and embracing, and being embraced by Him, if they but knew the secret way that led into His presence.

All of which was admirable and beyond reproach.

But Cabala went further and tried to tell how that union with God could be attained—and that was where it fell into pathetic error. It took to mumbling about imps and demons, about magic words and magic numbers, about lucky stars and guardian angels, about secret books and mystic seals. All the truck and imbecility of magic, all the nonsense about spells, amulets, evil eyes, and lucky stones, became part of Cabalistic lore.

It was a delusion and a snare, plunging and entangling the people in the crudest superstition. And generation after generation it bred False Messiahs.

3

To tell of all the Cabalists who set themselves up as Messiahs, would take many more pages than we can afford here. Of most of them it is enough to say that they suddenly appeared, preached, excited the people, and then disappeared. Many of them fell a prey to the civil authorities, and were either forcibly baptized or put to death. Some of them may have been plain impostors, and deserving of that fate. But the majority of them seem to have been poor, half-insane fellows who were fully as deluded as their followers. Long brooding over the woes of the Jewish people, coupled with years of staring into the glare of the Cabala, had hypnotized them into really believing themselves the "Anointed of God." Typical of their faith in themselves is the instance of one of them who actually asked to be beheaded so that he might prove that he could come to life again!

Their daring was almost incredible. For instance, a swarthy, emaciated, quick-witted adventurer named David Reubeni, managed to convince both the Pope at Rome, and the King of Portugal, of his pretensions. So great was the enthusiasm he aroused, that many Maranos in Portugal were suddenly impelled to declare themselves Jews once more. One of them was a handsome youth named Diogo Pires, who was royal secretary in one of the high courts. He cast aside all his honors, had himself circumcised, took the Hebrew name of Solomon Molko, and started off impetuously to meet the Great Day. He ran away to Syria, and became a leader among the Cabalists there. (Even Joseph Karo, the dry legalist who wrote the Schulchan Aruch, became one of Molko's disciples.) And then he went to Italy to proclaim to the world the immediate coming of the Messiah.

What adventures Molko had in Italy, how he was befriended by ambassadors and cardinals, was secretly smuggled out of his death-cell by the Pope, met David Reubeni once more and went off with him to convert the Emperor, and how finally he was burned at the stake, provide an abundance of material for a thrilling novel.

4

But even more fascinating is the story of Sabbatai Zevi, the greatest of all the False Messiahs.

Sabbatai was born in Turkey, and early distinguished himself as a pious Cabalist. He was known as a queer young fellow—queer enough, at least, to deny himself all pleasures, fast day after day, and bathe in the sea even in winter. These practices were the fashion among the extreme Cabalists: they starved and froze their bodies until they became delirious with the pain. And while in that delirium they believed they tasted the ecstasy of union with God.

Sabbatai was born into a world that was all a-tremble with panic and excitement. The year 1666 was approaching, and because of some curious manipulations of a verse in the New Testament Book of Revelation, 1666 was looked forward to by many Christians as the year of the coming of the Messiah. The Jews, too, had a calculation that pointed to his coming at about that time. The fact that for the Christians it was the Second Coming, and for the Jews the first, made very little difference. The exciting point was that He was coming!

With much of the world thus nervously awaiting the miraculous appearance, it was neither strange nor difficult for a youth like Sabbatai to get a fixed idea into his head that he himself was the one to appear. Neither was it difficult for him to get others to accept the idea, too. In Turkey and Syria, where the Cabala had been sapping the intelligence of the Jews for generations, he was very soon accepted with mad acclaim. In Poland, where the ghastliest massacres were just then decimating the Jews, he was just as eagerly hailed. Even in Germany, Holland, and France the Jews took him at his word. Their spirits had been so broken by long-continued suffering and unremitting torture throughout the world, that they were ready to believe in anyone promising early release. Pilgrims came to Sabbatai from all corners of the Diaspora, bearing rich gifts from their communities. Great rabbis in far distant lands, on hearing rumors of the "Messiah's" appearance, wrote to each other in bewilderment, not knowing what to believe or do.

Sabbatai himself was undoubtedly deluded and somewhat insane; but he directed his campaign with rare shrewdness. He did everything possible to win the allegiance of the people, from distributing candy among the children of the town, to giving himself solemnly in marriage to the Torah. He scourged his body publicly, sang mystical songs, distributed printed accounts of his visions, and sent messengers everywhere proclaiming his messiahship.

Finally, the Turkish officials took a hand, for the Sabbataian movement had begun to take on the semblance of a political revolt. But they did not exert themselves. After they had imprisoned Sabbatai they let his prison be turned almost into a throne-room by his frenzied admirers. The synagogues throughout Europe were decorated with his initials, "S. Z." In many communities, houses were unroofed and other preparations made for a new Exodus. Prayers were offered in Sabbatai's name, and good-luck charms were engraved with his initials. Pictures were drawn of the holy Sabbatai astride a lion crunching a seven-headed dragon in its jaws, leading the Twelve Tribes on their way back to the Holy Land. Even some Christians caught the fever, and thought they sighted mysterious vessels off the coast of Scotland with silken sails bearing Hebrew inscriptions.

30.—*The Wanderings of Sabbatai Zevi*

5

And then of a sudden the whole mad boom collapsed. A rival "Messiah" suddenly came out of Poland, and failing to come to terms with Sabbatai, denounced him to the Sultan. Sabbatai was taken from the prison in which bribed officials had permitted him to do as he pleased, and was dragged to Adrianople. There he immediately perceived that his end was approaching, for the government had lost its patience. Frantically he looked about for a means of escape, and found it—in conversion. When he was brought for judgment before the mighty Sultan he simply cast off his Jewish head-dress and put on a Turkish turban.

Awful was the consternation in all Israel when the news spread that the holy Sabbatai had turned Mohammedan. Great rabbis and scholars who had been deceived by the impostor, hung their heads in shame; and everywhere great sport was made of the Jews by their enemies. The Sultan, who might just as easily have been among the duped, now pretended great disgust with the credulous Jews. Seriously he spoke of converting or exterminating all of the hundreds of thousands in his realm; and only narrowly was the attempt averted.

But the marvel of it was that even then the belief in Sabbatai did not cease entirely. Jews by the hundred persisted in regarding him as the long-awaited Messiah. They told themselves that his conversion was but a part of the Messianic programme, and they quoted from the Prophets to prove it. And they, too, became Mohammedans with him.

Sabbatai himself encouraged these simpletons by telling them that God had commanded him in a vision to change his religion outwardly. He kept up a continuous agitation, lying and playing traitor to both Jews and Turks. Finally he was trapped at his deceitful game and exiled to a lone village in Albania. And there in shame and poverty he died.

6

But the storm Sabbatai Zevi had aroused did not die with him. A century later, great rabbis in Poland and Germany were still squabbling over him and his claims.

And to this day in many towns in Turkey descendants are to be found of those Jews who turned Mohammedan with the impostor. The "*Donmeh*" they are called by the Turks: the "Apostates." They keep themselves apart from the other Jews and make a great show of going to the mosques and keeping the Mohammedan holydays. But beneath it all, they are still Jews. They live side by side, or in houses which are secretly connected, marry only among themselves, have their own hidden meeting-places where they pray in Hebrew or Ladino, and still await the return of Sabbatai the Messiah. Somehow they have obtained a monopoly of the barber trade, so that in a town like Salonica to-day you can hardly have your hair trimmed save at the hands of one of these strange half-Jews. And sometimes the swarthy young foreigner who shines your shoes in an American barber-shop, is also one of them. . . .

It is all a bewilderingly strange story. . . .

CHAPTER XXXIII

HOW THE SECRET JEWS OF SPAIN FLED TO HOLLAND AND THE NEW WORLD

When the Jews were cast out of Spain in 1492, most of them found refuge in Turkey, Palestine, and Syria. And we have already seen what manner of adventures they had there.

But the story of the Maranos who remained behind is still to be told.

The Inquisition continued its work of persecution, and not alone in Spain, but later in nearby Portugal also. But somehow it completely failed to accomplish its purpose. The Maranos still remained Maranos, secretly observing the ancient Jewish rites, and training their children and their children's children to observe them. Not merely to the third and fourth generations, but to the ninth and tenth, the practices of the ancient faith were secretly transmitted. Though all Spain and Portugal reeked with the smell of burning Jewish flesh, the heresy could not be destroyed.

But as the years passed and the tyranny of the Inquisitors did not abate, the Maranos grew desperate. Though they had great wealth and high station, the strain of living in hourly danger of exposure became too great even for them. So they began to think of flight. Accordingly, in the sixteenth century some of them followed their Jewish brethren who had fled to Turkey, and there they returned openly to the ancient faith. And there they prospered and grew enormously powerful.

But as had happened so often before in the history of the Jews, in a little while their popularity began to wane. Perhaps it was because they had increased in numbers too rapidly in their new home and had become too prominently noticeable there. (When foreigners in a community are few, their presence is rarely resented. But when they so multiply that they seem to be always in the way, the attitude of the natives quickly changes.) So after the sixteenth century but few Maranos looked upon the Near East as a refuge.

They began looking to the north instead; to the Netherlands.

2

After one of the most heroic revolutions in the story of all mankind, Holland had just succeeded in freeing itself from the tyranny of Spain. Naturally, therefore, it attracted the Maranos. In greater and greater numbers they began to take refuge in the free-spirited republic, bringing with them their wealth and vast trading connections. And from then on the glory of Spain began rapidly to wane—and the might of Holland began to grow.

A distinguished Jewish community arose in Amsterdam. Many of its members had been rather lofty aristocrats in the land from which they had fled, and had held high positions there. Former priests and prelates were among them; perhaps even former inquisitors. There were statesmen and physicians, scholars and financiers. And many of them bore romantic Spanish names that rolled off the tongue like polite rumblings of thunder.

(It is interesting to picture a haughty Juan Martinez de Caballeria and a proud Roderigo Ramirez de Ribera, with their black little van dyke beards, their enormous ruffs, their silk doublets, huddling with their brethren in a little synagogue and reciting the Hebrew prayers of their forefathers. . . .)

3

And from this parent colony in Holland, many others were formed. The King of Denmark was induced by the prosperity which the Jews were bringing to the Netherlands, to invite them to settle in his country too. Far more important, England now reopened its doors to the Jews. In 1654 Oliver Cromwell was won over by the eloquent rabbi of Amsterdam, Menasseh ben Israel, and set aside the edict that had kept the Jews out of England for more than three and a half centuries. From then on Jews from Holland—and later Germany—began to filter into England in a steady stream.

4

Nor was that all. America too now became a refuge for the wandering Jews. By a strange trick of fate the very day after the Jews were ordered out of Spain was the day that Christopher Columbus set sail for the West. The coincidence was almost a prophecy. That voyage, made possible to a certain extent by the funds, the nautical instruments, and the man-power of the people who had just been made homeless, discovered for them a new home.

31.—The Flight of the Maranos

Maranos drifted over to the New World with the earliest Spanish and Portuguese conquistadors in such numbers that soon the dread Inquisition was set up there. Full half a century before the Pilgrim Fathers ever set foot on the continent, Jews were already being martyred at the autos-da-fé in Mexico and Peru.

But fortunately for the Jews, not all the New World fell into the hands of fanatical Catholics. In 1642 a group of six hundred Jews set sail from Holland for Brazil, which then was a possession of the Dutch. The community grew rapidly, so that twelve years later, when the Portuguese conquered the province, several thousand Jews had to flee. Most of them settled in the Dutch West Indies, but a shipload of twenty-three found their way to New York, which then was called New Amsterdam. The governor, Peter Stuyvesant, tried to keep the little band of fugitives from landing; but the Dutch West Indies Company, which was partly controlled by Amsterdam Jews, sent orders to him to let them in. Before the orders could arrive, however, several of the wanderers had gone on and taken refuge in Rhode Island, where full religious liberty had been granted all settlers.

And thus did the Wandering People cross the threshold of the New World.

5

At first it was only the Sephardic Jews from Spain and Holland who wandered to the new colonies. But soon the Ashkenazic Jews from Germany began to emigrate to them also. The Thirty Years War

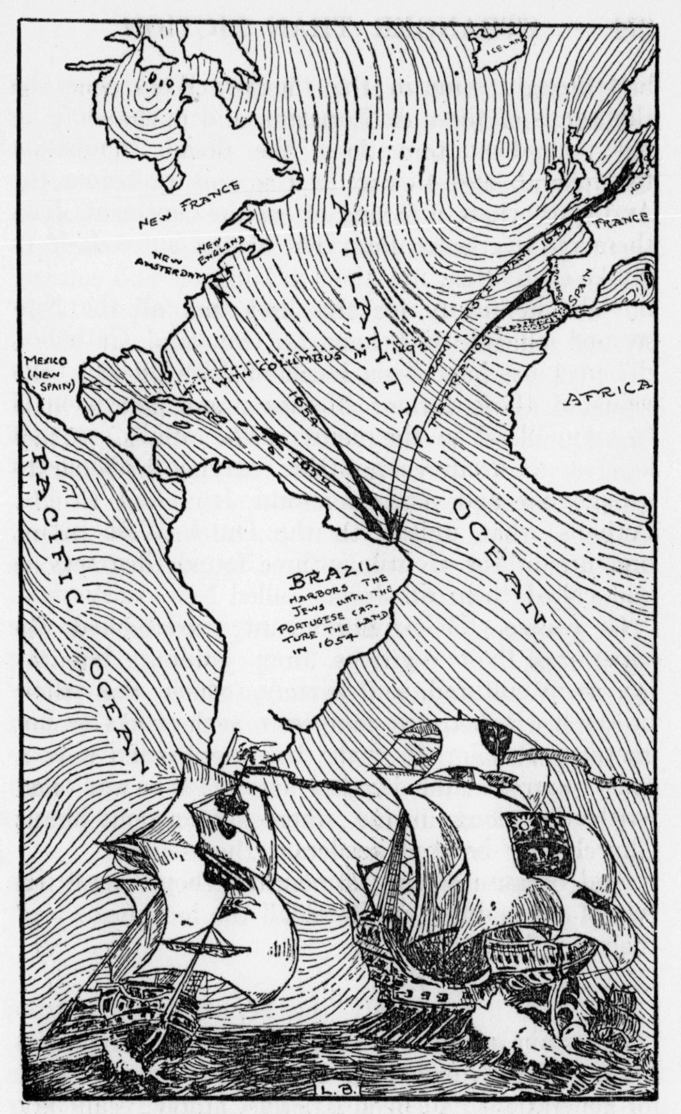

32.—*How the Jews Came to America*

had brought ruin in their homeland to countless thousands of these Ashkenazim, and in droves they now poured out to settle in freer places. They fled to Holland, and thence to England and America. And everywhere a feeling of coolness arose between them and the Sephardim. The two groups were quite unlike each other, not alone in language and culture, but also in stature, features, and complexion. They seemed almost to belong to two different races. (There must have been much Spanish blood in the veins of those former Maranos, and not a little German blood in the veins of the others.) They kept apart from each other, praying in separate synagogues and using somewhat different rituals. Perhaps what united them most was the silent pressure of the Gentile, who drew no distinctions and called them all Jews.

Of course, the Sephardim were considered the superior of the two groups, for they were far wealthier, more cultured, and better groomed than their brethren who had just escaped from the foul German ghettos. But for all that, those Sephardim were a sadly narrow and bigoted lot. They who had writhed so long in the clutches of an intolerant Church now became intolerant themselves.

And because of that intolerance they committed two of the saddest crimes in all the long history of their people. . . .

6

A certain scholarly young Spaniard named Uriel Acosta, though belonging to a Marano family that for generations had been strictly Catholic, suddenly fled away to Amsterdam to become a Jew. He had long been secretly studying the Holy Scriptures, and a mighty yearning for the religion of his forefathers had taken possession of him.

But no sooner did he reach Amsterdam than he discovered the religion of his brethren there was quite unlike the religion of his forefathers in Palestine. Hardly a trace of kinship was left between the two. The flaming faith of an Amos and a Jeremiah had died down to a smolder of petty law-keeping; the dreams of an Isaiah had been supplanted by the Shulchan Aruch. And a holy desire to reform the religion of his brethren was kindled in the heart of the young dreamer. Earnestly—and perhaps impatiently—he attacked the travesty on true Judaism which obtained among the Jews around him.

But those Jews were in no mood to allow any one to tamper with their hard-and-fast form of belief. Having suffered for it so many generations, they now insisted that it should be treated as perfect and unchangeable. So the rabbis complained to the police, and Acosta was thrown into prison as a public enemy to all religion. He fled to Germany, and for nine years lived in coventry there. Finally he could stand it no longer, and he returned, a broken man, to Amsterdam and begged to be forgiven.

He was readily taken back, and lived for a while at peace in the community. But then trouble began again. Acosta could not long remain a hypocrite and make a pretense of believing what he knew to be false and ridiculous. People began to complain to the rabbis that he was not observing all the laws of Judaism. He was summoned before the officials of the Synagogue and commanded to repent. And on his refusal he was excommunicated with awful oaths from the fold of Israel.

Seven long years he suffered in silence. Even his nearest relatives refused to speak to him. And then for the second time his spirit caved in, and he surrendered.

But this time he was not so readily taken back. First he had to make public confession of his sins in the crowded synagogue. Then he had to kneel and let his naked back be lashed thirty-nine times. Finally he had to prostrate himself on the threshold of that House of God and let himself be stepped over or trampled on by the mob.

It was too much. The proud spirit of the hidalgo, Acosta, who had sacrificed everything to throw in his lot with the Jews, could not live on after so terrible a humiliation. He went home, wrote a brief sketch of his stormy life, and then shot himself.

7

But Acosta's spirit of protest lived on after him. Hardly five years passed, and another young Jew was discovered to be a heretic. His name was Baruch Spinoza, and he seems to have belonged to one of the prominent Jewish families in Amsterdam. Born in 1632, he was reared in the religious school of the community. He studied the Bible and the Talmud, and toward the end of his course, the writings of the great Jewish scholars like Ibn Ezra and Maimonides. And also he studied Latin, the sciences, and mediæval philosophy.

This Baruch Spinoza was a brilliant lad, and

no doubt his teachers looked upon him as a future leader in the community. But gradually the story was noised around that he was thinking free and heretical thoughts. He was not molested, however, until after his father's death. Then he was brought before the officials of the synagogue to answer for his reputed heresies. And before those officials he freely admitted the truth of all that had been rumored about him. He did *not* believe in angels, or in heaven and hell, or in anything else that his reason declared impossible.

The rabbis were horrified. It was not merely that they could not themselves tolerate this young man's scorn of their beloved errors. It was more a terrible fear in them that if word of his heresies reached the Christian world, all the Jews might be made to suffer.

First the officials tried to buy his silence; but Baruch nobly refused to be bought. So then they cut him off forever. A mere youth of twenty-three, he was excommunicated and driven from the city. And from that day to the day of his death, Baruch Spinoza never again was spoken to by a Jew.

He wandered from one village to another, finally settling in The Hague. He earned a livelihood as an optician and lens-grinder; but most of his hours were spent in setting down his ideas about God, religion, and freedom. Learned Christians from many lands came to consult with him, or wrote to him on philosophic problems. And when he died at the age of forty-five, his lungs destroyed by the glass dust he had so long breathed at his daily toil, he was the most noted philosopher of his age.

This Jew, Spinoza, had but resurrected and carried on the grand tradition of Maimonides. He had sought to base all his thinking on reason, not on faith. He had refused to believe what the men of the Church or Synagogue commanded. He had tried to think for himself.

To-day no one remembers the names of the rabbis who hounded that young thinker out of Israel. But all our world knows the name of their victim. For he it was who helped lay the foundation of modern philosophy. He was one of the great light-bearers of human-kind, one of its immortal warriors against credulity and ignorance.

The pious rabbis of his day branded Spinoza as an enemy and a betrayer of Israel. (Which is just what the ancient priests always thought of the prophets of their time.) But his whole life and labor proved him to be infinitely truer to the spirit of Israel than they.

For Baruch Spinoza was a breaker of idols and a rebel against all them that would enshackle thought. He was a worker of Godly Mischief. In a very real sense he was the spirit of the Strange People incarnate. . . .

CHAPTER XXXIV

THE DARKNESS IN EASTERN EUROPE

The Jews met with relatively little ill-treatment at the hands of the non-Jews in Holland and the West; but it was far different in the East. The princes of Poland, as we have already seen, had previously welcomed the Jews in their flight from mob-ridden Germany. Those princes found them then of high value, for their activities brought commerce and a measure of prosperity to the Polish provinces. And the Jews, glad to find refuge and asylum anywhere, came in ever increasing numbers. They spread out and multiplied until there was a Jewish colony in almost every town and village. They did not till the soil, for there were already too many native peasants for that sort of work. Instead, the Jews functioned as traders and professional men, and thus became the middle class of the land.

That proved their undoing in the end. For generations they managed to live on in fair comfort, wedging themselves ever more firmly in between the serfs and the lords. And then suddenly they discovered themselves imprisoned. They were caught between two millstones, so that at every approach of bad times they were crushed. Whenever the lower class was hungry or the upper class was bankrupt, the Jews who formed the middle class were ground.

It was not until the middle of the seventeenth

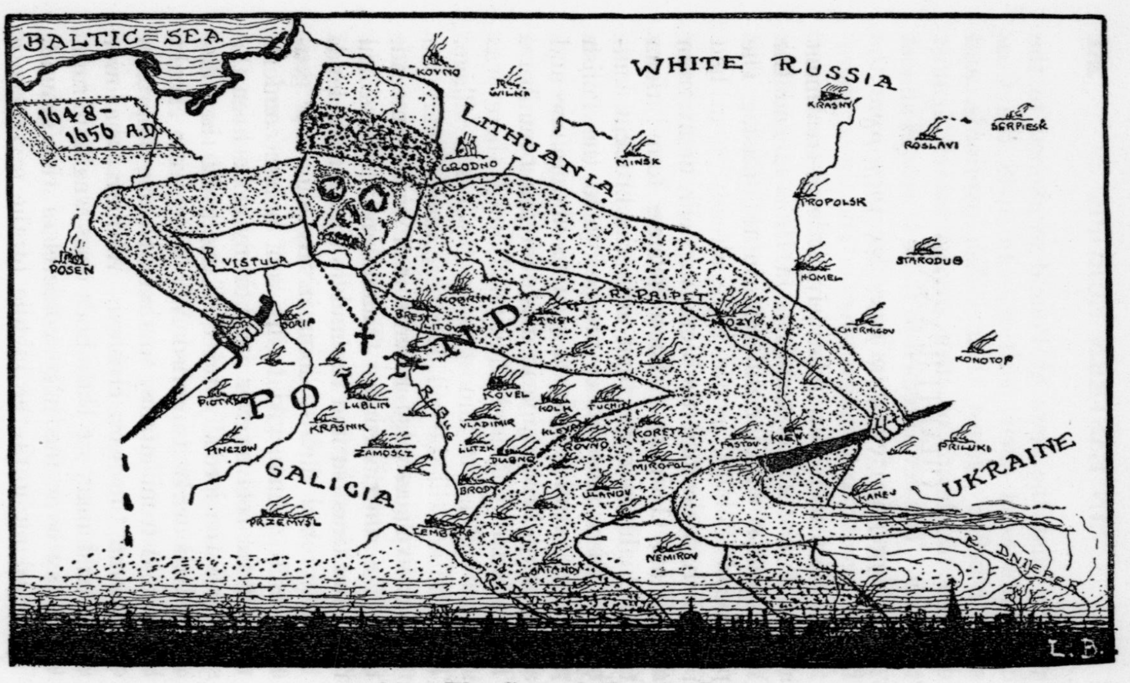

33.—*The Cossack Breaks Loose*

century that the Jews of Poland awakened to the dreadfulness of their position. In 1648 the Cossacks rebelled against their Polish overlords, and directed the brunt of their savage attack against the Jews. The Jews seemed to those Cossacks almost worse than the feudal princes, for they were the feudal agents and taxgatherers. The Jews, therefore, were tortured and plundered; they were almost drowned in their own blood. Over a half-million of them lost their lives before the uprising was crushed.

And that was but the beginning. From that day to this the Jews of Eastern Europe have known no rest. These upper and nether millstones have ground them, bled them, crushed them, generation after generation. For two hundred and twenty-five long and bloody years their life has been but a nightmare.

2

That explains why Eastern Europe became the center of the extremest Talmudism. When the Jews awakened to find themselves in a raging sea of hostility, they almost instinctively shot up their high wall of Law. And that wall became and remained the sole interest in their religious lives.

This was especially true in the north in Lithuania and what is called White Russia. Every male child from infancy was sent to the *cheder*, the "classroom," to learn Hebrew. And almost as soon as it could read, its little body was taught to bend and sway over the huge volumes of the Talmud. Day and night the child was forced to freeze or swelter in the stuffy *cheder* while it learnt to repeat in a peculiar sing-song tone the arguments of the ancient rabbis.

At thirteen each boy was confirmed, and he was then allowed to go to work if he had shown no particular diligence as a pupil. But very many of the boys went on with their studies. They went on to the *yeshivah,* the college, or in the smaller communities, to the *bes ha-medresh,* the house of learning. These boys were usually supported by the community, getting their meals each day in a different home, and sleeping on the hard benches in the study room. Until they were seventeen or eighteen they lived in that way; and then often they were married off to the daughters of wealthy Jews and were supported in the *yeshivah* perhaps for the rest of their lives by their fathers-in-law.

They never studied anything but the Talmud. The reading of a book of poetry, or science, or philosophy—especially one written in any but the sacred tongue—was considered a most serious crime. The students learnt only how to split hairs—how to divide and mangle and shred every little Talmudic rule so as to make a dozen new rules out of it.

Twice a year great fairs were held in the land, and along with the traders who came to them to exhibit their wares, came also the students to show off their cleverness. While the traders from different towns haggled with each other over prices, the students from different *yeshivos* disputed over Talmudic verses. And before the fair was over, the wealthiest traders picked the most brilliant students, and took them home to marry their daughters or sisters.

The old Jewish idea that the only genuine aristocracy is that of brains, was unchallenged among them. The scholar was the lord supreme. Everything—not alone wealth and station, but also native kindness of heart and even character—was counted far less important than learning.

3

This idolization of learning was not so intense, however, among the Jews in the southern provinces—in Poland, Galicia, and Ukrainia. There too the *cheder* and *bes ha-medresh* existed in every town and village; and there too learning was highly respected. But it was not looked on as the one thing exclusively worth respecting.

There was a marked difference in psychological background between the Jew of Poland and his brother in Lithuania. In Poland and the southern provinces generally, the emotions were esteemed and considered more important than mere intellect. The Jews there were more interested in extracting a wealth of feeling from their religion, than in producing by much thinking a host of arguments in its favor. Perhaps that explains why to this day the vast majority of the artists, writers, actors, and musicians among the East-European Jews, come from those southern provinces; while the astutest lawyers and keenest scientists among them, usually come from Lithuania.

No one can tell for certain how this difference arose. Perhaps it was due to the greater admixture of rich Tartar blood in the veins of the Jews in the south. Perhaps in that region more intermarriages

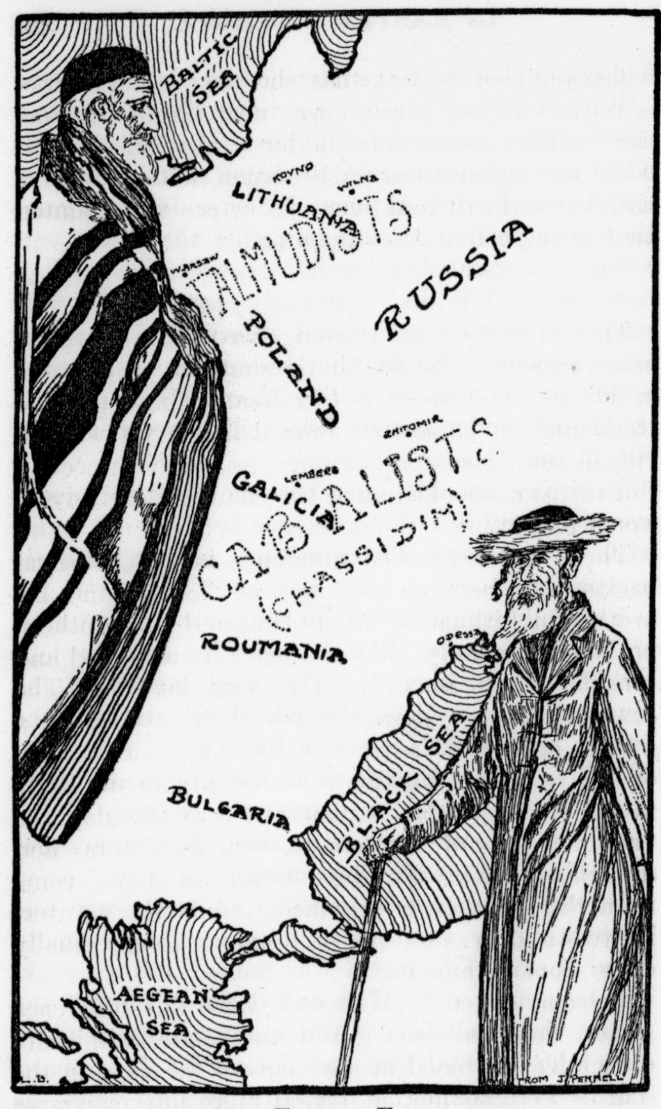

34.—*Eastern Europe*

had taken place with the descendants of the Khazars.

Whatever the cause may have been, however, the contrast was unmistakable. The Polish Jews could not and did not try to forget all their woes in dull Talmudic disputations. They preferred a game that gave their imaginations rather than their wits a chance to gambol and frolic. So while the northerners, the "Litvaks," patiently spun their holy rules, the southerners played with incantations and magic spells. While the Lithuanians set their minds to the task of boring through the Talmud, the Polish and Galician Jews let their fancies run riot in the Cabala.

In a way the difference between the two regions was strikingly like the difference between old Judea with its scholarly Pharisees and Galilee with its mystical Essenes. . . .

Naturally enough it was in the southern provinces of Eastern Europe that the ache for a miraculous Deliverer was keenest. The least rumor of the appearance of a new Messiah swept through the Jewish population there like the wind. The boom of Sabbatai Zevi carried them literally to the verge of hysteria. Even the disgraceful collapse of the boom, did not cure them altogether. Not for another century, indeed, were they cured.

It was another low impostor, a man very like Sabbatai, only even more impudent, who finally cured them. The rascal was named Jacob Frank, and he appeared in 1755 and declared himself the reborn Sabbatai Zevi. And many hundreds there were who believed him and flocked to his support. The second coming of Sabbatai seemed quite as credible to them as the second coming of Jesus still seems to millions of Christians to-day.

The coming of Frank caused a furor that shook all of East-European Jewry. The rabbis denounced him violently, especially in the shrewd, level-headed north; but nevertheless, his following grew.

Then, suddenly, like a pricked balloon, the furor collapsed. Four years after Frank first put forward his claims, he and his followers found themselves caught fast in the talons of the Church. And just as the Sabbataians, to save their lives, became Mohammedans, so the Frankists now became Christians.

That brought the Jews abruptly to their senses. Twice within a century they had seen great and much-vaunted "Messiahs" end up as cowardly apostates. Twice they had been duped.

They never were duped again.

CHAPTER XXXV

THE STORY OF THE GOOD SHEPHERD OF POLAND WHO WAS CALLED BAAL SHEM TOV

But the old hunger for religious excitement still lived among the Jews of Poland and Galicia. Struggling along in the semi-darkness behind their frowning rampart of Law, they had not lost their craving for the coming of a man who could bring them the sun.

And at last such a man came.

His name was Israel ben Eliezer, but the people soon learnt to call him *Baal Shem Tov*, "The Kind Master of God's Name." A strange and wondrous man was he—one who in his whole life and work seems to have been a true brother to that other "Kind Master," Jesus of Nazareth. And like Jesus, very little is definitely known about Baal Shem Tov, for he too left no writings. Only naïve and confused legends remain to tell us of his life, and it is not easy to decide just what in them is fact and what is fancy.

He was born in one of the southern provinces about the year 1700, and was left an orphan at an early age. Kindly townsfolk tried to rear him, sending him to *cheder* with their own children. But he was a difficult lad to bring up. He was forever playing truant, and wandering off alone to the woods. He was always dreaming—of just what, no one could find out. And he simply would not apply himself to his Talmudic studies. So indolent a student was he indeed, that finally he was expelled from the *cheder* and told to go and find work.

He was then a grown man of twelve, and he found a job as a helper in a *cheder*. He taught the little tots the alphabet; and part of his duty was to take them to and from the school. (The word "pedagogue" originally meant a Greek slave who used to do just such work in ancient Athens.) Then, when he grew older, he became the *shamosh*, the sexton, of a synagogue.

People did not know just what to make of him, he was so eccentric in his conduct. He would sleep most of the day, and spend the nights alone in the synagogue, where he would pray with terrible fervor. He would sway to and fro, shouting loudly and seeming in a trance half the time. Or else he would sit up and pore over huge volumes of Cabala.

For many years he lived in a lone village near the Carpathian Mountains where he eked out a living for himself and his wife as a clay digger. For a while he was a tavern-keeper, then a village Hebrew teacher, and then a *shamosh* again.

2

And then all of a sudden he started out among the people as a self-appointed magic healer, a baal-shem, a "Master of God's Name." Many other such healers were wandering about the countryside of Poland and Galicia at the time. They all claimed to be able to do wonders and work miracles with the aid of God's secret name. They were supposed to be able to cure diseases, cast out demons, foretell the future, and perform other such marvels for the superstitious folk.

But in one respect this Israel was quite unlike the other "healers." There was a kindliness about him, a saintliness that fast won him to the hearts of the downcast Jews. He was not at all like the ordinary baal-shem, who mumbled incantations for money. He never once asked for pay and he helped everywhere. There was a godly light in his eye and a godly sincerity in his heart. The people saw that he came and spent himself for them only because he truly loved them.

That explains why they called him "Baal Shem *Tov*," "the *Kind* Master of God's Name." Even Christian peasants were among those who came to him with woes and wounds for him to heal.

At first the orthodox Cabalists probably looked down on him as once the Pharisees had looked down on that other kindly healer, Jesus. And from first to last the aristocratic Talmudists of the north hated him as the aristocratic Sadducees had hated the Nazarene. But the simple folk, the tailors and the cobblers, the teamsters and the tavern-keepers—they and their sickly wives and their anæmic children all believed in Baal Shem Tov, and worshiped him.

And from him they learnt to look on the world in a new way. God, he told them, was everywhere and in everything—not alone in the synagogues, but also in the muddy roadways, the foul villages, in every dreary moment of their daily toil. So everywhere they could pray to Him and find Him.

And it was their duty to pray to Him wherever they might be—to count every moment holy. Not by praying at certain fixed times in a certain fixed way, could they be true Jews, but only by making all their lives a prayer. So declared Baal Shem Tov.

Fundamentally that was the valid element in the theory underlying all of Cabala. But Baal Shem Tov added to it a peculiarly attractive note of his own. He proclaimed that one's life must not be a sad or mournful prayer, but emphatically a gay and joyous one. Only thus could it be acceptable to God.

Now the ordinary Cabalist did not think this at all. He was rather afraid of God, and usually inclined to sidle up to him with a long, tearful face. That is why he believed in long fasting, great mourning, and fearful conjuring with magic words. He imagined it was the only way to secure God's favor.

But Baal Shem Tov declared that every one should whole-heartedly love God, and not be at all afraid of Him. No one should go to meet Him with tears and terror, but only with laughter and song. In prayer, one should not whisper, but shout and dance; in life one should not fast, but feast and make merry.

3

So did this new prophet assure the humble folk of Poland—and they believed him. They believed because they wanted to believe. Baal Shem Tov with this new doctrine of his, made their life worth living. He gave them back the right to laugh—a right they had not dared to exercise in many long dark centuries. He insisted that they sing and be happy. He brought back the sun to them.

So they listened to him intently and believed and obeyed him. He spoke in simple parables that they could understand without difficulty. And he healed them when they came to him, and comforted them in all their distresses. He drew no distinctions between rich and poor, between learned and ignorant. All were equal in his eyes, for all were equally part of the great God he loved.

Never did he speak of himself as the Messiah, however. On the contrary he was forever insisting that only when all Israel loved God truly would the Messiah come. He called himself merely a *tzaddik*, a "Righteous Man," and his followers he called *chassidim*, "Pious Ones." Every chassid, if he were but sufficiently earnest in his piety, could become a tzaddik. The difference was not one of kind but of degree. The tzaddik because of his tremendous piety was nearer the heart of God, and could understand God's intentions and interpret them to the folk. He was, as it were, a connecting link between God and the ordinary man.

Such was the gist of the teaching of that queer, lovable, loving mystic whom the people called Baal Shem Tov. For many years he taught it to the people, and spread it all through the land.

And when the kind baal-shem passed away he left that teaching as his legacy to comfort his brethren in Israel.

4

But they that came after Baal Shem Tov and undertook to carry on his mission, were smaller and less exalted men. Either they had not righly understood him, or they had understood and did not care to obey. For at their hands the noble belief of Baal Shem Tov sank from a prophetic yearning to a priestly cult. It became but a low means of personal enrichment for those who set themselves up as tzaddikim.

The leading disciples of Baal Shem Tov were the first tzaddikim, and after them others arose. They passed themselves off as professional holy men, and commanded the plain people to support them. And the plain people, being simple and superstitious, obeyed. They gave their last pennies to the tzaddik of their district—the "Gitter Yid," the "Good Jew," as they usually called him in Yiddish—and out of these he grew wealthy. He lived very much like a Polish prince, surrounded by a court of helpers and favorites. He had a palace, a stable of fine horses, and a cellar filled with the costliest wines. And in time a tradition arose that only the son of a tzaddik could be a tzaddik—that holiness was confined to a certain few families.

5

Of course, the rabbis of Lithuania attacked these tzaddikim and the whole Chassidic movement. They excommunicated its preachers, and when they found that was of no avail, they even had them imprisoned by the civil authorities. Perhaps it was asking too much to expect them to understand the great hunger inspiring and sustaining the new movement. Those northern rabbis, staid and severe in all their thoughts and deeds, were shocked at the gay spirit of the chassidim. Especially were they scandalized by the amount of gay drinking that was common among the members of the new sect at their many festivals. And perhaps, too, those northern rabbis were human enough to be a little jealous of the enormous power of the popular tzaddikim.

But despite all the opposition, the new movement lived and prospered. While it did not spread much beyond the borders of the southern provinces, Poland and Galicia, inside of these it became supreme. The few *misnaggedim*, "opponents," who persisted there, were accorded scant tolerance indeed.

To this day Chassidism is supreme in those provinces. There are still tzaddikim to be found there, trying to live off the starving Jewish masses. And many of them have come to America, here to live off the immigrants from those provinces. They can sometimes be seen to this day in the larger American cities: long-bearded men with curly locks hanging down over their temples. They dress usually in fine silk gaberdines, black during the week, but a spotless white on the Sabbath. They wear their trousers stuck into their long stockings, probably because in the time of their great-great-grandfathers it was the fashion to wear knickerbockers. Their heads are covered with huge, round fur hats. And for a little gift they will shower you with blessings and promise that your every wish will be fulfilled.

So low as that has the teaching of Baal Shem Tov fallen. . . .

CHAPTER XXXVI

THE DAWN OF TOLERANCE IN EUROPE, AND WHAT IT WON FOR THE JEWS

In the middle of the eighteenth century it was still Night; and it seemed as dark as ever it had been in Jewish history. Persecutions were not so bloody as in earlier years; but they were still cruel and embittering. The world had outgrown its savagery a little, and no longer lashed the body of the Jew. But it still sought to crush his spirit.

That explains why the Jew cut himself off from the world. He hid behind his high wall, and created there a life all his own. Necessarily it was a narrow and ingrown life: an unhealthy groping in the Talmud, or a piteous groveling at the feet of the tzaddik. But at least it was life, not death.

Soon, however, the light of the Dawn began almost imperceptibly to creep up over the horizon. A new spirit stole its way into the heart of the world, and of a sudden whisperings were heard of a strange thing called Tolerance. It was as if mankind were emerging from a stupor. The world sat up in aching bewilderment and wondered what could have possessed it all these years. Men began all at once to realize that "differentness" was not necessarily sinful! They began to see that human beings were human beings, no matter what their race, or religion, or station in life. In America, revolutionists were declaring that men are created free and equal. In France they were crying "Liberty, Fraternity, Equality!"

The world was waking up.

2

Of course it was the Jew who benefited most markedly by the change.

In 1782 the emperor Joseph II of Austria passed the famous "Edict of Toleration" which abolished the wearing of the badge of shame by the Jew, and also the insulting poll-tax. And then in 1791, France went further and abolished *all* laws against the Jew. For the first time, in all the history of Europe, the Jew was put on a footing of equality before the law with other men.

Holland followed in 1796, and even Prussia, one of the most reactionary of all the European lands, finally began to grant civil rights to the Jews in 1812.

The Era of Emancipation had at last set in for the long outlawed people. Ghetto walls were torn down and with them the ghetto fears. Stooped shoulders straightened themselves a little, and downcast eyes now began to look straight forward. At last the Jew became a citizen of the world.

And hard on the awakening of the world came the awakening of the Jew. Indeed, almost before the first gleam of Dawn had shot its advancing spears up over the horizon, a few—a very few—among the Jews were already craning their necks over their wall to welcome the light.

3

Most prominent among the awakening Jews was a sickly hunchback who stands out as one of the real heroes in the history of his people. The life of this hunchback, Moses Mendelssohn, reads strikingly like fiction. He was born in 1729, the son of a poor Torah-scribe in Germany. At the age of fourteen he tramped on foot to Berlin, to continue his education there. For years he starved and studied. And then slowly he began to climb to the heights. Lessing, who was one of the foremost dramatists of the day, became his intimate friend. ("Nathan the Wise," a popular play by Lessing, was written around the gentle character of the hunchback; and in its day it exercised a profound effect in softening Christian prejudice against the Jew.) And Emanuel Kant, the greatest of German philosophers, gave Mendelssohn his genuine admiration. (He had once been defeated by the Jew in a prize essay competition held by the Berlin Academy of Sciences!)

And the whole world stared in amazement. The acceptance of a professing Jew into the highest literary and scientific circles of the land, had never been dreamed of as possible before the coming of this man. And slowly, reluctantly, the world began to reverse itself and revise its opinion of the alien tribe. It began to concede that at least *some* Jews might be acceptable.

But Mendelssohn was not content with that partial concession. He desired that *all* Jews should be considered eligible. Yet he was not blind. He saw only too well that the vast majority of his brethren hardly deserved to be graded as more than aliens. The terrors of the Night had put them four hundred years behind the times. Their rabbis, themselves products of benighted *yeshivos* in Lithuania, had kept them in ignorance of all save the Talmud and the Shulchan Aruch. Even though their ancestors for centuries had lived in the land, they knew little German. They spoke only the ghetto jargon, that lawless mixture of ungrammatical German and mispronounced Hebrew which later came to be called Yiddish.

So Mendelssohn set himself to the task of stirring his brethren out of their four-hundred-year slumber.

4

It was far from an easy task, for many there were who did not wish to be stirred. They had dozed off beneath their smothering blankets, and they asked only to be let alone. But Moses Mendelsshon would not heed that request. With patient but firm hands he began stripping off the ancient and moldy coverings.

He translated the Scriptures into pure German so that his Ghetto brethren might learn at last the language of the people around them. And even more important, he edited a new commentary that was printed together with the translation. Scores of commentaries had already been written on the Scriptures, but almost all of them were filled with distinctions that were far-fetched or stupid, and that confused the meaning of the Holy Writ rather than made it clear. Only Ibn Ezra's commentary had previously made any genuine attempt to be critical and intelligent; and that was already antiquated. So Mendelssohn found himself simply compelled to edit the new commentary.

And when in the year 1783 the "Mendelssohn Bible" was completed and published, it caused great excitement. The old-fashioned rabbis violently combated it and commanded their followers not to dare to look at it. They feared that the German translation might lead the Jews to forget their Hebrew altogether; and they were certain the new commentary would lessen the respect for all the old laws that had been read into and foisted upon the Scriptures.

But the earnest little scholar was not daunted. He refused to stop long enough to engage in argument with his opponents. He simply went on with his Godly Mischief. Very like his idol, old Maimonides, he tried to give a rationalistic explanation of Judaism. He did his best to make the religion of his people seem reasonable in the eyes of free-thinking and critical men. Of course, that meant stripping off a great deal of the superstition and protective ignorance in which the Talmudists and Cabalists had wrapped their faith. And consequently it meant the incurring of more hostility from the orthodox.

5

But nevertheless Mendelssohn went on with his work, never pausing even to the day of his death. And when he died others were forthcoming to take up the work after him. A new generation of Jews arose, thanks to Mendelssohn's labors, and it proved to be a generation readier to meet the Dawn that just then was breaking. In many lands Jews began to look out over their imprisoning wall. The idea of translating the Bible into the vernacular of the land became common throughout Europe. Dutch, English, Italian, and other versions appeared in rapid succession, all of them written by Jews and for Jews.

The movement spread even to Poland and Russia. It was called there the *Haskala*, the "Enlightenment," and it stormed the gloomy *yeshivos* and *chedarim* much as the Renaissance had stormed the Christian colleges and monasteries four hundred years earlier. Jewish humanists arose, earnest scholars who sought with all their might to pull the weeds that had sprung up in Jewish thought and practice.

Hebrew began to flourish again—not the corrupt and distorted Hebrew of the Talmudists, but the ringing, exalted Hebrew of the Prophets. And it was used now not to write more codes of Law or new blatherings of Cabala, but poems and novels and essays of real worth.

Along with the rebirth of Hebrew literature, a Yiddish literature came quite unexpectedly to birth. The brawling, ill-sounding gibberish of the ghetto somehow accomplished the miraculous, and became a genuinely literary language. Poetry, fiction, and drama of high quality were written in it.

Thus the Jewish scholars were provided three different ways of approaching their brethren. They could use the language of the land—German, Dutch, or whatever it was—or they could use Hebrew or Yiddish. And since even the humblest Jew could usually read at least one of these languages, the ideas of the scholars were able to spread. Still no lowering of the high wall of Law around the Jew had taken place; but gradually there began a mighty straining to clamber over the wall, or at least to climb to the top and peer out at the new Dawn.

Gradually, very gradually, the Jew began to look out again at the world.

CHAPTER XXXVII

THE STRUGGLE FOR FREEDOM IN ALL THE NATIONS, AND HOW IT DESTROYED THE WALL OF THE GHETTO

Dawn broke in the last years of the eighteenth century. Moses Mendelssohn, who died in 1786, saw no more than the first shafts of the light. But the next generation actually felt the warmth of the rising sun. Napoleon and his victorious armies had largely destroyed the wall of the Ghetto. Only the wall of the Law was left; and the new generation by standing on the "Mendelssohn Bible," could look right out over that wall with little difficulty.

So now at last the outside world was revealed to the Jews in all its inviting splendor. It was a vast world full of exciting uniforms, romantic titles, enormous fortunes, and enticing honors. The very sight of it set the blood pounding in their veins. At last they were free to take part in that world. At last they were—emancipated.

2

But they were mistaken. They had no more than ventured out into that sun-lit world, when utter darkness closed down on them again. The sun disappeared. The Dawn of a sudden sank back into Night.

For reaction had followed revolution. Napoleon

had been defeated; his empire had been destroyed. And the nations of Europe had immediately rebounded to their old ways. Some immediately repealed all the laws granting the Jews full freedom; and others simply forgot they had ever passed such laws. In Rome the rule of the pope was reinstated, and all the old oppressive measures were put in force again. In Germany there were even wholesale massacres and expulsions.

Thus the Jews, who but a few years earlier had escaped from the Ghetto, now discovered themselves being forced back there again. And they were most unwilling to go. They had already played in the world of the Gentiles, and it was not easy for them to leave it. Indeed, many of them were ready to surrender everything, even their names and their faith, rather than lose that Gentile world.

So throughout Western Europe there was a great flocking of Jews to the baptismal font. One after another the most learned and prominent among them fell away to Christianity. In England the descendants of the very Maranos who had braved all the tortures of the Inquisition for the sake of their religion, now sidled into the Church for the sake of retaining political equality. In Berlin one-third of the entire Jewish population—and the most cultured third—turned apostate. Moses Mendelssohn's own children were the leaders among the deserters. . . .

3

It was not at all from choice and real change of heart that the Jews deserted. Their intolerable position drove them to it. There they were, men and women steeped in the highest culture of the age, leaders in thought and society, yet at the same time political outcasts. Simply because they called themselves Jews, the world called them aliens. They could not enter many of the professions; they could not hold office; they could not even vote. As one of them, Heinrich Heine, the great German poet, said bitterly: "If the law had permitted the stealing of silver spoons, I should never have been baptized."

So they ceased to call themselves Jews. With a sneer or a leer on their lips, they had themselves sprinkled with holy water—and then proceeded to call themselves Christians.

Very soon, however, they discovered that despite the holy water, they were *still* counted aliens. Only in the sight of the law had they become Prussians, or Austrians, or Englishmen; in the sight of men they were still Jews. Even though they could, as Christians, hold office and enter the professions, the Christian world still discriminated against them. Perhaps the best known instance is Benjamin D'Israeli (Lord Beaconsfield), who was always attacked as a Jew, even though he had been baptized in infancy, and was all his days a conforming Christian.

So slowly the truth dawned on the apostates that they could not elude the prejudice of the Christians by deserting their fellow-Jews. For their fellow-Jews simply could not be deserted. One seemed shackled forever to the people among whom one had been born. Once a Jew, always a Jew!

And with the realization of that truth, a new

spirit took possession of the hearts of many of the apostates. Since they could not gain freedom by flight, they determined to wrest it by battle. They went back to their as yet unbaptized brethren, and standing shoulder to shoulder with them, they tried to *force* the world to accord them their human rights. They no longer tried in some cowardly way to change themselves; instead they tried fundamentally to change the world.

And thus was the Jew brought to enlist in the modern revolutionary movement.

4

It was not difficult for the Jew to enter the revolutionary movement. He was a rebel by heritage. From the time of the ancient Prophets, all his ancestors had been "troublers" and revolutionists. The spirit of protest, the hunger for something better, had always been part of his life.

He had no hand in the earlier revolution—the one that brought on the short-lived Dawn enjoyed by his people at the end of the eighteenth century. (That had been kindled in France, and the few Jews then in the land had been poor pedlars or shopkeepers.) But in the revolutions of 1830 and 1848, the Jews was in the very thick of the fighting.

Many Jewish names stand out prominently in those history-making revolutions. There are first of all the names of several Berlin Jewesses, Henrietta Herz, Rahel Levin, and Moses Mendelssohn's daughters. The homes of these women were centers of the cultured life of Mid-Europe—and at the same time centers of its liberal and revolutionary thought. Almost every great man of the period—for instance, Goethe, Schleiermacher, Victor Hugo, and Schlegel—seems to have made the acquaintance of these Jewesses at one time or another.

Then, of course, there are Ludwig Borne and Heinrich Heine, two men who by their merciless wit and sarcasm became leaders among the revolutionist writers. Karl Marx, Ferdinand Lassalle, Johann Jacoby, Gabriel Riesser, Adolphe Cremieux, Signora Nathan—all these of Jewish lineage played important rôles in the social struggle that went on throughout Europe in this period. Wherever the war for human liberty was being waged, whether in France, Germany, Austria, Hungary, or Italy, there the Jew was to be found. It was little wonder that the enemies of social progress, the monarchists and the Churchmen, came to speak of the whole liberal movement as nothing but a Jewish plot.

5

Of course, the liberal movement was far more than that. Essentially it was a heroic effort to drive away the Darkness and cast out its lords. It was a movement to crush the tyrants so that the people might be free. It was the Protestant Reformation in the world of politics.

Incidentally, however, it brought complete release at last to the Jew. Within a generation after 1848 there was hardly a country in Europe—save Russia—where in the eyes of the law the Jew was not accorded complete equality with all other men.

In Norway even temporary residence had always been forbidden to Jews; but complete freedom was granted in 1851. For over a century the Jews had been fighting in England for the right to sit in Parliament—and the way was at last cleared in 1858. Nine years later, Austria removed all Jewish disabilities. Two years after that, Germany did likewise. The next year the ghetto gates in Rome were torn down.

And so one land after the other finally granted the Jew his rights as a citizen. To be sure, they were granted to him only reluctantly. He was still "different" and the world still could not quite forgive him for it. In almost every land he had to fight long and bitterly before full freedom was given to him in practice.

But finally he triumphed.

And then the long Night seemed to be at an end forever. The New Day had really dawned now, and the Jew was free at last.

At least, so he imagined.

CHAPTER XXXVIII

THE STRUGGLE FOR REFORM IN JUDAISM, AND HOW IT BEGAN THE DESTRUCTION OF THE WALL OF LAW

And while one army of Jews was struggling to destroy the wall of the ghetto, another was striving just as strenuously to lower the wall of Law. It is usually said that Moses Mendelssohn was the leader of this second army; but that is hardly true. Mendelssohn never entertained the intention of lowering the wall of Law. His whole aim had been merely to supply a ladder by which his fellow-Jews could climb up and peer over the wall. To the very end he had himself scrupulously kept the laws of the Talmud and Shulchan Aruch. He had freed himself only in thought. In practice he had remained altogether orthodox.

Undoubtedly that explains why the next generation so readily fell away to Christianity. Mendelssohn had fondly imagined his followers, after he had helped them to the top of the wall, would be content to do as he had done. He had imagined they would be content merely to *look* at the outside world.

That was his fatal mistake. Of course it was impossible for them to rest content with merely looking. Soon, very soon, they were burning with the desire to leap off and take active part in the carnival.

And they did. The moment Mendelssohn's steadying hand was removed, off they toppled like so many Humpty-Dumpties. And then not all the king's horses nor all the king's men could put them back over the wall again. For once having danced in the sun of the open world, they would not go back to grope and stumble again in the gloom of the prison yard. No matter what it cost them, they would not go back.

2

During the first years of the nineteenth century, when the followers of Mendelssohn first slipped down off the wall of Law into the great open world outside, there was little said. They disappeared so quietly that their fellow-Jews behind the wall hardly noticed what had happened. But with the reaction following the defeat of Napoleon, and the re-establishment of the ghettos, the sweep of apostacy became an open scandal. For the Jews who had slipped away, now discovered themselves trapped in a sort of No-Man's land. In front was the rampart of the ghetto shutting them off from the world; in their rear the rampart of the Law. And they had to make an open choice between the two.

Now although the rampart of the ghetto was high, cut into it was a wide and inviting gateway. And though it was a Church gateway guarded by a crucifix, nevertheless it was attractive, for it led out into the world. The rampart of the Law, on the other hand, had no breach in it whatsoever. Only by clambering back over its very top could one get back within its protection. And when one got there, only the gloom of the prison yard was the reward.

So hundreds of Jews in making their choice between the two walls, turned to the one with the wide gateway. There was an epidemic of baptisms in Western Europe in the period from 1815 to 1848. And that epidemic shocked Western Jewry into wakefulness. It was evident that something drastic had to be done, and done immediately. Young Jews—and usually the most cultured and gifted in their communities—were still balking at the wall of Law and being forced over to the Church gateway. It was clear that the wall would have to be lowered at once, and the prison yard made more attractive, if the best blood in Jewry was to be saved.

And thus arose the Reform Movement in Judaism.

3

Already for over a generation brilliant Jewish scholars in Germany had been busily laying the foundation for that movement. They had been investigating scientifically the vast rampart by which the Jews had walled themselves in. Then they had gone further, and made a critical survey also of all the life going on behind the rampart. A new field of research had come into being—the Science of Judaism it was called—and learned Jews had been laboring on its problems for several years.

As a result, it had become more or less possible to begin the Reformation. It was tentatively known what was ancient and fundamental in Judaism, and what was recent and unimportant. So the reformers set to work.

At first they centered their attention on the synagogue ritual, seeking to simplify and beautify it. Rabbi after rabbi for eighteen hundred years had been adding to the length of the services. The prayers were all recited in Hebrew or Aramaic, so that exceedingly few of the Jews understood what was said. In fact, with its Oriental chanting and its noise and confusion, the whole ritual had grown foreign and unattractive.

A new generation of Jews was arising in Germany, a generation that had been out in the world and had come to admire certain of its fashions. It was no longer Oriental, but Occidental—Western! It no longer felt at home in a house of prayer where the men, clad like desert wanderers in head-coverings and vast striped shawls, sat in the main pews, while the women, like harem slaves, sat hidden behind a thick curtain in a little back-room or up in a gallery!

So in Hamburg and other cities new synagogues using a modernized ritual began to appear. Prayers were recited partly in German; an organ was used; mixed choirs replaced the old-fashioned cantor; men and women sat together in family pews; and no noise or conversation was permitted during the services.

4

Of course, a storm of protest went up from the orthodox, and there ensued a war very much like that now raging in the Church between the Modernists and the Fundamentalists. Attempts were made by orthodox rabbis to excommunicate the daring reformers. But Jewry had advanced too far for that. The leaders in the new movement—for the most part, rabbis themselves—were reviled and denounced and opposed and threatened. But they were not driven from the fold. The mistake that had been made eleven hundred years earlier, when the Karaites were cast out, and seventeen hundred years earlier, when the Nazarenes were cut off, was not repeated.

And the reformers went on with their work. Their movement, which was confined at first to Germany, began to spread to England and other lands. Especially it spread to America, where through the energy and ability of young immigrant rabbis from Germany—most prominently, Isaac M. Wise—it became almost dominant in Jewish life.

5

Changes in ritual, however, were but the beginning. Soon far more drastic reforms followed. Judaism in its entire practice was liberalized and brought into harmony with the life of the day. The Shulchan Aruch, the Talmud, even sections of the Torah, were laid aside as law-codes that had long outlived their usefulness. The dietary laws were held to be no longer binding, and the rabbinic regulations concerning marriage and divorce gave way to the civil regulations of the land. The whole aim was to free the Jew, to level the high rampart of Law, so that his going out into the world would not necessarily mean deserting Jewry. During the long Night the protecting rampart of Law had been terribly necessary; but now that Day had dawned, it was seen to be only a hindrance.

For by the time these major changes were put on trial by the Reformers, Day had indeed dawned. The wall of the ghetto it seemed had been razed to the ground forever, and the Jew had become a citizen of the world. He no longer had need of ramparts to protect him from his enemies. His enemies were gone. Peace covered the earth as the waters covered the sea, and all bigotry, hatred, and stupidity had been banished forever and aye.

At least, so thought the Reformers in that ecstatic hour of release.

6

And thinking so, they went on even to new extremes with their work. They sought to revolutionize the whole traditional outlook of the Jew.

During twenty-four hundred years the eyes of the Jew had been turned yearningly toward Jerusalem. All those years he had been clinging stubbornly to one hope—that the Messiah would some day come and lead him back to his holy land.

The great Prophets who were the first to conceive the dream of an "Anointed One," had hardly been in agreement as to just what was to be His nature. Some—for instance, Isaiah, and Haggai—considered Him a person, a descendant of the royal house of David, who would restore the people to their home, inaugurate there a reign of perfect justice, and be called the Prince of Peace. Others—for instance, the Unknown Prophet of the Babylonian Exile—seem rather to have considered Him a spirit. With them He was a great hunger for Right, for world-wide Justice and Peace—a hunger embodied in Israel, and one that would be appeased only when Israel and its ideals of Right and Justice and Peace were triumphant.

Later writers, embittered by continued oppression, were drawn of course to the former conception. It was far more satisfying to their bruised and persecuted souls. So they made it the center of all their thinking.

This dream of a personal Messiah ran something like this: In God's own good time a wondrous Person would suddenly appear and miraculously destroy all Israel's enemies. Then He would gather the Jews from the four corners of the earth, and mounted on a white ass or a lion, He would lead them back in triumph to the Holy Land. There they would be joined by all the righteous souls of the past, for these would in the meantime have rolled underground to Zion and been brought back to life. The Temple would be restored, and sacrifices would be offered again. And thereafter the Messiah would reign supreme and all would be well with the Jews and the world forever and aye!

There was much more to the dream—innumerable minor fancies and extravagant details. Generation after generation the fantasy had grown until it had become almost incredibly naïve and childish. Yet never in over two thousand years was it doubted by the Jew. Every day in his prayers he had begged for its realization, and regularly on his festivals he had cried: "Next year in Jerusalem!"

And it was that dream more than anything else that had made the Jew's life bearable during twenty terrible centuries. . . .

7

But great as was the worth of that dream during the Night, it seemed to lose it all with the coming of Day. The Reformers of the nineteenth century, cultured men with critical minds, could deem it little more than a crude and superstitious vagary. They spurned it utterly. Yet a little of the old yearning for the Messiah still lived on in them—only it was for a nobler, a higher, a more spiritual Messiah than the one dreamed of by their fathers. These Reformers went back to the Scriptures and took up the conception of the Messiah that had long been neglected—the conception of the Unknown Prophet of the Babylonian Exile. The Messiah, they therefore held, was not a person, an individual, but a spirit. He was the Spirit incarnate in Israel, the "Suffering Servant of the Lord," who had been divinely anointed to redeem the whole of mankind. Israel had a Mission. It was to be God's most ardent champion in the struggle to bring Peace and Light into the world!

So did the leaders of the Reform Movement reinterpret the old dream of their fathers. The whole ideal of the "Anointed One" was reft of its patriotic, its nationalistic, import. Instead, it was made purely religious and universalistic.

For the first Reformers contended that the Jews were no longer a nation. In their estimation the Jews were purely a religious group, like the Protestants or the Catholics. The more pompous among them liked to call themselves "Germans (or Americans, or Englishmen) of the Mosaic Persuasion." They no longer considered the Holy Land as their home, but whatever land they happened to dwell in. Zion was everywhere, they claimed. Every synagogue in every land was a rebuilt Temple—the

Reformers always called them "temples" for that reason—and the languages of all peoples were equally worthy to be used in prayer. The God they worshiped was no tribal horde, no limited little Yahveh whose jurisdiction was confined to the ancient Land of Israel. He was the Lord of the Universe!

It was all very advanced and exalted thinking that the Reformers indulged in during those years. But as some of them soon discovered, in certain ways it was perhaps *too* advanced and exalted. . . .

CHAPTER XXXIX

THE MISSION OF REFORM JUDAISM—AND THE STORY OF THOSE WHO PRACTICED IT

Reform Judaism—or Liberal Judaism as it is coming to be called to-day—is so new a movement that as yet it can hardly be judged fairly. People are still arguing its pros and cons with such heat that we all are forced to look on the movement out of somewhat prejudiced eyes.

The accusation most commonly brought against it was that it tended to lead the Jews away from Judaism toward Christianity. And the first half of that accusation was unquestionably true—that is, if by Judaism is meant the religion that grew up among the Jews during the ghastly Night. The Reform Movement was an almost ruthless attempt to cut away from all that—to get back to the Judaism of the Prophets and begin growing and building all over again. In certain respects it may have failed in its attempt. But at least the attempt was honestly made.

The second half of the accusation, however, seems to be quite false. The Reform Movement had its origin in an effort not to lead the Jew *to* the Church, but rather to keep him *from* it. If the Church, either Protestant or Catholic, had seemed to the Reformers at all superior to the Synagogue, their movement might never have come to the birth.

They were strikingly clear-minded and courageous men, and it is unlikely that they would have balked even at outright apostasy if they had thought it would bring them nearer the Truth. But they saw only too well that the Christianity of the day was not one whit freer of superstition, bigotry, fear, and spite, than the mediæval Judaism they were fleeing. To go from the Orthodox Synagogue to the Orthodox Church meant to them going not forward but sideways—no, backward. For though contemporary Judaism spent all its time regulating one's action, contemporary Christianity was worse, for it devoted itself rather to shackling one's thought.

What the Reformers were really seeking was not merely some *other* creed than Orthodox Judaism, but some *better* one. They wanted a belief that did not bind them either with petty rules or stupid dogmas, but one that set them utterly free. They sought a religion that rested not on the authority of a book or a priest, but on the great human hunger for Truth and Righteousness. And after they had fashioned that creed as best they could, all danger was past of their ever being lured to adopt Christianity.

2

Significantly, but few of the Reformers or their children ever went over to the Church. Some of them, to be sure, have since gone over to Unitarianism; but that doctrine can hardly be classed in with the religion of the Church. (Indeed, it is almost as far from the Church as is the Synagogue.) And in very recent years, some have gone over to Christian Science—but that doctrine too is many worlds removed from the religion of the Church.

No, the vast majority of the Jews who were baptized came from the ranks of those who had never entered the Reform Movement. They went over from Orthodox Judaism, which because of its very orthodoxy, its "fundamentalism," is far closer to Orthodox Christianity than the religion of Reform Judaism. For instance, it was the colonies of Sephardic Jews in Holland, England, and America, which were most reduced by apostasy. And the Sephardic Jews with but rare exceptions were most rigidly orthodox in their Judaism.

3

Liberal Judaism has grave faults, and perhaps they will be shown up pointedly enough a little later in this story. But it also has its virtues. For instance, there is its unfaltering opposition to any return to what is usually called "authority." Like Orthodox Judaism, it has no pope, living or dead, in control of its freedom. Its rabbis hold office not because of any official "ordination," but by virtue of their reputation for learning and religious zeal. And unlike Orthodox Judaism, it has not even a "printed pope," for it accepts neither the Shulchan Aruch nor the Talmud as binding.

Even the Bible is not allowed to play tyrant over its thinking. Liberal Jews cherish the Bible for the nobility of its prophetic protests, the beauty of its psalms, the grandeur of its books of wisdom. They pore over it because they see in it the epic of their early search for God. But they refuse to believe it utters the last word on that theme, or that the search ends with its last page.

That is a wondrous advance—the more so because it was made after four centuries of retrogression. Christianity, which began its forward march three hundred years earlier, is only now being stirred to hazard a similar advance.

And it was not the only one made by Liberal Judaism. Another advance lay in the ideal it preached of the Prophetic Mission of Israel. For according to this ideal, the essence of religion lay not in praying for the health of one's soul, but in striving for the well-being of mankind. The truest Jew was seen to be the person who labored most earnestly to bring on a Reign of Peace among men.

That was and is an overwhelmingly high ideal, and Reform Judaism deserves abundant praise for lifting it out of the writings of the Prophets and preaching it anew. Unfortunately, however, Reform Judaism seemed able to do exceedingly little to put that preaching into practice. In every "temple" in Germany and America there was fulsome talk of Israel's Mission—but little effort actually to carry it out.

Perhaps that is the severest criticism one can make of the new movement: it knew exactly what the Jew *ought* to do, but failed to induce him to *do* it.

4

There were indeed Jews who were carrying out the historic mission of Israel, who were serving as true messiahs among men, but exceedingly few of them seem to have been inspired by the Reform Movement. The exceptions were commonest perhaps in Hungary, where certain Reform rabbis like Ignatz Einhorn and Adolph Huebsch made their "temples" notable centers of the revolution of 1848. But save for such exceptions, the Jews who led or participated in the heroic efforts to remold the world of the last century, were neither Reform or Orthodox. Indeed, they were often not professing Jews at all.

For instance, there was Heinrich Heine and Ludwig Börne, both unfaltering champions of freedom. And even more conspicuously, there was Karl Marx, one of the great prophetic geniuses of modern times.

Jewish histories rarely mention the name of this man, Karl Marx, though in his life and spirit he was far truer to the mission of Israel than most of those who were forever talking of it. He was born in Germany in 1818, and belonged to an old rabbinic family. He was not himself reared a Jew, however, but while still a child was baptized a Christian by his father. Yet the rebel soul of the Jew flamed in him throughout his days, for he was always a "troubler" in Europe. He was banished from one land after another, and he was arrested and imprisoned many times. He had to flee from Germany to France, then to Belgium, then back to Germany, again to France, and finally to England.

He was so persecuted simply for not holding his peace. Very like the ancient Prophets in that respect, he could not abide the sight of injustice and corruption. He was forever protesting in behalf of the "underdog." He was one of the founders of Socialism, and his book entitled "Capital," is called the Bible of the Socialist movement. He believed in equality, in democracy, not alone in the domain of politics but also in the domain of industry. He sought to win for every man the right not merely to vote as a citizen, but also to thrive as a human being. He warred to banish poverty, and all the vice and disease and ugliness that poverty breeds.

There may be some question whether Karl Marx waged that war in the most desirable or the most effective way. But none can question that the war itself was worth waging. It was an earnest effort to remold the society of men into a true brotherhood, and though there may still be those who insist it was misguided, none can deny it was holy.

5

Significantly enough, however, those who most fervidly talked of the Mission of the Jew, had little love for a Karl Marx who tried to live it. Almost as soon as they were emancipated and could mingle as equals before the law with other men, the need for a newer and better world was forgotten by them altogether. All of a sudden the world as it was, began to seem quite good enough.

From reaching up, the Jews now turned to reaching out. From fighters they changed to "climbers." . . . Not all of them—but many. Too many. . . .

Reform rabbis still continued to tell the occupants of the pews that they were chosen for mighty works, that they were all messiahs. But those who really essayed those mighty works, those who were the *true* messiahs, rarely sat in the pews to listen.

CHAPTER XL

THE ANTI-SEMITIC REACTION IN EUROPE, AND HOW IT HELPED GIVE RISE TO ZIONISM

Liberal Judaism was—and still is—a movement of a small minority. It attracted only those of the broadest "worldliness" in the lands of the greatest enlightenment. In Russia and Roumania where lived half the Jews of the world, it made no headway whatever. In all of the Orient it was utterly unknown. The Wall of Law still towered high in those lands, and the Jews behind it still dreamed on of a Messiah who would lead them bodily back to Zion. To have told them to look on the land where they dwelt as their Zion would have appeared to them but an unfeeling and blasphemous jest.

The Reformers in the West knew that full well; but they were not in the least dismayed. To them it seemed but a question of time before their movement would take root also in the East. For Day seemed to be dawning there too. Emancipation was spreading Eastward, and with it, enlightenment and courage.

And in the second half of the nineteenth century it did indeed seem as though Day were about to reach the East. The most tolerant monarch that Russia had ever known, Alexander II, ascended the throne in 1855. . . . Turkey in 1876 accepted a constitution which gave all citizens, no matter what their religion, full equality before the law; and in the first Turkish parliament elected the following year, there were three Jews. . . . The Treaty of Berlin, signed by the nations of Europe, in 1878, included a clause compelling Roumania, Servia, and Bulgaria, to cancel all laws discriminating against the Jews. . . . It did indeed seem indubitable that light was seeping into the East.

2

And then of a sudden came a reverse. The advance all at once changed to a retreat, and the growing light turned again to darkness. Alexander II was murdered, and after his assassination, the Jews were the victims of the ghastliest cruelties throughout Russia. In Turkey, the new parliament was dismissed and the constitution forgotten. By a trick, Roumania evaded the clause in the Treaty of Berlin compelling her to grant equality before the law to the Jews. Instead still heavier burdens were piled on them, afflicting them so severely that they fled by the thousands.

Even in the West the clouds gathered to blot out the sun. A new movement arose against the Jews, an unholy mixture of crude prejudice and false science, which called itself Anti-Semitism. Warnings were spread far and wide that the Jew was an enemy and a menace, for once more it was discovered that he was "different." Not "different" merely in religion, but even more in blood. It was clamored that the Jew belonged to an alien race. He was not an Aryan, a real European, but a Semite, a native of Asia. Because the first languages spoken by Aryan and Semite had been distinctly different it was concluded that the bloods of Aryan and Semite must likewise be distinctly different.

It was all sheer nonsense. Aryan and Semite were indeed different in their psychology, in their thinking, but not at all in blood. Quiet intermarriage had constantly been going on between the two groups. Every war between the two, every invasion, deportation, oppression, and trading connection, had left children of Aryan fathers among the Semites, or children of Semitic fathers among the Aryans. It was altogether untrue that the two races were still scrupulously "pure" and unrelated in blood.

But though untrue, still the charge was repeated. And the Anti-Semites went further and declared that the two groups were not merely unrelated, but racially also unequal. The Aryans were far the superior of the two races—so they claimed. Indeed, all that was good in civilization had been contributed by them, just as all the evil had been dragged in by the Semites. And all the great men of history, no matter where born and reared, were claimed by the Aryans as their own. Even Jesus of Nazareth! . . .

3

And then quite naturally a movement arose to stamp out the "inferior" race. In Germany a party was organized for the express purpose of robbing the Jews of all their political and social rights. In other lands similar parties sprang up—in Austria.

Hungary, and France. Anti-Semitic newspapers appeared in which all manner of crimes were laid at the door of the newly-emancipated people. In France they were accused of being German spies, and in Germany of being French spies. And in all these lands the Jews were said to be plotting against all Aryan civilization, seeking to ruin it so as to set up Semitic anarchy in its place.

Even the stupid old mediæval "blood accusations" were revived again. In the Hungarian town of Tisza-Ezlar in 1882, a peasant girl disappeared just three days before the Passover. Immediately the Jews were accused of murdering her to procure blood for the festival, and only with great difficulty were they protected from the fanatical mobs. Similar accusations were made in other towns and in other lands—in Germany, France, Roumania, and Bohemia. There were riots and massacres, fiendish assaults and heartless expulsions. It seemed almost as if the dread Night were returning.

4

The reaction culminated in one scandalous affair that shook all of Western Europe and that had its effect on all the world. There was deep unrest among the people in France because a corrupt government was rapidly dragging the country down to ruin. Panically that government looked around for a way to save its skin—and pounced on one of the Strange People. That was nothing new. Kings and governments had often found it convenient in days gone by to stave off revolution by turning the wrath of the masses against the defenseless Jews.

A young Jew named Alfred Dreyfus, an officer in the French army, was accused of selling military secrets to the Germans. Undoubtedly it was done in the hope that his trial and condemnation would arouse such a furor of Anti-Semitism that the corruption of the government would be entirely forgotten in the excitement.

But Dreyfus did not prove a good scapegoat. He showed fight, and he had a wealthy family to support him. Dreyfus was condemned and sentenced to a living death on Devil's Island; but immediately his people began an agitation for a new trial. Protests were made, mass meetings were held, articles and pamphlets and books were written in defense of the innocent man. France was convulsed to its very depths, and all the civilized world became aroused. Twelve long years the excitement lasted, and finally, after the true criminals committed suicide, and the corrupt government had been overthrown, Dreyfus was exonerated.

It was a frightful ordeal, not alone for Alfred Dreyfus, but for the whole Jewish people. With him they all stood on trial, for he had ceased to be *a* Jew, and had become *the* Jew. And though in the end he and his people were declared innocent, the lesson of the "Affair" sank deep into their memories and remained there. From then on, the Strange People were a far sadder but wiser lot. It had put the horrible old Fear of the Goy back into their hearts. They suddenly found out that despite all the long years they had fought for liberty, they still had not gained their end. They were still gypsies. They had been telling themselves that they were at home everywhere, but now they knew again that they were at home nowhere at all.

They were still in *Golus*, in Exile. . . .

5

And then arose that most dramatic movement called Zionism. The old Messianic ache began to throb again, and once more Jews even in the West began to long for their ancient homeland. The hasty optimism of the Reformers who had called every land their Zion was at an end. And with it almost the whole Reform Movement in Europe came to an end. Only in America, where the lash of Anti-Semitism had not yet been laid on the back of the Jew, could the "temples" thrive. In Europe their harried kinsmen were content to worship in synagogues, and wait for the redemption of the Holy Land before talking any more of grander sanctuaries.

Once again the ancient vow of the Wandering Jew was to be heard in the world:

> "If I forget thee, O Jerusalem,
> May my right hand forget its cunning;
> May my tongue cleave to the roof of my mouth,
> If I remember thee not, O Zion!"

Only now that vow was not uttered in a whisper as of yore. It was no longer a timorous prayer but a fierce cry of defiance, a ringing battle cry. The Jew was no longer willing to retreat and cower behind his ramparts, to pray tremblingly for the Messiah to come. He himself would be the Messiah! He himself would retake the old home-land! . . .

The Zionist movement started first in Russia during the dread days following the murder of Alexander II. But it was vague and powerless there. Its Russian adherents were enthusiastic over it, tremendously enthusiastic—but that was all. Zionism with them remained a dream, a thing to talk about. They utterly lacked the worldly ability required even to attempt to realize it.

But then came Theodore Herzl.

6

Herzl was a Western Jew, born in Budapest in 1860. During his youth as a university student, and his young manhood as a journalist and dramatist, he took no interest whatsoever in Jewish life or thought. He was a typical member of the generation of Jews then growing up in Central and Western Europe. Alfred Dreyfus belonged to the same type—a Jew solely by virtue of his birth.

At the time of the first Dreyfus trial, Herzl was in Paris, serving as the foreign correspondent for a Vienna newspaper. And the sight of a young officer being disgraced and betrayed to the mob simply because he was a Jew, set a train of thought running in the journalist's mind that was destined to change the whole future of the Jewish people.

Herzl had such poor Jewish training that he knew little of the Messianic Hope reaching back to the Exile in Babylon, and nothing at all of the feeble Zionist agitation that had just started up in Russia. All he had discovered was that though thoroughly a European in training and conduct, he was nevertheless without a real home in any

European land. No matter how hard he might deny it, he was still regarded as an alien and an intruder wherever he lived. There was therefore but one thing for him to do: go to some land where he would *not* be an alien. There presumably he would be let alone to live his own life in peace and develop his own talents in quiet. There he would be able to give his Jewish genius free scope, and be his own self.

There, in his very own home, he would be free!

And hardly conscious of what consequences might follow, Herzl set down his ideas in a book entitled "The Jewish State." It was not a book of exceptional merit. Zionists in Russia had written on the same subject a generation earlier with better understanding, greater feeling, and more originality. Nevertheless, that book made a world-wide impression. Almost immediately Herzl's reputation was made and his whole career was transformed. At the age of thirty-six he suddenly discovered that he was no longer a care-free, religionless literary man, but the head of a vast and intensely religious movement. Here and there little groups of Zionists sprang up, for the most part refugees from Russia and Roumania, and they madly hailed Herzl as their leader.

Herzl's life now became one unceasing round of labor. His supporters in the beginning were largely dreamers, enthusiastic but penniless. The Jews of wealth frowned on his movement, for they still cherished the idea of working out their salvation in the lands of the Exile. So Herzl found his task was twofold: he had to win the Jews for a home and win a home for the Jews.

Eight years he wrestled with those two tasks—eight years of incessant writing and speaking, of pleading and rebuking, of running to and fro in all the lands of Europe and the Orient, of meeting with sultans and emperors and popes and ambassadors, of unabating, feverish agitation.

And then he died. After eight years of superhuman effort, Theodore Herzl crumbled in the prime of life. It had been too much even for him. Dissension had broken out among his own followers. The Westerners among the Zionists were willing to locate the new home anywhere—in Argentine or the heart of Africa. The Easterners, with the old Messianic dream far mightier in their souls, would have the home nowhere save in Palestine.

And torn between the two Zionist factions, assailed by the Anti-Zionists, thwarted by the Christian Powers, the great leader was destroyed.

But his Zionism lived on. Other men leaped into the breach and carried on until to-day Zionism looms in importance above every other movement in all the life of the Strange People.

CHAPTER XLI

THE GREAT EXODUS FROM EASTERN EUROPE

The head and the directing intelligence that guided the Zionist movement, belonged very largely to the West; but its heart from first to last was Eastern. That was natural, for full half of the whole Jewish people dwelt in those lands in the east of Europe. By the end of the nineteenth century, almost six million Jews were penned in there, groping in the darkness of Night behind the outer wall of Christian persecution and the inner wall of Talmudic Law.

The Polish overlords who in the fourteenth and fifteenth centuries had so gladly welcomed the Jews, were now no more. All their lands had been taken from those overlords late in the eighteenth century by three neighboring powers: Prussia, Austria, and Russia. And as ill-luck would have it, the portion taken by Russia contained the vast majority of the Jews.

A greater misfortune for the luckless people could hardly have occurred. Russia was perhaps the most backward nation in Europe. Her czars were the most despotic of rulers, and her subjects the most barbarous of serfs. When Poland was conquered the Jews fell into the paws of the Russian bear, and they suffered indescribably. And the more they suffered from the ever greater lengths to which their oppression was carried, the more they degenerated.

They shut themselves off so completely from the outside world that they lived almost in utter darkness. In the provinces of the north they buried themselves still further in Talmudism, and in those of the south they plunged even deeper into Chassidism.

2

Only during the reign of Alexander II, from 1855 to 1881, was the oppression lightened a little; and

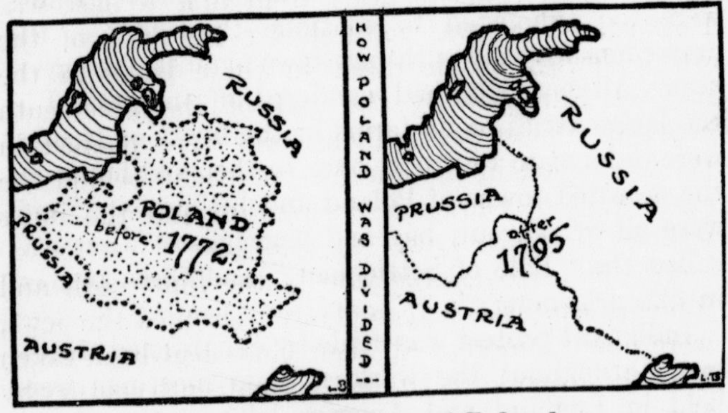

35.—The Partition of Poland

immediately Jewish genius began to bloom again. Russian universities were thronged with Jewish students glad to escape the gloom of the *cheder* and *yeshivah*. Ambitious merchants closed and left their little shops in Polish towns, and moved off to Moscow and St. Petersburg. Jewish newspapers and periodicals appeared in Russian and Modern Hebrew. Yiddish newspapers began to flourish. Musicians like Anton Rubenstein, and sculptors like Marc Antokolski, made their appearance.

The very Dawn seemed to be breaking at last in dark Russia.

And then swift reaction followed. Alexander II was murdered in 1881, and with his successor came back all the terrors of the Night. The revolutionary unrest that was seething in the masses, was turned against the Jews. Bloody riots went on everywhere, so that it seemed the whole of Russian Jewry would be destroyed. And when the fury of the mob was spent, and Cossacks and peasants were too exhausted to continue the carnage, the czar came forward with new laws against the survivors. All Jews who had wandered off and settled in the larger cities or on farms in the heart of Russia, were ordered to return at once to their old homes in the crowded towns of Poland and Lithuania. They were all driven out, bag and baggage, to what was called the "Pale of Settlement," and there penned in like prisoners.

Indignant protest was made by enlightened statesmen throughout the world. Mass meetings were held in England and America. The outrage was decried in the press of many lands. But the czar and his ministers paid no heed. They were determined to get rid of the Jews once and for all. They openly admitted that they hoped to convert a third of the Jews by their persecutions, drive out another third, and murder all the rest.

So persecutions continued. From 1903 to 1906 indescribable massacres occurred. (*Pogroms* they were called in Russian.) Thousands of Jews were slaughtered in the streets of Kishineff, Odessa, and other cities in the Pale.

36.—What Happened in the Pale of Settlement

But it was all to little avail. The czar and his counsellors found themselves still unable to get rid of the Jews. Hundreds of thousands were killed off, and millions of others fled—but still more millions remained on in the land. And the more they were afflicted, the more stubbornly they lived on; the more they were hounded, the more they multiplied. They refused utterly to change their ways or their thoughts; rather they sought to change the ways and thoughts of the Russians. Their sons and daughters were the most desperate and violent of the nihilists and terrorists. Wherever in the land there was talk of revolution, young Jews were to be found among the leaders.

3

The fleeing millions scattered to every corner of the globe. They poured out of the foul Pale in droves and scurried to every imaginable place of refuge. They settled in France, England, South America, China, Australia, Canada, South Africa—everywhere. But most of all they settled in the United States.

Unfortunately the exodus was altogether without direction. There was none to tell the fugitives where to go. As they were used to town life in the "Old Country" they naturally made for the towns in the new countries. They settled in swarms in the larger cities, in London and, especially, in New York.

Only at the twelfth hour was an heroic attempt made to provide channels for the streams of emigration. In 1891 a German Jewish banker named Baron Moritz de Hirsch, set aside the huge sum of

$45,000,000—the largest gift in the history of the world—for the sole purpose of directing the emigrants away from the cities toward the open countryside. He bought vast tracts of land in Argentine and other countries, on which to settle the fugitives. His aim was to put the Jews back on the soil, to make them farmers instead of merchants.

But despite the money and zeal back of the effort, it failed. Somehow the Jews could not feel at home outside the cities. Two thousand years of town dwelling had estranged them from the soil. Theoretically they could see all the advantages of rough, healthy, outdoor life—but practically they could not take to it.

Perhaps the root of the failure lay in the fact that the whole scheme of Baron de Hirsch was not a thing of their own creation. The emigrants weren't settling themselves on the land; they were *being* settled there. It was not their own hunger for the soil that was drawing them to the agricultural colonies, but the thousand doles which a kindly millionaire offered them.

Many, therefore, even of those who took the doles and went out to the colonies, soon tired and moved in to nearby cities.

4

And in the cities new problems arose. They became most acute, of course, in the United States, for about a million Jewish immigrants took refuge there between 1881 and 1905 alone. The port cities on the Eastern coast—New York, Boston, Philadelphia, and Baltimore—developed vast ghettos and dread ghetto evils.

Those ghettos and their evils are still in existence to-day, and they will continue to exist probably for many years. All the efforts made by benevolent German Jewish millionaires have failed to end them. And the chances are that they will continue to fail. The ghetto masses themselves must work out their salvation.

And they will. They are already doing it.

There is tremendous vitality in those masses, and in some slight measure they have already lifted themselves out of the lowest depths. On their first arrival in America, they were despised and rather scorned by their brethren who had preceded them from Germany. Just as previously there had been a coolness between Spanish and German Jews when first they came together in Holland and America, so now a coolness arose between German and East-European Jews. And just as that first coolness was dispelled by time, so the second is being dispelled.

5

Most of the German Jews in America emigrated to the United States during and after the Napoleonic wars. They came over in rags, for they had been robbed of everything in the wars and the subsequent reaction in Germany. And these newcomers were treated by the Sephardic Jews, already well at home in the New World, very much like "poor relations."

But not for long. The destitute wanderers from Germany, despite their foreign ways and guttural accents, soon began to improve their lot. They started out as pack-pedlars, then opened little country shops, grew up with the towns, and finally became owners of huge department stores and factories. And their children, who had no foreign ways and spoke without an accent, became people of influence in the middle-class life of America. So that what few Sephardic Jews had not drifted off to Christianity, were now glad to intermarry with them. Compared to the wealth which the energetic newcomers from Germany had managed to amass, the somewhat effete descendants of the Spanish Jews were almost paupers.

Thus is summed up the whole story of Jewish social life in the United States—and in a measure also in England—up to 1881.

6

And then almost to a detail that story began to repeat itself. The Russian Jew, poor, full of foreign peculiarities, a stranger speaking a strange jargon, became a pack-pedlar in the country or a sweat-shop worker in the city slum. The German Jew, quite a bit proud of his Americanism and his refinement, looked down on this poverty-stricken immigrant with his outlandish ways. This German Jew belonged to a "temple," and had liberalized his religion almost out of all recognizable likeness to the rigid Talmudism of the newcomers. And he was wealthy. He mixed and mingled in what he considered the highest of Gentile society. So he could not but be a little ashamed of his Russian relatives.

Of course, he was benevolent to them. With characteristic Jewish generosity, he aided them with loans and alms, and built "settlement houses" and other charitable institutions for them. Nevertheless his attitude toward them was snobbish. He considered them hopelessly "foreign" and low, and therefore his inferiors.

But gradually the more ambitious or more fortunate of the Russian Jews began to lose their "foreignness," and showed themselves anything but inferior. From pack-pedlars they became storekeepers, and from sweat-shop hands they turned into "bosses." They began to attain wealth, and to move from their ghetto tenements to fine homes in the suburbs where the German Jews lived. They either became Reform Jews and joined the "temples," or else they refined their synagogue ritual and called themselves Conservative or Modern-Orthodox Jews.

In Chicago and New York, hundreds of thousands of them who did not attain wealth but were compelled to remain in the working class, organized themselves into powerful trade-unions.

There was no holding them back. All the energy pent up in them during their long Night in the Pale of Settlement, broke loose and simply swept every obstacle out of their way. Their keen intelligences, whetted from long study in the Talmud, simply gashed a path for them.

And the dominance in American Jewish life which once passed from the Spanish Jew to the German Jew, now began to pass from the German Jew to the Russian Jew.

That second process is going on to-day—and going on most rapidly. Another generation or two, and the transfer will be complete.

And then it will be the turn of the Russian Jew to show his mettle. Like his brother in Germany or Spain, he was well able to live through all the terrors of the Night.

But what is going to happen to him now that his Night has passed? . . .

CHAPTER XLII

THE NIGHT OF WAR, AND THE NEW DAWN

The Exodus from Eastern Europe which began in 1881, continued without interruption until 1914. And then there came an ominous halt.

The World War had begun. Of a sudden all the nations of Europe found themselves leaping at each other's throats—though just why, no one of them really knew. They acted rather like those pathetic maniacs who are so genial and sane and industrious for months on end, and then suddenly, bewilderingly, without all trace of reason, run amuck.

The savage in the heart of man broke loose and slashed all the bonds of civilization.

In a way the War can be understood as another convulsive effort of the Night to get the world back into its clutches—an effort that succeeded only too well for a while. Epidemics of savage intolerance of all that was "different" became common everywhere. And as might be expected, it was Jews, the universally "different" people, who were its sorriest victims.

The severest sufferings were inflicted on them of course in Eastern Europe, and almost half the Jews of the world still lived in that region. There they lay helplessly in the path of vast armies rushing to blow each other to fragments. Just as in ancient times the Jews occupied the bridge between the empires of the Orient, so now they dwelt on the main highways between Germany, Austria, Russia, and Roumania. And the armed hosts of the powers came thundering over those highways, attacking and counter-attacking, rolling each other backward and forward, murdering and pillaging and burning their way, and leaving East-European Jewry prostrate and broken.

The ordeal of the Belgians was as nothing compared with what was thus suffered by the Jews on the Eastern front. For the Jews were not ordinary noncombatants going through the ordinary hell of war. They were Jews, and as such were marked out for an especially fiendish torment. They were the prey of both sides, so that no matter which won, they invariably lost.

2

It is not easy to tell of the atrocities committed against the Jews during all four years of the World War on the Eastern front, and all five years of civil war that followed in Russia. The story is too ghastly! There were wholesale deportations of women and old men and children. . . . Cattle trucks were filled with the sick and helpless, and were abandoned on railroad sidings in the forests. . . . Carts and sleighs were loaded with starving women and children, and sent off into oblivion in the dead of night. . . . Everywhere there was terror and flame and carnage. . . .

Of all the lurid chapters in the long story of the martyrdom of the Jews, the one enacted there and then in Eastern Europe was the worst. It began in

August of 1914, when Russia battered her way into Galicia; and it went on without a moment's pause until 1923. The Revolution and downfall of the czar brought no relief, for civil war then broke out. Anti-revolutionary generals let their Cossack armies cut down the Jew without mercy, on the assumption that the hated folk were all friends of the Revolution. And roving bandits calling themselves Bolsheviki, plundered and murdered these same Jews on the ground that they were all *against* the Revolution.

There in southwestern Russia a whole people was beaten almost to death. Hundreds of thousands of Jews were murdered or starved, and hundreds of thousands more went wandering through the land vainly seeking a hiding place.

3

But even after the War the sufferings of the Jews were not confined to Russia. Poland had been made a nation once more, and drunk with its new glory, it celebrated its triumph with wholesale massacres of the homeless folk. Roumania and Hungary, even Germany, were the scenes of Anti-Semitic riots and murders.

And in lands further west, although Anti-Semitic passion could not culminate in lynchings and massacres, it nevertheless brought sore evil to the Jews. A flood of malicious propaganda swept through France, England, and America. Fresh currency was given to old slanderous stories which recounted how the Jews were all secretly united under the leadership of certain mythical Elders of Zion and were plotting to conquer all the world. Anti-Semitic parties and fraternities were organized in many lands, even in America; and Anti-Semitic books and newspapers were published and widely distributed.

All the forces of reaction everywhere let loose after the War, turned with the old venom upon the Jew. Wherever custom made it possible he was stoned and murdered, and elsewhere he was reviled and despised.

4

And out of the bitterness of his experiences during and after the War, one dread lesson was brought home again to the Jew: he was still in *Golus*, in Exile.

Even in America that lesson was well learnt at last. It came first through the sight of the holocaust of his brethren in Eastern Europe. Ever since 1881 the Jews in America had been answering the call for aid from their brethren in the Pale. And year after year they had been solacing themselves with the hope that the horrors there would soon, very soon, abate.

But the horrors only increased. In 1914 they forced the first of a series of enormous relief drives to be launched in America to rescue East-European Jewry. Incredibly large sums, millions upon millions of dollars, had to be sent over to feed and clothe the victims of war and prejudice. Year after year the Jews in America, poor as well as rich, were thus forced to tax themselves to relieve their afflicted brethren. In 1922, in one supreme effort, as much as seventeen millions of dollars was subscribed!

But while all those funds were being gathered and distributed, a doubt began to creep into the minds of the American Jews as to the worth of their efforts. Slowly it began to dawn on them that the fortunes they were sending across were going merely for relief, and were doing nothing at all to effect a cure. Even more: they began to come to the conclusion that a cure could *never* be wrought if their people were left to live in Eastern Europe.

5

For a whole century they had been deluding themselves that the full solution of the Jewish world problem lay in obtaining complete recognition of the Jews as citizens in every land where they dwelt. But the World War made it clear that in at least one region, Eastern Europe, the Jewish problem could never be solved by the removal of their civil disabilities. Because of their vast and huddled numbers, their alien religion, their hateful position as middlemen, their age-old unpopularity, the Jews could never possibly feel at home there. They would have to migrate. Inevitably they would have to flee.

But whither? The more attractive lands in the west were no longer willing to receive them. Like America, they had closed their doors. And to send the fugitives to Mexico or to one of the South American republics, was but to drag out the misery. For those lands, generous and hospitable to-day, might grow bitter and hostile to-morrow.

No, it was clear that what these people needed was not another *nachtsyl*, another "night's lodging," but a real *home*. That secure haven was needed most obviously for the persecuted in Eastern Europe; but no less certainly was there need of it for the sensitive, the creative, the artist Jews everywhere else. For the latter, though now perhaps physically comfortable, were spiritually lost. As they themselves put it, they did not feel "at home" anywhere in the Diaspora. They could not express fully and joyously the Jewish genius astir in their souls.

Moreover, ordinary Jews, the merchants and the professional men everywhere in the world, also needed a home; not a home for their bodies but for their cowed and Exile-broken spirits. They needed a spiritual world center, a dynamo radiating courage and strength to them wherever they happened to live. With the wall of the Ghetto almost demolished, and the wall of Law fast wearing away, they stood in desperate need of some new rampart of protection if they desired to survive. They needed a spiritual home.

And where in all the world could they expect to find such a home, physical or spiritual, save—in Palestine?

6

By such a process of reasoning were American Jews won over at last to make the dream of Theodore Herzl their own. Only in the interval it had come to be something more than a dream. The incessant labors of Herzl's successors had by this time been crowned with victory. On November 2, 1917, the British Government officially declared its intention of helping to make Palestine—which it was just then wresting from the Turks—a "national home for the Jewish people."

And thus at one stroke was a fantastic dream made almost a reality.

There still remained some Reform Jews in America and "Britishers of the Mosaic Persuasion" in England who continued to labor under the old delusion. Some of them still believed that Zionism was a step backwards, an inglorious retreat into a narrow nationalism. There are still some who believe that to-day. . . .

But rapidly even they are being won over, for they are coming to see that Zionism is not at all an effort to corral all the Jews in the world within the borders of Palestine. Not even the most fanatical Zionist dreams of doing that. The Jews in the Diaspora now number over sixteen millions, and they never could be crowded into a land four times the size of Palestine. All that Zionism proposes to do is to secure a home for the Jews who now are homeless—and for the Jewish spirit which for almost two thousand years has been without a haven.

7

That home has now been secured. In 1922 the League of Nations ratified the British Mandate over Palestine, and thereby the Powers of the world signified that the declaration first made by Great Britain had their indorsement. All that is left—but it is a mighty task—is to furnish the home so that the wanderers may return there and live. And that task is now being done.

8

So to-day, eighteen hundred and fifty-four years after their expulsion from Palestine at the hands of Rome, the Wandering People are on their way back. Not all of them. Only those go back who are most conscious of their race, who have been beaten in body or harried in spirit until their whole life has become a matter of race. For the most part thus far they are young people, youths and maidens from East-European universities, and with their staffs and knapsacks they go back on foot. The *Chalutzim*, the "pioneers," they are called, and in legions they are trooping back to redeem the land of their fathers.

Two distinct urges have been basic in all the story of the Jews: the prophetic dream and the priestly way of realization. The one has given the people a *reason* for living, and the other has sought to provide a *way*. One thinks of them almost as two vast spiritual back-drops on the stage of Jewish history—the one a stirring red, the other a sober gray—in front of which the whole drama has been enacted. No matter to what corner of the world the action has shifted, always one or both of those drops have lent the basic color. *It is the clash between prophetic hunger for the ideal and priestly resort to the expedient that lies at the bottom of every advance and every retrogression in the spiritual life of the Jewish people.*

Zionism, of course, belongs quite clearly to the gray. It is essentially a priestly movement—not a reason for living but a way to keep alive. It is a means, not an end. And if prophetic spirits to-day are leading the *chalutzim*, the Zionist pioneers, it is solely because they realize this. They look on the rehabilitation of the homeland but as the prelude to something far greater. To them it is but a clearing of the way for the rehabilitation of the old prophetic spirit. They abide the gray back-drop now, but only because they dream of seeing the red one hung in its place in a little while.

And perhaps they will not be disappointed.

There were only forty-two thousand *chalutzim* who returned from the Babylonian Exile in 536 B. C. Yet from their loins there sprang a people that gave a new idea of God to half the world—the idea that He is the Father of all Mankind.

What these thousands of newer *chalutzim* may give, no one can tell. Perhaps a new idea of Mankind. No, not a new idea of Mankind, but an old one reëmphasized—the idea of the ancient Prophets that Mankind is one great Fellowship.

For the rebel spirit of the Prophets is mighty in the bones of these young pioneers. They are no timorous band fleeing in a panic from an evil world, but hardened warriors intrenching themselves for a new assault on it. They are aflame with the passion to redeem not solely Palestine, but through Palestine all the world. The Messianic dream is still with them. They still believe, even though but half-consciously, that the mission of their people is to bring on the Kingdom of Heaven.

So who can tell what may yet come forth from the new-old land of Israel? . . .

9

Yet one forecast may indeed safely be made. With the going back of these *chalutzim*, the Jews everywhere go forward. They go forward in history, taking on a new lease of life. A new rampart has been thrown up to supply the protection afforded by the old one of Law. And behind it Jews are making ready to go on with their work, their historic work of Godly Mischief.

So that even our day can see no end to the life of the Strange People, but again only a new beginning. Even here one cannot write "Finis" to this long story, but only

TO BE CONTINUED

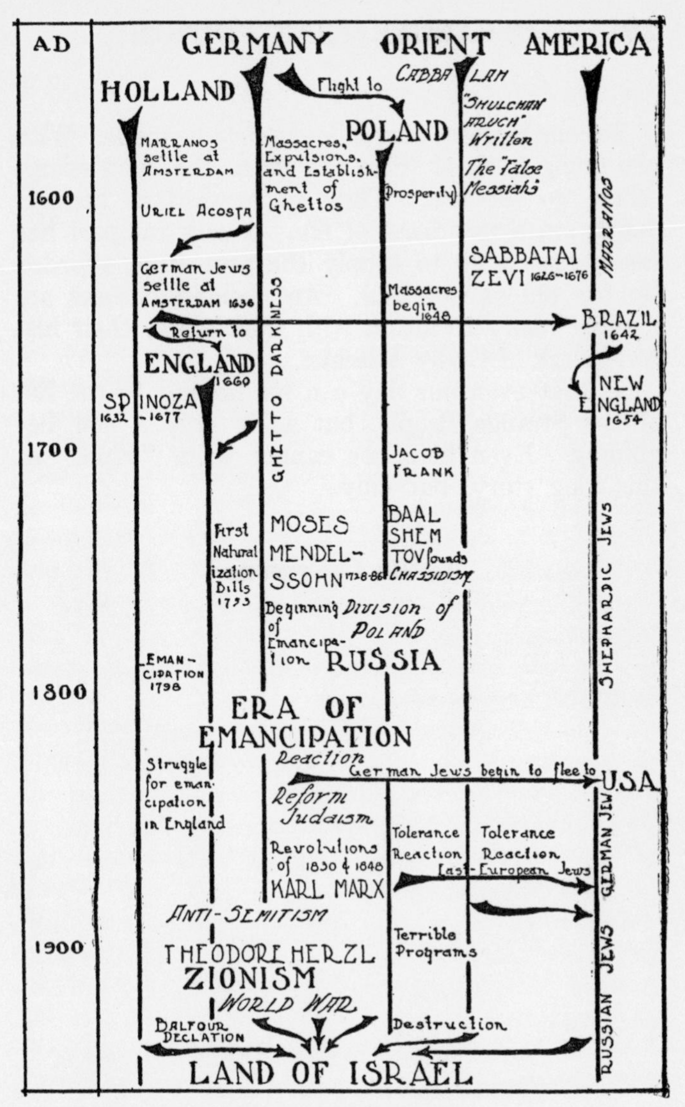

Chart F. The Adventures of the Jews, Part VI

GLOSSARY

GLOSSARY

AHL UL KITAB: Arabic for "People of the Book." The name applied by the Arabs to the Jews because they had written the Bible.

ARAMAIC: The popular dialect used by the Jews after the return from the Babylonian Exile. It is a corrupt form of Hebrew.

ASHKENAZ: The mediæval Hebrew for Germany.

ASHKENAZIM: Jews living in, or belonging by ancestry to Germany and the rest of Northern Europe. Used in contradistinction to Sephardim, the Jews from Spain and Portugal.

BAAL (pl. BAALIM): Hebrew for "Master." Any of a number of local gods worshiped by the Canaanites.

BAAL SHEM: Hebrew for "Master of The (God's) Name." Term applied to a magic-worker and healer among the Jews of Poland and Galicia. The most famous of them was Baal Shem Tov, "The Kind Master of God's Name."

BES HA-MEDRESH: Hebrew for "house of learning" or rabbinical school.

CABALA: Hebrew for "tradition." A system of magic and mystical thought that was popular among the Jews in the Middle Ages. It was based on peculiar Bible interpretations which it was believed had been secretly handed down by the ancient rabbis.

CHASSID (pl. CHASSIDIM): Hebrew for "Pious One." A follower of Chassidism, the religious movement which arose among the Polish Jews in the eighteenth century, and which won over nearly half of the Jewish masses.

CHANNUKAH: Hebrew for "dedication." The Jewish Feast of Dedication instituted by Judas Maccabeus in 165 B. C., to commemorate the rededication of the Temple altar after its pollution by Antiochus Epiphanes of Syria.

CHEDER: Hebrew for "room." The name applied to an elementary Hebrew school.

CHRIST: From the Greek word *christos*, meaning "anointed." The same word in Hebrew is *mashiach*, or Messiah. Paul called Jesus of Nazareth "Christ" because he thought him the Messiah, or "God's Anointed."

DIASPORA: Greek for "dispersion" or "scattering." The term used to describe the world outside of Palestine inhabited by the Jews after the Exile.

DÖNMEH: Turkish for "Apostates." A sect of secret Jews descended from the followers of Sabbatai Zevi who went over to Mohammedanism with him. Most of them now live in Salonica, in Turkey.

ELOHIM: Hebrew for "God" (originally "gods").

ELOHIST: Name given to the ancient historical document set down in the ninth century B. C. by the chroniclers of the Northern Kingdom, and now to be found in fragmentary form in the Bible.

ESSENE: Name of Hebrew or Aramaic origin applied to one of a sort of brotherhood or monastic order among the Jews of Palestine from the second century B. C. to the second century A. D.

GAON (pl. GEONIM): Hebrew for "Illustrious One." Head of the chief rabbinical academy in Babylonia during the early Middle Ages.

GITTER YID: Yiddish for "Good Jew." A Tzaddik, or wonder-working rabbi, reverenced by the Chassidim.

GOLUS: Hebrew for "Exile."

GOY (pl. GOYIM): Hebrew for "Gentile."

HASKALAH: Hebrew for "Wisdom." The movement begun in the late eighteenth century in Germany, and afterwards in Poland and Russia, to liberalize Jewish life and thought.

HEBREW: From the Hebrew *ivri*, the original meaning of which is not definitely known. Properly the word should not be applied except to Israelites and Judeans *before* the Babylonian Exile. After that event the term "Jew" (from *Judah*) became the accepted one.

HELLENISM: From the Greek word *Hellas*, meaning Greece. The word is used to describe the culture and civilization of ancient Greece.

ISRAELITE: From the Hebrew *Yisrael*, meaning "Champion of God." A descendant of Israel or Jacob. Specifically, one belonging to the Northern Kingdom.

KARAISM: The "Religion of the Bible." A Jewish sect originating in the eighth century, which rejected the Talmud and tried to base its religion and life altogether on Biblical Law.

KEDOSHIM: Hebrew for "Holy Ones," or "Saints." The term often applied to the Jewish martyrs.

LADINO: Spanish for "learned" or "cultured," evidently from the word *Latin*. It is the name for the curious jargon made up of mixed Spanish and Hebrew, which is spoken by the Sephardic Jews in the Orient. It is sometimes called Spagniolish.

LITVAK: Yiddish for a Lithuanian Jew. Often it is used to connote shrewdness and cunning, because the Lithuanian Jews were great adepts at Talmudic argument.

MARANO: Spanish for "Accursed." A Jew professing Christianity in order to escape persecution.

MESSIAH: Hebrew for "Anointed." The expected king and deliverer of the Hebrews.

MISHNA: Hebrew for "Repetition." The code of civil and religious law compiled by Rabbi Judah a little before 200 A. D. It was called by that name because it repeated, with many changes and enormous elaborations, the laws of the Pentateuch.

MISNAGGEDIM: Hebrew for "Opponents." Those who opposed the Chassidim, and disbelieved in the "wonder-working" Tzaddikim.

MOREH NEVUCHIM: Hebrew for "Guide for the Perplexed." A philosophic study of the creeds of Judaism written by Moses Maimonides (often called Rambam) in the twelfth century.

Nevim: Hebrew for "prophets." Originally it may have meant "shouters."

Pharisee: From the Hebrew *pharash* meaning "to interpret," or according to many scholars, "to separate." The Pharisees destroyed the power of the Jewish priests by "interpreting" the Holy Law in new ways.

Piyyutim: Mediæval Hebrew for certain synagogue hymns.

Pogrom: Russian for "devastation." An organized massacre, usually of the Jews.

Rabbi: Hebrew for "My Teacher." A Jewish title of respect for a teacher of the Law. Later it came to mean the spiritual leader in a synagogue.

Rashi: Name coined of the initial letters of *Ra*bbi *Sh*elomoh (bar) *I*tzchak, the famous commentator on the Bible and Talmud who lived in France 1040–1105.

Resh Galutha: Aramaic for "Prince of the Exile." The leader of the Jews living in Babylonia. The office was hereditary in a family that claimed descent from King David, and was abolished by the Mohammedans in the eleventh century.

Sadducees: From Tzaddok, who was Solomon's high priest. The Sadducees formed the priestly and aristocratic party in Judea from the second century B. C. almost to the end of the first century A. D.

Sanhedrin: Greek for "assembly." The parliament and supreme court of the Jews during many centuries.

Seforim: Hebrew for "books," but sometimes used with special reference to the Holy Books of the Bible.

Semites: One of the descendants of Shem. A member of the race which seems to have originated in the Arabian Desert, and which to-day is represented chiefly by the Jews and Arabs.

Sepharad: Mediæval Hebrew name for Spain.

Sephardim: Descendants of the Jews who were expelled from Spain and Portugal, and who settled in the Orient, Holland, and the New World.

Shamash: Hebrew for "servant." The word now has come to mean a sexton or beadle of a synagogue.

Shulchan Aruch: Hebrew for "Set Table." Title of the most popular compilation of the rabbinic laws regulating the practice of Judaism. It was written by Joseph Karo in 1555.

Synagogue: Greek for "a gathering." A Jewish religious organization, or the building in which such an organization worships.

Talmud: Aramaic for "learning." The collection of Jewish civil and religious laws drawn up by the rabbis in Babylonia in the fifth century. (There was also a Talmud drawn up in Palestine a century earlier, but it never attained great importance.)

Targum: Aramaic for "interpretation." A translation or paraphrase of the Old Testament in the Aramaic dialect popular in Judea after the Babylonian Exile.

Torah: Hebrew for "law." The name given to the "Five Books of Moses" which contained the Biblical Law.

Tosafists: Writers of Tosafos, which is the Hebrew for "additions." The Tosafists flourished in France in the twelfth century, and wrote little critical and explanatory notes on the margin of the Talmud.

Tzaddik (pl. Tzaddikim): Hebrew for "Righteous One." A rabbi claiming the power to work miracles.

Yahveh: Original name of the God worshiped by the Hebrews. Through the mistake of an ignorant translator, the word is now usually spelled *Jehovah*.

Yeshivah: Hebrew for "session." A rabbinical college.

Yiddish: From the German *jüdisch*, meaning "Jewish." The vernacular of East-European Jews. It is the Middle High German language of the sixteenth century, mixed with Slavic and Hebrew.

Zohar: Hebrew for "Splendor." Title of a Cabalistic work introduced into Spain in the thirteenth century by Moses de Leon.

SIX CHARTS TELLING THE ADVENTURES OF THE JEWS

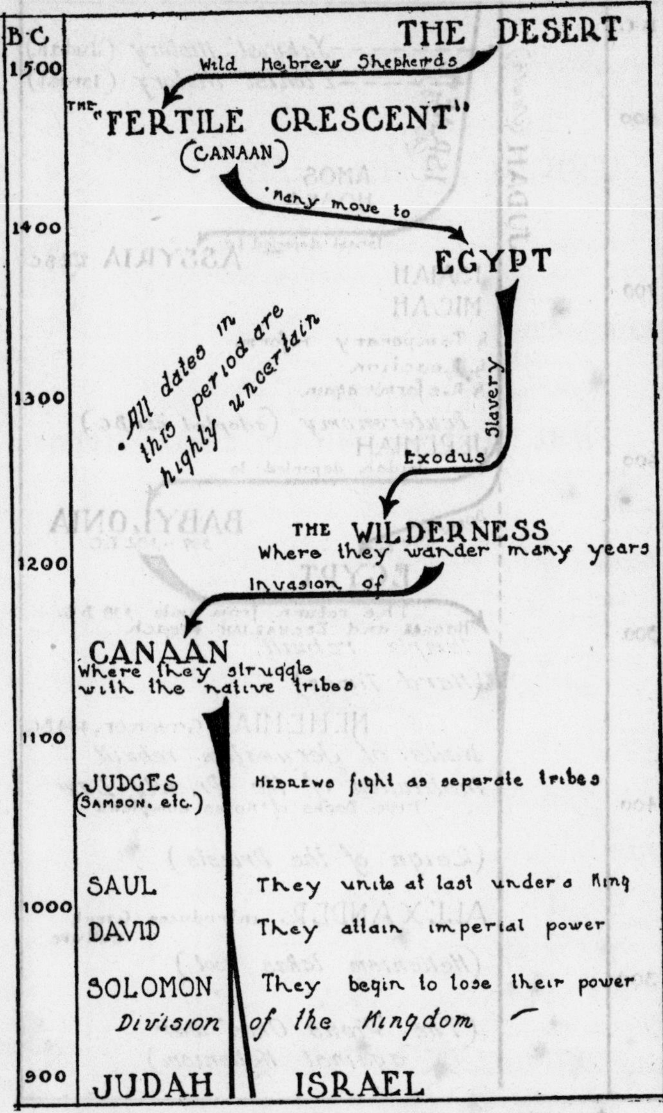

Chart A. The Adventures of the Jews, Part I

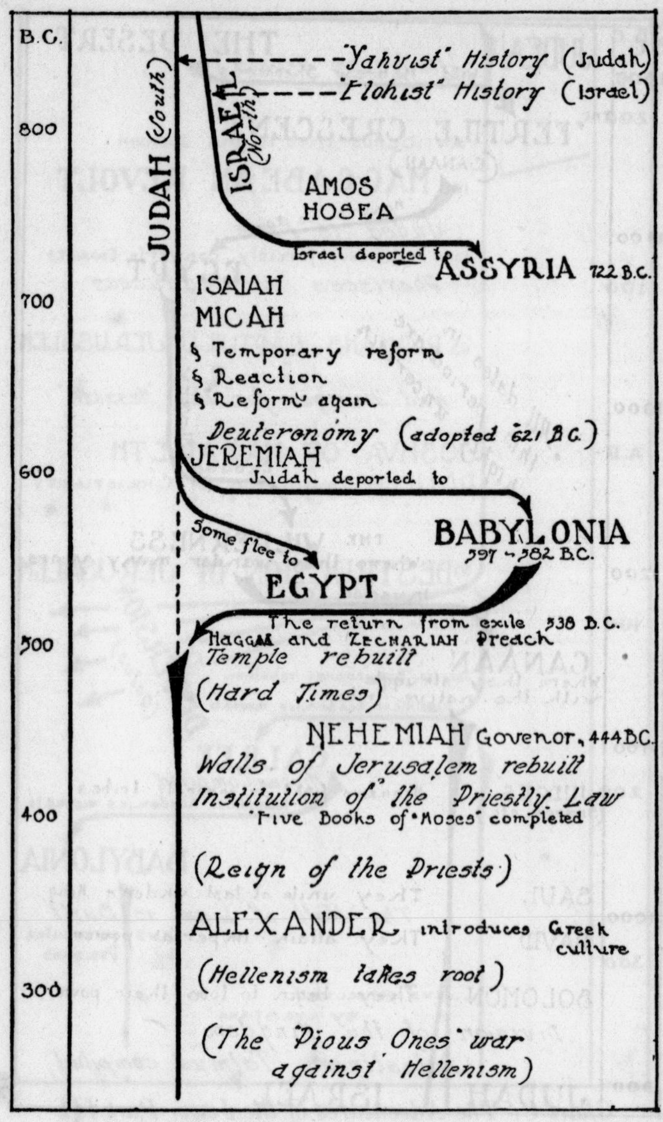

Chart B. The Adventures of the Jews, Part II

B. C.

JUDEA

(Hellenism grows)

200

ANTIOCHUS tries to end JUDAISM

168 MACCABEAN REVOLT

Judea is Free

JOHN HYRCANUS forcibly converts IDOMITES

100

Pharisees vs. Sadducees

63 ROMANS CAPTURE JERUSALEM

Wild Hunger for the "Messiah"

A. D.

JOSHUA OF NAZARETH

PAUL – Begining of CHRISTIANITY

70 DESTRUCTION OF JERUSALEM

100

SANHEDRIN meets in JABNEH

THE DISPERSION (Golus)

132–135 BAR KOCHBA rebellion

RABBINICAL Academies moved to

GALILEE

200

Mishna Compiled

RABBINICAL Academies moved to

BABYLONIA

The Wall of Law is Built

300

JEWS persecuted by PERSIANS

...JEWS* persecuted by CHRISTIANS

..Palestinian Talmud compiled

Chart C. The Adventures of the Jews, Part III

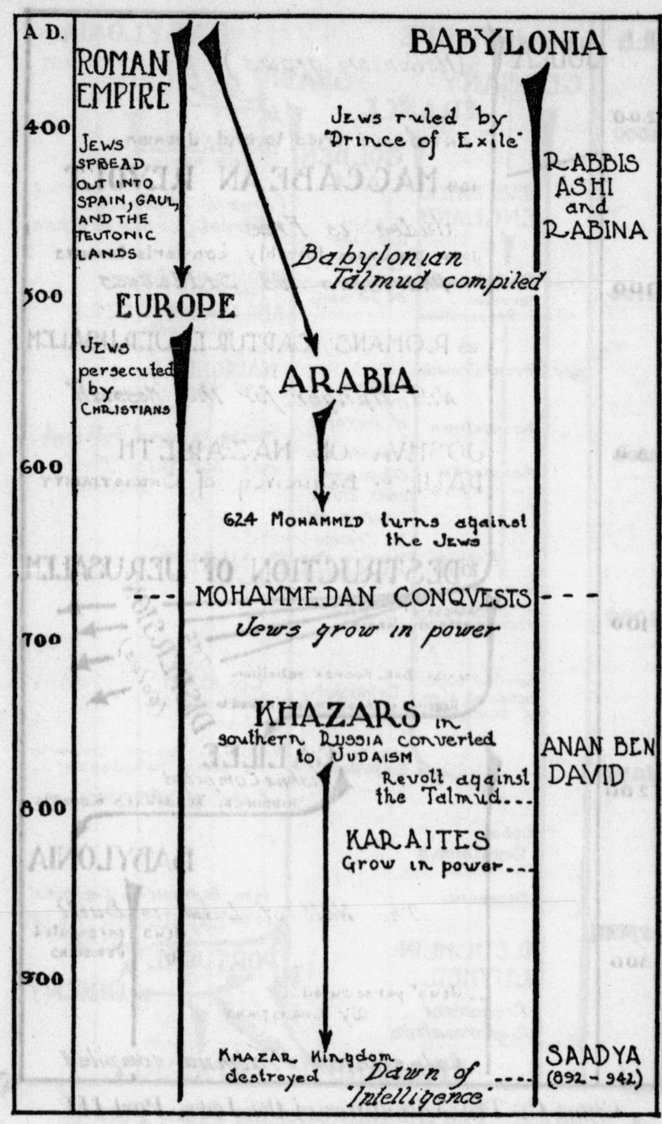

Chart D. The Adventures of the Jews, Part IV

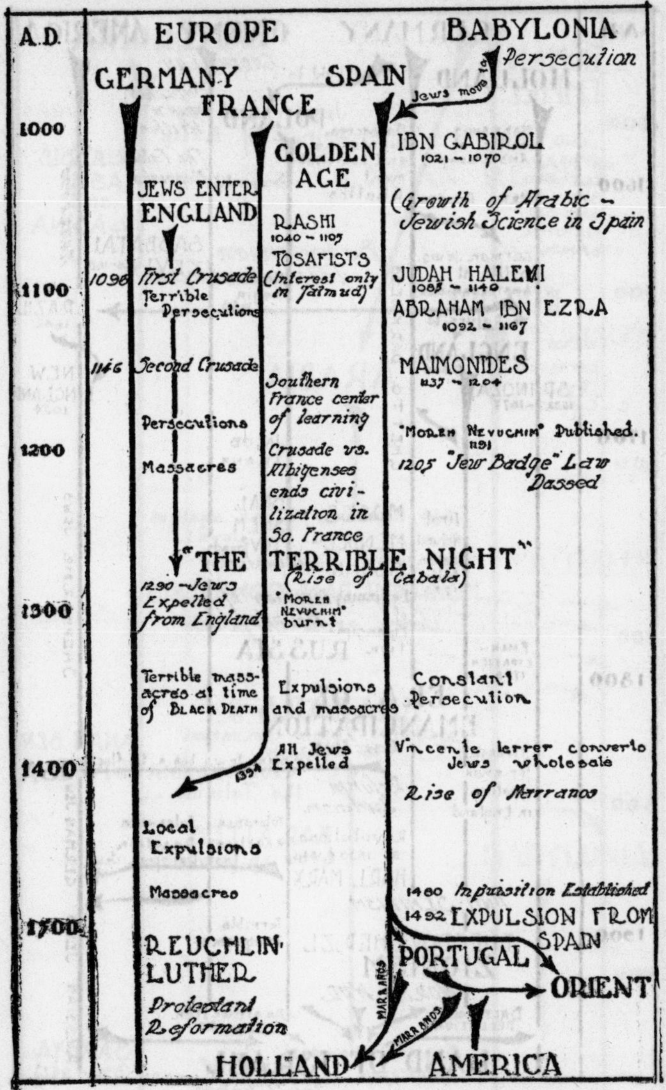

Chart E. The Adventures of the Jews, Part V

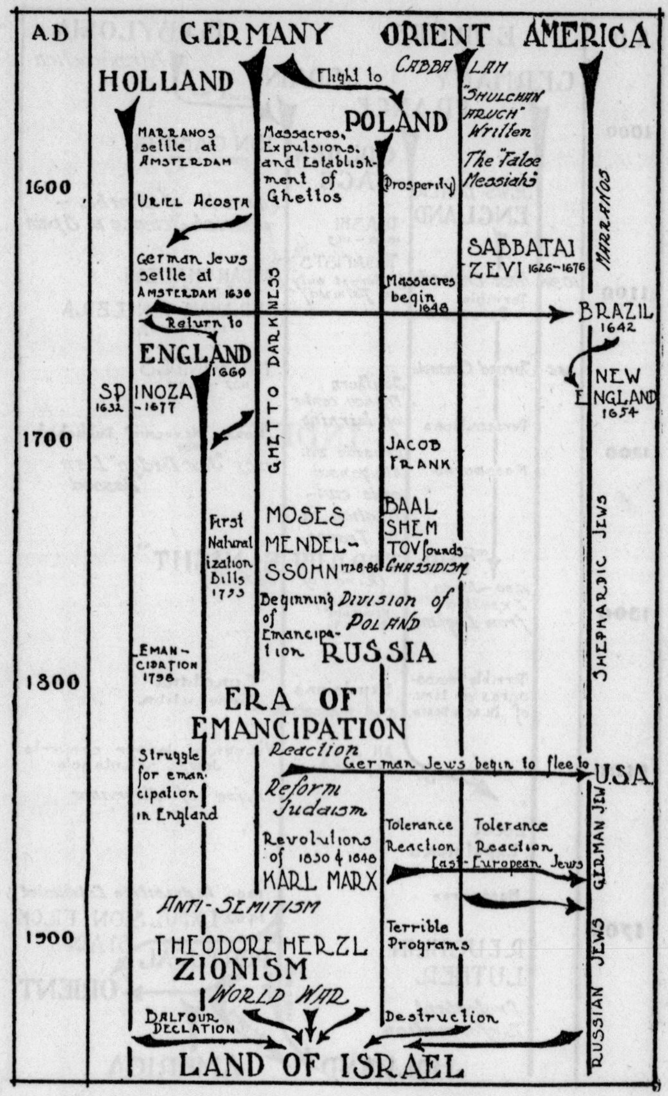

Chart F. The Adventures of the Jews, Part VI

INDEX

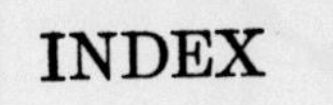

INDEX